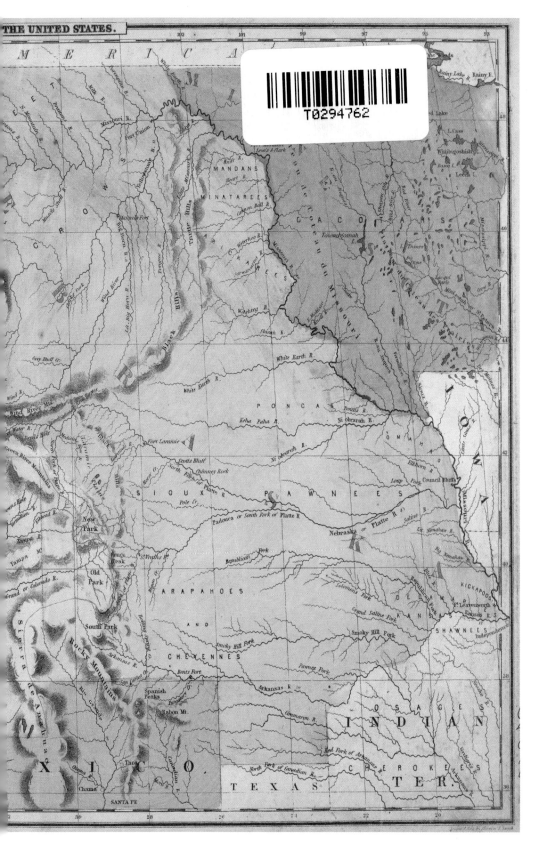

THE UNITED STATES.

A Winter with the Mormons

The 1852 Letters of Jotham Goodell

NUMBER FIFTEEN IN THE SERIES
UTAH, THE MORMONS, AND THE WEST

This series seeks to make available both
unpublished manuscripts and out-of-print classics that
enhance our understanding of
Utah, the Mormons, and the West.

An early portrait of Jotham and Anna Goodell.
—*Courtesy Naomi B. Baker of Delevan, N.Y.*

A WINTER WITH THE MORMONS

The 1852 Letters of
Jotham Goodell

EDITED BY DAVID L. BIGLER
Preface by George Miles

The Tanner Trust Fund
J. Willard Marriott Library
University of Utah
Salt Lake City, Utah
2001

ALSO BY DAVID L. BIGLER:

The Gold Discovery Journal of Azariah Smith, 1990

*Forgotten Kingdom: The Mormon Theocracy in the
American West, 1847–1896*, 1998

Army of Israel: Mormon Battalion Narratives, with
Will Bagley, 2000

Maps illustrated by Thomas Child

Library of Congress Cataloging-in-Publication Data

Goodell, Jotham, 1809–1859.
 A winter with the Mormons : the 1852 letters of Jotham Goodell / edited
and with introduction by David L. Bigler ; preface by George Miles.
  p. cm.–(Utah, the Mormons, and the West ; v. 15)
  Includes bibliographical references (p.) and index.
  ISBN 1-56085-161-9(alk. paper)
  1. Goodell, Jotham, d. 1859. 2. Mormons–Utah–History–19th century. 3.
Utah–Description and travel–Sources. 4. Utah–History–Sources. 5. Overland
journeys to the Pacific–History–Sources. 6. Pioneers–Oregon. I. Bigler, David
L., 1927- II. Title. III. Series.
F826.G66 2001   979.2'02–dc21
    For on-line cataloging information, see http://www.loc.gov/catalog/

For the descendants of
Jotham Weeks and Anna Glenning Bacheler Goodell

CONTENTS

ILLUSTRATIONS

MAPS

The first three columns of the front page of *The Oregonian*, 8 May 1852, printed J. W. Goodell's third letter (see page 45) describing his winter among the Mormons.

PREFACE

Few Americans of the twenty-first century can grasp the violent conflicts that marked the early years of the Church of Jesus Christ of Latter-day Saints, whose members are generally known as Mormons. How was it that a church and community now regarded as highly patriotic as well as socially and politically conservative were involved in not one but three civil wars in the first thirty years of their existence? What happened in Missouri, in Illinois, and again in the country of the Great Salt Lake that found the Mormons embroiled in open combat with their neighbors, the state militia, and ultimately the army of the United States?

Obscured by the passage of 150 years, the Mormon conflicts have been overshadowed in historical accounts by the stories of the Mexican and Civil Wars. Compared to them, the violence associated with early Mormonism appears minor. But the cost of the Mormon disturbances, the political consequences, and the lives and property lost in them were significant. They were, for example, greater than those associated with the Branch Davidian tragedy in Waco in 1993. Clearly, for nineteenth-century Americans, the new church presented great challenges that disrupted the established order. A close scrutiny of the tensions that lead to the Mormon civil wars would reveal much about the conventions of American religious and political ideology (including the boundaries beyond which creativity and imagination were seen as deviant), about the relationship of American identity to the federal union and the limits of American nationalism, and about the extraordinary religious and social bond that inspired and enabled the Mormon effort to make the desert bloom.

Jotham Goodell's letters, originally published in *The Oregonian* in 1852 and republished here for the first time, offer considerable insight into the origins and character of the animosity in between Mormons and those they called "Gentiles" in early Deseret and Utah Territory. Goodell's observations, made at a time of uneasy truce, help us understand fundamental conflicts that came to a head in 1857 when President Buchanan sent one-third of the federal army marching toward Salt Lake City in what has ever since been known as the Utah War.

A perceptive if hostile observer, Jotham Goodell spent the winter of 1850–1851 living among the Mormons. His letters about that experience are polemic, not analytic. Convinced of his rectitude, Goodell does not soften his criticism of the Mormons with dispassionate prose. Presuming that most readers share his values and basic attitudes, Goodell offers neither apology nor defense of them. At the same time,

Goodell worries that his reports may strain his readers' credulity. He takes care to support his assertions about the evils of Mormonism by providing considerable detail about his personal experiences.

The mixture of self-revelation and eyewitness testimony in Goodell's letters makes them an extraordinary resource. Their expression of his values and prejudices illuminates the cultural environment that led the Mormons to leave the settled regions of the United States. Goodell is not a sympathetic reporter, but his harsh tones and sharp judgements make clear the obstacles that Mormons faced in gaining respect for their religious beliefs and social values. The letters' detailed observations provide an unusual perspective on the society that was emerging in the Salt Lake Valley; they are among the few reports of life in early Deseret not left by Mormons. Goodell's descriptions allow us to appreciate more fully the ways in which Mormon millennial enthusiasm and defensive attitudes toward Gentiles helped convert religious differences into social and political conflicts.

A Presbyterian minister leading an emigrant party to Oregon, Goodell decided in September 1850 that it was more prudent to settle temporarily in Utah than to risk crossing the mountains in the fall. He appears to have had no previous experience with Mormons, writing in his letter number 4 to *The Oregonian* that "all my knowledge of them was derived from the testimony of others." Goodell's ignorance did not deter him from judging the Mormons: "I knew indeed that they were deluded," but he claimed that he had always thought them "a persecuted people."

Goodell's experiences soon transformed his attitude. The practice and general acceptance of polygamy astonished and infuriated him. Suspicion of Mormon leaders as "imposters" and a condescending view of the general community as misinformed dupes gave way to contempt for all of Mormon society. Mormons no longer seemed a merely misguided group whose theology was unsound; they were, in his eyes, deeply immoral. No matter how Mormon religious ceremony and civil practice regulated the exercise of polygamy, it was, for Goodell, nothing more than an expression of sexual depravity and a surrender of individual and social restraint. From such corruption no good could come.

Goodell's religious vocation might have made him more sensitive to polygamy than most Americans. Consider, however, that the editor of *The Oregonian* began the serial publication of Goodell's essays not with his general apology for sharing the story of his experiences among the Mormons, but with letter number four, which contains his lengthy observations about the "spiritual wife" system. Whether Americans were outraged or titillated by Mormon polygamy, they were clearly intrigued by it.

Goodell's broad critique of Mormon society built upon his contempt for polygamy. His observations of Mormon legal, economic, and political relations continually return to the theme of expedient self-indulgence as the primary engine of Mormon behavior. Whether they are making cowardly deals with "savage" Indians, selling goods at inflated prices to hard-pressed travelers, using the courts to extort money from unfortunate outsiders, or seeking to obtain federal funds for irregular purposes, Goodell's Mormons are undisciplined, selfish, and unprincipled. When confronted with evidence of the sacrifices the pioneers have made to emigrate to Salt Lake or with their willingness to subordinate individual comfort to the needs of the larger community, Goodell sees not nobility but craven fear of the Danites, the Church's secret militia.

Goodell's depiction of a corrupt, authoritarian society reflects a broader theme in American popular culture of the ante-bellum years, the fear that powerful conspiracies were undermining American freedom. Critics castigated the Freemasons, Roman Catholics, the slave-power conspiracy, and the abolitionists as secret, self-serving organizations whose ambitions were incompatible with American democracy. In such an era, Mormon social cohesion was seen not as an inspiring expression of community but as a political, economic, and social threat.

As much as Goodell's letters tell us about the attitudes that made it difficult for many Americans to accept Mormonism, it would be a mistake to regard them as merely vindictive diatribes. Goodell was a careful observer who supported his critique by thorough descriptions of specific incidents. While his interpretations may at times be simplistic and are uniformly unsympathetic to the Mormons, his letters contain rich details about life in Deseret. Time and again they reveal the intriguing way in which the Mormons' millennial confidence, consciousness of past wrongs, and fear of outsiders shaped society at Great Salt Lake.

By 1850, when Goodell's overland party paused among the Saints, the pioneer settlers of Deseret could take justifiable pride in all they had accomplished since leaving Nauvoo in the winter of 1846. The efficient migration of more than 5,000 settlers during the summers of 1847 and 1848 had vindicated Brigham Young's leadership. By 1852 the number of

settlers would rise to 20,000. Following the construction of
Great Salt Lake City, outlying settlements were quickly established and parties dispatched to establish a colony in southern
California. The church, which had seemed on the verge of
disintegration following the assassination of Joseph Smith,
was convinced that it had emerged from a time of trial and
was entering a period in which the prophecies of *The Book
of Mormon* would be fulfilled. What Gentiles might have
seen as an exile, Mormons saw as an exodus. Though they
considered themselves persecuted, by 1850 the Mormons of
Deseret were a self-confident community looking forward to
their political as well as religious ascension.

Goodell's report of the celebrations that accompanied the
blessing of the sanctuary in Utah Valley reveal the community's optimism. He may have been scandalized that the
Mormons would hold a ball to mark a sacred occasion, but
we learn from him that the Saints partied enthusiastically
throughout the night. He cites the presence of numerous
infants as evidence of Mormon sexual lasciviousness, but
many sociologists would see a high birth rate and interest in
children as a sign of a community's health and confidence in
its future.

Mormon self-confidence could become arrogant and
immodest. Goodell reports conversations in which settlers
and officials expressed the conviction that the United States
would soon pass away. Mormon courts refused to be bound
by Anglo-American precedents, as judges and prosecutors
proclaimed the right to rely upon "higher laws." Emboldened
by the success of their migration, the Mormons were

prepared to create not only a new settlement but also a new polity with its own jurisprudence.

Despite its positive outlook, the Mormon community of Deseret cultivated the memory of past injuries. As Goodell observes, the Saints held Missourians in particular contempt. Public speakers decried them as "mobocrats" and reminded their audiences of the violence they had inflicted upon the Mormons. The Saints were also skeptical of federal officials and politicians in general. They blamed them, as a class, for failing to protect church members in either Missouri or Illinois. Past experience left the Mormons wary of outsiders in general and highly sensitive to criticism. They were especially suspicious whenever Gentiles met together or formed associations. Goodell observes how quickly Mormon acquaintances forgot the assistance he had rendered them when they learned that he was serving as secretary for the "emigrant community."

Mormon self-confidence did not lead them either to forgive past enemies or to trust unfamiliar people. It apparently contributed to a belief that retribution for their past suffering was not only just but imminent. Sometimes this attitude was expressed in vague, hypothetical terms about what might happen to a federal appointee so bold as to attempt to assume office in Utah. Other times it took the form of direct threats like the ones Goodell reports he received. Most often, however, the combination of millennial zeal and anger over past injustice appeared in the arbitrary and capricious use of power to monitor and harass travelers. Whether it was forcing emigrants to pay property taxes the same day they were assessed, compelling emigrants acquitted in court to nonetheless pay costs, insisting that an entire wagon party travel seventy miles in the midst of winter to stand trial for allegedly harboring a fugitive, or sending an "agent provocateur" to push the emigrants into foolish, illegal behavior, the Mormon authorities seemed willing to make disproportionate use of their power for little reason other than that they could.

Goodell's critique of Mormon religion led him to insist that there could be no reliance placed upon the civil institutions that the Mormons had created in Utah. In similar fashion, Mormon mistrust of Gentiles made them wary of any institutions they did not control. Brigham Young could defend Mormon patriotism by citing the service of five hundred Mormons during the Mexican War, but neither he nor the Mormon community at large believed that the federal government would treat them honorably. Protected by distance and terrain, Young and his people felt justified in resisting any effort to compel their subservience to federal norms.

Most historical accounts of early Utah Territory blame grasping, inept federal officials for creating the crisis that eventually led to the Utah War. President Fillmore's decision to appoint Lemuel Brandebury, Perry Brocchus, Broughton Harris, and Henry Day to territorial office was not wise, for the four men were principally interested in their own political careers. They were ill prepared to preside over one of the most volatile cultural and political fault lines in the country, but Goodell's letters make clear that the Mormons were ready to resist any appointments not drawn from their own ranks. The treatment the federal officers received in Utah was not a response to their personal faults. Their conduct exacerbated the crisis, but it is unfair to see them as the cause.

Having spent four years building a community that could isolate itself from the institutions and authority of the United States, the Mormons of Deseret were not prepared to surrender lightly their autonomy. It would take five years for the initial crisis to come to a head and an additional forty years before the Mormons and the country could agree upon Utah's admission as a state. The letters of Jotham Goodell help explain the enormous gulf that both sides had to bridge.

GEORGE MILES
New Haven, Connecticut

ACKNOWLEDGMENTS

I became interested in the 1852 letters of Jotham W. Goodell while conducting research for a paper on the impact of the Gold Rush on early Mormon settlements in the American West. Most of the California-bound emigrants who passed through Salt Lake Valley during the massive population shift to the West that began in 1849 commented favorably about the religious community Brigham Young and his followers established in 1847. But many of those who remained in Utah over the winter of 1850–1851 afterward expressed exactly opposite opinions. Their sharply negative reaction stands in surprising contrast to the generally positive impressions of emigrants who stayed only a few days in these raw frontier settlements before pushing on.

Among the most outspoken of such sojourners was Jotham Goodell. Unlike most overland emigrants of 1850, he was taking his family to Oregon to make a new home, not rushing to seek a fortune in California. His nine letters, published in 1852 by *The Oregonian* newspaper at Portland, open an important window on the nature of the theocratic society that existed at that time in the Great Basin. They also reflect the militant posture of the young millennial movement toward the American republic during the period of transition from the State of Deseret, an independent nation-state created in 1849 by Brigham Young, to a territory of the United States in 1850 with the unasked-for name of Utah.

In preparing Goodell's letters for publication, I have benefited from the kindness and assistance of many longstanding associates and some esteemed new friends, a few of whom I would like to mention with appreciation.

To Margene Goodell of Amherst, Ohio, and Naomi B. Baker of Delevan, New York, I am especially indebted. They have generously shared their abundant knowledge of Goodell family history and resources in their possession, including letters, pictures, and other information. Teresa Goodell of Beaverton, Oregon, and Helen Goodell and Sharon Smith of Puyallup and Auburn, Washington, have also made helpful contributions to the final manuscript. The interest of these friends in Goodell family history and their concern to preserve it has truly made this work possible.

John and Vanessa Call of Derby, Kansas; Addie Rickey of Salem, Oregon; and Dr. Jim Tompkins of Beavercreek, Oregon, have contributed biographical information, journals, and pictures of Oregon and California pioneers whose stories validate Goodell's accounts. Their help is greatly appreciated. To Oregon Trail authority Arlie H. Holt and historian Robert Marsh of Dallas, Oregon, I am grateful for giving so freely of their time and knowledge to provide information about Goodell's activities in Oregon from 1851 to 1853.

Above all, I acknowledge with profound appreciation the constant support of Will Bagley, editor of the major new Arthur H. Clark Company series, "Kingdom in the West: The Mormons and the American Frontier," who read the manuscript, made many useful suggestions, and discovered several journals of great value. Copyeditor Dawn Corrigan's attention to detail was remarkable. I also wish to thank Gregory C. Thompson, Judith F. Jarrow, Floyd A. O'Neil, and Peter H. DeLafosse for their encouragement and advice.

Finally may I never take for granted the kindness and service of the professional archivists and librarians at the Utah State Historical Society; J. Willard Marriott Library, University of Utah; Merrill Library, Utah State University; Stewart Library, Weber State University; Harold B. Lee Library, Brigham Young University; Utah State Archives; Ohio Historical Society; California State Library; Sacramento City Archives; Oregon State Historical Society; and the Washington State Historical Society.

EDITORIAL NOTE

The Jotham Goodell letters in this volume have been literally transcribed from the pages of *The Oregonian* from April to June 1852 using the original spelling and grammar. Editorial additions are presented in square brackets, [thusly]. Words such as "defence" and "connexion" whose spelling differs from current usage are only noted by "sic" on the first occurrence.

This volume contains three appendixes presenting documents mentioned in or closely related to Goodell's letters. Appendix A is a complete republication of Millard Fillmore's

January 1852 report to Congress, "The Condition of Affairs in the Territory of Utah." Appendixes B and C contain letters from emigrants who also spent the winter of 1850–1851 as uncomfortable guests of the Mormon Kingdom.

To my knowledge, none of these documents has appeared in print since their original publication.

DAVID L. BIGLER
Roseville, California

INTRODUCTION

On 7 June 1851 *The Oregonian* newspaper at Portland announced the arrival of the first emigrant party that year, "commanded by Capt. Goodell." The story continued: "There are several families, among which are 16 females.[1] They left Salt Lake on the 28th of March, and arrived at the Dalles, May 29, making the journey in sixty-two days. The health of the company has been good during the journey. They were attacked by the Indians on Snake River, but lost none of their party. The Indians kept up a fire across the river upon them for two hours, which the emigrants returned, killing several Indians during the fight.

---

1. In a letter to the *Oregon City Spectator*, published on 12 June 1851, Jotham Goodell said his train from Utah consisted of one hundred five members, forty-eight men, nineteen women, and the rest children. See Clark, *My Goodell Family in America, 1634–1978*, copy courtesy of Margene Goodell of Amherst, Ohio, 13, 14.

1

"The Mormons at Salt Lake are represented as a very immoral and desperate set of men. They practice polygamy to a great extent. Some of their prophets are represented as having as many as sixty wives; all take unto themselves as many as may please their fancy, and their means will enable them to support. The above information was derived from several of the party who appear highly intelligent and respectable."[2]

For this news to spread did not take long. In less than three weeks it reached California where *The Daily Union* at Sacramento reported: "The first of the emigration across the plains recently arrived in Portland: they tell a sad tale of their sufferings by the way, they wintered at Great Salt Lake, where the Mormons imposed upon them, put on the charges heavily and treated them harshly."[3]

For Jotham and "Annie" Goodell the announcement ended a 2,500-mile journey that saw them and their children spend the winter of 1850–1851 camped in tent and wagons on the northern fringe of the new Mormon settlements in Salt Lake Valley. But it was not the end of the story for the captain of the year's first emigrant company to reach Oregon. In nine highly detailed letters to *The Oregonian,* published from 10 April to 26 June 1852, he scathingly described the Great Basin theocratic society and protested the persecution his family and other emigrants to Oregon and California had suffered that winter at the hands of Mormon authorities.

---

2. *The Oregonian,* Portland, Oregon Territory, Saturday, 7 June 1851, Vol. 1, No. 27, 2.

3. *The Daily Union,* Sacramento, 26 June 1851, Vol. 1, No. 86, 2/3.

Rev. Jotham Weeks Goodell
was an 1850 overland pioneer and a Presbyterian minister in
Washington Territory. — *Courtesy Naomi B. Baker.*

Goodell was motivated to write his series by the publication early in 1852 of reports and correspondence on the earliest fight between Mormon leaders and so-called "Gentile" officials of the newly created Utah Territory that broke out during the summer of 1851.[4] His accounts throw new light on a controversy that historians usually blame on the incompetence or arrogance of federal bureaucrats. They are also important in understanding Utah's theocratic society, which existed in its purest state prior to 1859, and later sources of conflict between a defiant territory and the United States. They must be considered in any evaluation of the reasons that President Buchanan in 1857 ordered an American army to Utah to assert federal authority.[5]

The author of these letters, Jotham Weeks Goodell, was born at Templeton, Massachusetts, on 23 April 1809, the eleventh and youngest child of William and Phebe Newton Goodell. He was a direct descendant of Robert and Catherine Kilham Goodell of Suffolk, England, who arrived at Salem in 1634 on the ship *Elizabeth*.[6] He was also a cousin of early northwest mountain man and trail guide, Timothy Goodale, who gave his name to the Oregon Trail's Jeffrey/Goodale Cutoff between Fort Hall and Fort Boise in present Idaho.[7]

---

4. These are contained in President Millard Fillmore's report to Congress on 9 January 1852, "Information in reference to the condition of affairs in the Territory of Utah," House Exec. Doc. 25 (32-1), 1852, referred to hereafter as House Exec. Doc. 25, Appendix A. Also see "Utah Territory," *Congressional Globe* (32-1), 9 January 1852, Vol. 100, App. 84–93.

5. For the story of this conflict, see Bigler, *Forgotten Kingdom: The Mormon Theocracy in the American West, 1847–1896.*

6. Williams, *A Genealogy of the Descendants of Robert Goodale/Goodell of Salem, Mass.*

Goodell was known to be "a well-educated man, a fluent and eloquent speaker; often called on to give orations and speeches."[8] Since his older brothers had attended Phillips Academy, Dartmouth College, or Andover Theological Seminary, he may have received at least some education at one of these institutions.[9] At age eighteen he moved to Ontario, Canada, opposite Niagara Falls, New York. There he married Anna Glenning Bacheler and became a minister and a founder of the Niagara Presbyterian Church of Canada. The couple resided at Ancaster and Beamsville, where five of their eleven children were born.

A deeply religious man, Goodell wrote his children's names and birth dates in the family Bible with this prayer: "Believing in a covenant keeping God these children have been solemnly consecrated to God by placing upon them the *token* of God's covenant mercy. O thou God of Abraham; who keepest Covenant with Thy people forever; Pardon the sins of Thy servant and hand maid, & grant that these *Thy* children, may have grace, to lay hold of the covenant of *Thy*

---

7. Timothy Goodale had his own run-in with the Mormons in July 1847 when Sgt. Thomas Williams and a party of Mormon Battalion soldiers, who had joined Brigham Young's pioneer company on Green River, seized Goodale's horse at Fort Bridger. Williams said he took the horse because one of the mountaineer's men had stolen a battalion mule at Pueblo, but Young made him return the animal "in the neatest, quietest, prettiest way possible; for which Goodale expressed his thankfulness to 'Captain Young'," wrote Thomas Bullock. See Bagley, ed., *The Pioneer Camp of the Saints: The 1846 and 1847 Mormon Trail Journals of Thomas Bullock*, 205, 221–22. For more on Goodale, see Harvey L. Carter's biographical sketch in Hafen, *The Mountain Men and the Fur Trade of the Far West*, 7:147–53.

8. Hargrave, *Goodale–Goodell Forebears*, 91.

9. Margene Goodell to David Bigler, 1 March 1999.

mercy for themselves and their children, and their children's children for a thousand generations!"[10]

Goodell also possessed a strong sense of loyalty to the young American republic. According to family tradition, he and his family had to leave Canada because he favored a move to join that part of Ontario to the United States. William L. Goodell, a grandson, said Elder Goodell "ran up the flags with the American flag above the British flag. This seemed to have angered the Canadians and they were going to lynch him so he and the family took refuge in a church and then rowed across Lake Erie to reach the American side." The descendant, a retired history teacher now deceased, told a relative to take all this "with a grain of salt,"[11] but other evidence tends to confirm the story, which probably survived because it reflected how Goodell felt about his native land.[12]

From Canada, Jotham Goodell and his family moved in 1837 to northern Ohio where they settled in Erie County on the shore of Lake Erie. There he served as second minister of the First Congregational Church in Florence Township, which was organized that year as a Presbyterian Church. In 1843 he served as a Congregational Church pastor in Medina County, south of Cleveland, where he wrote and published a forty-seven-page pamphlet, *The nature, design and mode of baptism, or Campbellism exposed.*[13] That December, he preached the dedication sermon for the First Congregational

---

10. Clark, *My Goodell Family in America, 1634–1978,* 13.
11. Portion of a letter from William L. Goodell of Puyallup, Washington, to Margene Goodell, undated.
12. Clark, *My Goodell Family in America, 1634–1978,* 12.

Church at Vermilion, Ohio, where he and his family lived until they moved west.[14]

Goodell's own reasons for going to Oregon may be best expressed in a letter he wrote in 1852 to his future daughter-in-law, Anna Maria Pelton, who remained in Ohio with his oldest son, William Bird. The couple moved to Washington Territory in 1854.[15] Referring to his son, Goodell wrote: "I know it would be vastly to his advantage, so far as temporal matters are concerned, to come to Oregon. Here with prudence, industry and economy he might in a short time, with God's blessing, become rich, while in Ohio, with no means to begin with, it will require a hard and long struggle."[16] That Goodell chose at the flood tide of the Gold Rush to go to Oregon, rather than California, indicates that he valued land as a source of wealth more than gold.

In 1850 Jotham, now forty-one, and Annie Goodell gathered seven of their ten living children—Mary Weeks, a

---

13. Alexander Campbell was the founder of the primitive gospel movement known as Disciples of Christ, which rejected other denominations and believed in a restored gospel and the imminent return of Christ. Many early Mormons, including Parley P. Pratt and Sidney Rigdon, had been Campbellite ministers.

14. Allen T. Price, Temporary Assistant Librarian, The Ohio Historical Society, Columbus, to William L. Goodell, 11 April 1968. Sources listed are Aldrich, *History of Erie County, Ohio* (1889), 452; The Ohio Historical Society Library; and H. L. Peeke, *The Centennial History of Erie County, O.* [1925], 630. The editor is also indebted to Teresa Tarnowski Goodell of Beaverton, Oregon, for other information about this period.

15. See Anna Maria Godell [sic] and Elizabeth Austin, "The Vermillion Wagon Train Diaries, 1854," in Holmes, *Covered Wagon Women: Diaries & Letters from the Western Trails, 1840–1890,* 7:78–130.

16. Jotham W. Goodell to Maria Pelton, 15 June 1852, letter in possession of Margene Goodell, Amherst, Ohio.

twin, eighteen; Melancthon Zwingle, fourteen; Emeline
Davis, twelve; Nathan Edward, ten; Henry Martin, seven;
Charlotte Elizabeth, four; and Jotham, Jr., barely one—and
headed for Oregon. They were accompanied by Holden A.
Judson, husband of their other twin daughter, Phoebe
Newton, who remained in Ohio, as did their oldest son,
William Bird. Another child, Joel Brigham Goodell Baker,
sixteen, lived with Jotham Goodell's sister, Phoebe, and her
husband, Jonas Baker, who resided in Lockport, New York.

If the Goodells traveled by wagon to the head of the
Oregon Trail on the Missouri River it would explain their
relatively late arrival in Utah. But it is probable that the only
segment of this journey they did not cover by water or rail was
some twenty miles from their home at Vermilion, Ohio, to
Sandusky on Lake Erie. It would have shortened their travel
time by a month or more to take a steamboat from this port
to Detroit, then another through the Straits of Mackinac to
Chicago. Here the Illinois-Michigan Canal connected to
steamboats on the Illinois and Mississippi rivers, which sailed
from St. Louis up the Missouri River to Independence and
St. Joseph, Missouri, and Council Bluffs, Iowa.[17]

A more costly alternative would have been to board the
Mad River and Lake Erie Railroad at Sandusky and travel by
rail to Cincinnati, transferring at Xenia, Ohio, to the Little
Miami Railroad for the final leg of the trip. At Cincinnati, a
major Ohio River port, steamboats offered transportation to
the four main jumping off places of the Oregon Trail along

---

17. By this route forty-niner William Swain went from Sandusky to
Independence in three weeks. See Holliday, *The World Rushed In: The
California Gold Rush Experience*, 64–79.

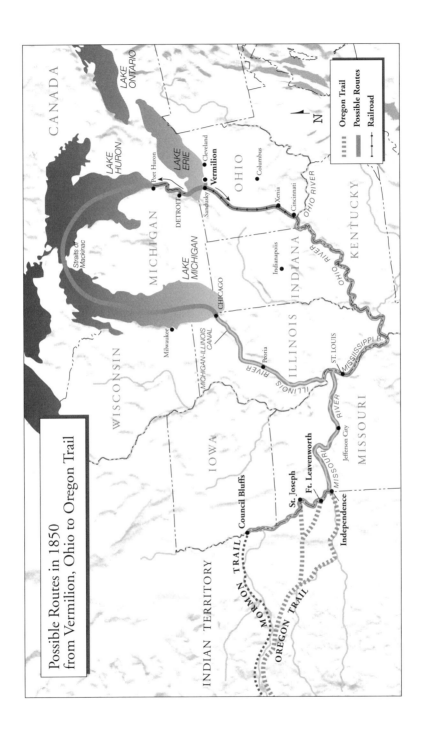

Possible Routes in 1850
from Vermilion, Ohio to Oregon Trail

the Missouri River, where they could purchase oxen, wagons, and supplies before heading west in late May or early June.[18]

Either way, three months and a thousand miles by ox team found them in present western Wyoming, still far short of their destination, where Goodell probably decided it would be safer to spend the winter in Mormon settlements than attempt a Blue Mountains crossing that season. Rather than take Sublette's Cutoff, near today's Farson, and go due west to Bear River and meet the Oregon Trail to Fort Hall, he chose instead to follow the original road to Fort Bridger. There the family took the Mormon Trail to reach Salt Lake Valley in September with two wagons, four yoke of oxen, and four milk cows. They came near the end of an emigration season that witnessed record numbers pass through the new "free and independent" State of Deseret.[19]

In 1850 from fifteen to seventeen thousand Gold Rush emigrants stopped at the "Mormon halfway house," as one

---

18. As the railroad pushed west more migrating Americans covered portions of this journey by rail. In 1853 Goodell's daughter Phoebe and son-in-law Holden Judson rode the train to Cincinnati and took steamboats down the Ohio and up the Mississippi and Missouri rivers. Only a year later, his son, William and his wife, Anna Maria, took a steamer from Sandusky to Detroit and went from there by rail all the way to Alton, Illinois, on the Mississippi River, opposite St. Louis.

19. The word "Deseret" from *The Book of Mormon* means "honey bee" and complements the communal symbol of the Beehive on today's Utah flag and seal. The State of Deseret, a synonym for the theocratic Kingdom of God, was established in 1849 and lasted in visible form until President Millard Fillmore on 9 September 1850 signed legislation that created Utah Territory. After that, it existed as an invisible system of government that operated behind the scenes until 1896 when Utah became a state. During the Civil War it reappeared for eight years to function as a "ghost government" in parallel with territorial rule until 1870. See Morgan, *The State of Deseret*, 91–119.

called it, to rest and make ready to go on to California, outnumbering by about seven times that year's Mormon emigration. Most were energetic, robust young males in a hurry, hell-bent to reach the gold fields and "see the elephant."[20] In contrast, the Goodells and about one hundred of the other emigrants that wintered in Utah that year were headed for Oregon with their families to make new homes. Unlike gold seekers, they could not choose to take the all-season southern trail to Los Angeles if an extended stopover in the Great Basin settlements did not suit them. And not all would find the communal religious society to their liking.

Only three years before, after years of conflict in Missouri and Illinois, the people of Israel in the Last Days, better known as the Latter-day Saints or Mormons, had moved to the Great Basin of North America, then in Mexico, to establish the Kingdom of God as an earthly state. Governed by God through inspired men, its followers believed, the new theocracy was destined during its founders' days on earth to sweep to world dominion. Said its leader, Brigham Young: "We will roll on the Kingdom of our God, gather out the seed of Abraham, build the cities and temples of Zion, and establish the Kingdom of God to bear rule over all the earth."[21]

Those who undertook this visionary endeavor were unlike any other emigrants in America's move west to California or Oregon. Faith and destiny drove them, not a quest for homesteads or gold. Like their leaders, most were young. The average age of the eight highest officials in the first 1847

---

20. A popular expression that roughly meant, "to see it all."
21. Brigham Young, 8 July 1855, *Journal of Discourses*, 2:317.

Mormon pioneer company, all apostles of the Church of Jesus Christ of Latter-day Saints, was just under thirty-nine. Revolutions are made by the young, and their crusade, "to reduce all nations and creeds to one political and religious standard," was a revolutionary purpose.[22]

Yet even as they surveyed their new millennial city, events elsewhere in 1847 would overtake and forever change their dream to establish God's Kingdom, prior to Christ's imminent return. An American army was moving that summer against Mexico City. And in Upper California, Swiss entrepreneur John A. Sutter and his partner, James Marshall, began to build a sawmill on the American River's South Fork, east of present Sacramento. On 24 January 1848, workmen turned the river into the new mill to test the flow of water on the wheel. That night, Henry W. Bigler, one of six Mormon Battalion veterans hired to work on the mill, wrote the words that would set off a population shift west: "This day some kind of mettle was found in the tail race that looks like goald."[23]

Less than two weeks later, Mexico on 2 February under the Treaty of Guadalupe Hidalgo surrendered to the United States the entire Southwest. The second largest land acquisition in American history encompassed all of five present

---

22. *Proclamation of the Twelve Apostles of the Church of Jesus Christ of Latter-day Saints to All the Kings of the World, to the President of the United States of America; to the Governors of the Several States, and to the Rulers and People of All Nations.*

23. Paul, *The California Gold Discovery: Sources, Documents, Accounts and Memoirs Relating to the Discovery of Gold at Sutter's Mill*, 33.

states, Utah, California, Nevada, Arizona and New Mexico, and large parts of Wyoming and Colorado.

So it happened that less than one year after its first pioneer company landed in Salt Lake Valley, latter-day Israel was right back in the United States, and the ramparts of its new Kingdom were about to be overrun by a horde of curious outsiders rushing to the placer diggings along the Sierra Nevada. After weeks on the trail, these overlanders were usually awestruck by their first glimpse of the city the Mormons had built in only two or three years. "For a moment not a word came from a single member of the company," said an Ohioan, "all were speechless at the grand scenery before us."[24] Most spent only a few days to rest and resupply before rolling on and took with them favorable impressions of their short visit. For Ansel McCall, the memory of his first meal with a Mormon family would live forever. It was a "sumptuous feast of new potatoes, green peas, bread and butter with rich, sweet milk," he said.[25] As forty-niner James Hutchings got ready to go, he lamented, "Tomorrow we leave civilization, pretty girls, and pleasant memories."[26]

The longer some remained, however, the more their attitudes turned against their Mormon hosts. And many of those who stayed over the winter of 1850–1851, numbering as many as a thousand, afterward protested bitterly the alleged

24. From Lake Erie to the Pacific: An Overland Trip in 1850–51, quoted in Madsen, *Gold Rush Sojourners*, 34.

25. McCall, *The Great California Trail in 1849*, 57.

26. Sargent, *Seeking the Elephant, 1849: James Mason Hutchings' Journal of His Overland Trek to California*, 156.

injustices they suffered in the faith's new Great Basin
settlements.

One of this number was Jotham Goodell, who camped
near Farr's settlement on the north side of Ogden River, near
the mouth of the canyon, about forty miles north of Great
Salt Lake City. Thirty-three-year-old Lorin Freeman Farr, a
Vermont native, had selected the location earlier that year
because it was an ideal place to build water-driven lumber and
grist mills. When Goodell arrived, the settlement was a single
row of cabins inhabited by several families. After Indian
hostilities that fall, settlers added rows of houses to create a
three-sided fort, enclosing some five acres, with the open side
facing Mill Creek. Here as an ordained minister, on 13
December 1850 Goodell married his daughter Mary Weeks,
by now nineteen, to Nathan Melory of Pennsylvania, twenty-
five, another wintering emigrant.

Some three miles from Farr's settlement was a larger
Mormon colony on Weber River, named Brownsville after its
founder, James Brown, a former Mormon Battalion captain
during the War with Mexico.[27] Before spring, Goodell and
about one hundred other emigrants to Oregon and California
would move a dozen miles north to Willow Creek, now at

---

27. President James Polk in 1846 authorized the enlistment of a battalion of
five hundred Mormons during the War with Mexico to assist the faith's western
migration. Brown established the first Mormon settlement on the Weber River
in November 1847 when he purchased Fort Buenaventura from mountain man
Miles Goodyear for $1,950 from the mustering-out pay he had collected for
discharged battalion veterans who had served at Pueblo. Later moved to higher
ground, Brownsville with Farr's settlement would come within the limits of
Ogden City, incorporated in February 1851.

Willard, Utah, to place as much distance between themselves and their Mormon neighbors as they could.

Goodell's account of this period, while angrily resentful, is significant because it identifies the earliest sources of controversy between Mormon theocracy in the West and other Americans. Among others, these included arbitrary court actions, disloyalty to the United States, denial of free speech, lack of political freedom, control of markets, and discriminatory taxation. Common to many causes of conflict between radically different forms of government was the issue of law, which many emigrants described as "informal, illegal, and unjust."[28] The system of justice exercised in Utah during this period appeared to offer some ground for this complaint.

The "free and independent" State of Deseret, established by Mormon settlers in 1849, provided that judges of its courts would be named by the legislature or chosen by election.[29] The same generally applied in Utah Territory, created by Congress in 1850, except that the territorial organic act required the president to appoint justices of the three federal district courts. These men were usually not Mormons.[30]

---

28. Slater, *Fruits of Mormonism, or A Fair and Candid Statement of Facts Illustrative of Mormon Principles, Mormon Policy, and Mormon Character, by More than Forty Eye-Witnesses*, 12.

29. See Morgan, *The State of Deseret*, 121–27.

30. See "An Act to Establish a Territorial Government for Utah," *The Statutes at Large and Treaties of the United States of America from December 1, 1845, to March 3, 1851*, Vol. 9, 453–58. The organic act is also published in *Acts, Resolutions and Memorials, passed at the Several Annual Sessions of the Legislative Assembly of the Territory of Utah, from 1851 to 1870 Inclusive*, 26–28.

On its face, the system appeared eminently democratic, but it rested on elections that were either never held or in which voters could not cast their ballots in secret. Hosea Stout became a legislator in 1849 "by what process," he wrote, "I know not."[31] Utah lawmakers later ruled that laws not approved by themselves and the governor could not be "read, argued, cited or adopted" in any court. They further directed that "no report, decision, or doings of any court" could be "read, argued, cited or adopted as precedent in any trial."[32] These laws removed two traditional cornerstones of American justice—legal precedence and common law. Finally, Mormon legislators ignored the intent of Congress and vested original criminal and civil jurisdiction in the probate (county) courts, ruled by Mormon judges, which effectively left appointed federal justices with empty courtrooms. In a society where perfect justice is bestowed by inspiration, one does not place one's trust in the rulings of men.

In most cases, Mormon judges or justices of the peace, usually local church leaders, settled disputes between quarrelsome emigrants with common sense and good judgment. But it was hardly any wonder that many travelers found the exercise of law by inspiration "informal, illegal and unjust."[33] Even before his series of letters appeared, Goodell expressed his contempt for theocratic law, to which he had been

31. Brooks, ed., *On the Mormon Frontier: The Diary of Hosea Stout, 1844–1861,* 2:358.

32. *Acts, Resolutions and Memorials, Passed at the Several Annual Sessions of the Legislative Assembly of the Territory of Utah, from 1851 to 1870 Inclusive,* 32.

33. Slater, *Fruits of Mormonism,* 12.

exposed more than most emigrants. In a letter to *The Oregonian* soon after his arrival in Portland, he wrote:

> To the Editor of the Oregonian—
>
> Sir: Perhaps some of your readers may be interested to know the manner in which the Mormons do business in their Courts of Justice. I therefore send you the following, as being the form of an Oath administered to a Jury in the County Court of Weber County, State of Deseret, by the Clerk of the Court, Louis [Lorin] Farr, Esq., a prominent member of the Latter Day Saints.[34] The writer was present when the Oath was administered—and was interested in the suit about to be tried, and vouches for the truth of the statement he makes in relation to it. There are other persons in this Territory, who were present at the same Court, who will at once recognize the oath as there administered.
>
> The jury were standing, each holding up his right hand, the Clerk also holding up his, with his eyes resting on the floor, and pausing at each part of the sentence: You do each of you in the presence of these witnesses, solemnly swear, that what you shall say to this Court concerning the case wherein A.B. is plaintiff and C.B. is defendant, shall be in accordance to the best of your knowledge, information, understanding and belief, in the name of Jesus Christ. I believe that is all. Amen!
>
> This was the oath verbatim. And this was the Court which robbed me of $70—not by any verdict rendered against me in said Court, for in three distinct trials the jury decided in my favor; rendering a verdict of "no cause of action," and yet my property was attached to pay the costs.[35]

---

34. This was Lorin Freeman Farr, who came to Utah in 1847 and became first president of the Weber Stake of Zion. In 1851 he became Ogden's first mayor, an office he held for over twenty years; today's town of Farr West, Utah, is named for him.

Goodell may have made himself the target of what he considered to be arbitrary lawsuits and discriminatory taxation. He agreed at a supposedly secret meeting of emigrants to serve as chairman of a committee to draw up a memorial to Congress on the injustices they had suffered in Utah Territory. If so, he paid a heavy price for accepting this obligation. Not a wealthy man to begin with, he would become so impoverished by spring that he was unable to move his family without assistance from fellow emigrants. Eloquently he expressed his indignation: "Were Brigham Young to come in person and tender back the money he robbed us of, there is not a man among us but would exclaim: *'Your money perish with you! In our distress and anguish of soul, you robbed us of our all, and exposed our wives and little ones to the danger of perishing with famine, amid the wastes of the desert!* Never, *never,* NEVER!'"[36]

Even before his letters appeared, others had protested what happened that winter. In 1851, one hundred fifteen emigrants to California called on Congress to replace Utah's new territorial government with military rule. They looked to Nelson Slater, a member of Goodell's committee, to expose the injuries they had endured in the Mormon theocracy. The forty-five-year-old New York seminary teacher and his wife, Emily, who wintered in Salt Lake Valley with their three children, ages fourteen, twelve, and nine, carried out this assignment in even greater detail.

---

35. *The Oregonian,* Portland, Oregon Territory, 26 July 1851, Vol. 1, No. 34, 1.

36. Ibid., 12 June 1852, Vol. 2, No. 28, 1.

Published at Coloma, site of Sutter's Mill and the 1848 California gold discovery, Slater's book compiled the personal accounts of dozens of outraged emigrants. In calling for the imposition of military rule in Utah, they endorsed ten resolutions charging that the court system was "a mockery"; that freedom of speech was "greatly abridged"; that "treasonable" opinions were often expressed against the U.S. government; and that "the policy of mormonism as a system, is oppressive, unjust, and unworthy of confidence."[37]

These and other allegations find outspoken affirmation in the series of letters presented here for the first time since it was published in 1852. Not for nearly a year after arriving in Oregon was the author in a position to write them. Then events in Utah, which took place shortly after he left, prompted Jotham Weeks Goodell to carry out the commitment that he had made to fellow emigrants to Oregon and California during the winter of 1850–1851.

---

37. Slater, *Fruits of Mormonism*. A graduate of New York's Union College and Auburn Theological Seminary, Slater later became school superintendent for Sacramento County. His book was the first copyrighted in California.

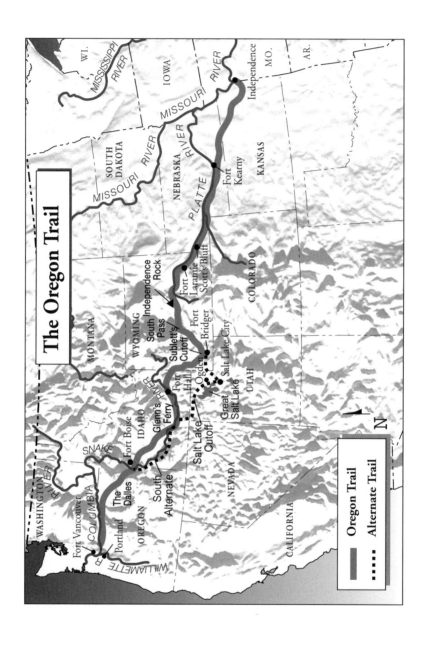

LETTER 1

"Credulity Is Staggered"

The first of Jotham Goodell's nine letters on Mormon
society in the Great Basin appeared in *The Oregonian* at
Portland soon after the publication of reports and correspondence on the 1851 clash between the American republic and
its theocratic territory, the earliest of many to come over the
next forty years.[1] Goodell sought to discredit Mormon ver-
sions of the fight and support charges by the first of many
federal officials who took flight from Utah during that period
out of fear, frustration, or a mixture of such emotions.

The seeds of the controversy had been planted the year
before. In September 1850, the month the Goodells arrived
in Salt Lake Valley, Congress ignored Mormon petitions for
entry into the Union as the State of Deseret and created
instead a territory with the unwanted name of Utah.[2] To allay

---

1. These are compiled in House Exec. Doc. 25, which is presented in full as
Appendix A.

the disappointment of its citizens, President Millard Fillmore appointed Brigham Young to a four-year term as first governor. But three of the six other appointees to territorial offices came from the outside and were not members of the new territory's dominant faith.[3]

One who did not belong was twenty-seven-year-old Broughton D. Harris from Vermont, the new territorial secretary, who came in July 1851 with $24,000 in federal gold to pay the expenses of the legislature. He also expected to certify the census, required by law to apportion representatives, as well as the elections that year. To his surprise he found that the census had already been conducted before he arrived. Harris considered the count "so false and exaggerated that a correct census would have betrayed the fraud."[4] And he viewed the elections as no more than "a burlesque upon the order and decorum required by the organic act."[5] So he defied Brigham Young's repeated attempts to lay hands on the federal gold and stoutly refused to turn it over.

Another non-Mormon, Chief Justice Lemuel G. Brandebury from Pennsylvania, came early that summer to

---

2. Some members of Congress thought *The Book of Mormon* name Deseret sounded too much like "desert."

3. Besides Young, other Mormon appointees were forty-nine-year-old Vermont native Zerubbabel Snow, an older brother of Mormon apostle Erastus Snow, associate justice; Missourian Seth M. Blair, a former Texas ranger, age thirty-one, U.S. attorney; and thirty-five-year-old Joseph L. Heywood from Massachusetts, U.S. marshal.

4. The source of this charge may have been the counting of emigrants to inflate the population and qualify for statehood. One emigrant said that the Mormons "followed the emigrants 100 miles to take the census." Unruh, *The Plains Across: The Overland Emigrants and the Trans-Mississippi West, 1840–60*, 325.

swear in Young as governor, but discovered on his arrival that the attorney general of the State of Deseret, Daniel H. Wells, had already performed that necessary ceremony. Soon after, Brandebury was outraged at the 24 July 1851 Pioneer Day celebration in Great Salt Lake when Governor Young said, among other seditious-sounding remarks, "[President] Zachary Taylor is dead and gone to hell, and I am glad of it!"[6]

Harris and Brandebury both took offense at the charge, also leveled at the July 24th event, that the call for Mormon volunteers during the Mexican War was part of a plot by government to exterminate the young faith as it began its move west into the wilderness. Although Utah's first delegate to Congress, John M. Bernhisel, who was also present at the observance, appeared to deny their claim, there can be little doubt that the federal officials accurately reported the patently false charge or that the speaker was echoing the views of Brigham Young.[7]

The third newcomer, Associate Justice Perry E. Brocchus of Alabama, was last to arrive and hardly proved to be a peacemaking influence. When he tried to "correct erroneous

---

5. Secretary Harris listed seven violations of election procedures to justify his refusal to pay legislative costs. See House Exec. Doc. 25, Appendix A, page 189. Oddly not mentioned in these irregularities was that all candidates in the 1851 elections, except one, were elected unanimously, 1,259 to 0. A single ballot, probably cast by mistake, spoiled this otherwise perfect record. See Jack, "Utah Territorial Politics: 1847–1876."

6. See Exec. Doc. 25, Appendix A, page 155.

7. For other examples of the false charge involving the Mormon Battalion enlistment, see Long, *Report of the First General Festival of the Renowned Mormon Battalion, which came off on Tuesday and Wednesday, Feb. 6 and 7, 1855, in the social hall, G.S.L. City, U.T.*, 10–19, and Tyler, *A Concise History of the Mormon Battalion in the Mexican War, 1846–47,* 348–55.

opinions in regard to the Government," he only appeared to impugn the patriotism of the Mormon congregation, some three thousand strong. At this imagined insult, emotions erupted and Brigham Young reportedly warned, no doubt referring to Brocchus, "some persons might get their hair pulled or *their throats cut.*"8

Now badly shaken, the three appointees, plus Indian Agent Henry Day, took flight back to the states to tell the president that the inhabitants of the territory were disloyal to the United States and did not appreciate the "blessings of the present form of government established for them."9 To the dismay of Governor Young, Harris returned the gold to the U.S. Treasury office at St. Louis.

Hardly novices when it came to public controversies, Mormon leaders fired back. Governor Young told the president that if the "run-away" officers had discharged their duties faithfully, "all would have been well." The combative mayor of Great Salt Lake City, Jedediah M. Grant, a possessor of formidable verbal skills, rushed to the nation's capital to assist Utah's erudite delegate to Congress, fifty-three-year-old Pennsylvanian John M. Bernhisel, in counterattacking the offending officials.10 Typical of most fights involving Mormons in the nineteenth century, the two sides so squarely contradicted each other that it was virtually impossible for an impartial observer to figure out where the truth

---

8. See Exec. Doc. 25, Appendix A, page 172 and page 157.

9. Ibid., page 184.

10. For more on Grant's role, see Sessions, *Mormon Thunder: A Documentary History of Jedediah Morgan Grant,* 86–110.

lay. President Fillmore's report to Congress, reprinted as Appendix A, simply sets forth both sides without comment.[11]

In his first letter, Goodell introduced a "distinguished officer" of the U.S. Army, who wintered near his own tent and afterward described conditions in Utah to his friends in Missouri. The *St. Louis Intelligencer* published portions of the officer's letter in 1851. While both Goodell and the newspaper withheld the writer's name, there can be no doubt that he was thirty-three-year-old Major William Singer, an additional paymaster at Santa Fe during the Mexican War.[12]

The recently discharged officer and his family started for California in 1850 but failed to reach Fort Hall before late August, too late to attempt a crossing of the Sierra Nevada. At the Snake River trading post, Hudson's Bay factor Richard Grant advised Singer either to take the Oregon Trail to the Northwest and go by sea to California or to go south over the Fort Hall Road to Great Salt Lake and winter in the Mormon settlements. To his later regret he took the latter course and settled on the Ogden River near the wagons of the Oregon pioneer who later related their experiences. His letter (from which Goodell quotes) is published as Appendix B.

In his initial installment, Jotham Goodell makes clear at the outset what motivated him to write his series.

---

11. The above quotes are from House Exec. Doc. 25, Appendix A. For more on this controversy, see Bigler, *Forgotten Kingdom: The Mormon Theocracy in the American West, 1847–1896*, 56–61.

12. See 1850 Utah Census for Weber County; *San Francisco Morning Call*, 29 June 1901, 14/3; and *Marysville Daily Appeal*, 30 June 1901, 1/7.

THE OREGONIAN

PORTLAND, OREGON TERRITORY
SATURDAY, 10 APRIL 1852, VOL. 2, NO. 19, 1.
THE MORMONS.

TO THE EDITOR OREGONIAN:

Sir:—Recent intelligence from the city of Washington informs us that the delegate to congress from the territory of Utah has placed among the executive archives, his prompt, unqualified, and peremptory negation of the truth of the statement of the returned officers, respecting that most deluded people.[13] To persons not familiar with the mysteries of that abomination, this may appear strange and unaccountable; but to those who, with the writer, spent the winter of '50 and '51, shut up in that den of infamy, each denial will not appear at all strange. Nor do I marvel that persons should be found among us whose credulity is staggered by the disclosures which these persons have made, who have become conversant with the affairs of the Mormons. A few months ago, a distinguished officer of the United States Army,[14] with his amiable lady, was compelled to spend the winter that I did among the Mormons, in a familiar letter to some of his friends, in St. Louis, briefly narrated some of the events which transpired during our eventful sojourn among them. This letter found its way into the St. Louis Intelligencer, the editor of which remarked in relation to it thus:

"It describes a most deplorable state of things at Salt Lake, so much so that it might be difficult to believe some portions of the account, were it not for the unimpeachable character of the gentleman who penned it. He is well known to nearly all of our citizens as the occupant of a responsible station in the United States Army. Considering the writer, the circumstances under

---

13. See Bernhisel to Millard Fillmore, 1 December 1851, House Exec. Doc. 25; Appendix A, page 151.

14. This is Goodell's first reference to Major William Singer.

which the letter was written, we are not permitted even to suppose that its statements are exaggerated."[15]

Doubtless, however, notwithstanding the character of the writer, multitudes who have read the letter have thought it was an exaggeration. And I will freely confess, that had I not been an eyewitness to the abominations he describes, I should have been slow in giving credance [sic] to the report. I could not have believed that in the 19th century, in enlightened christian America, a community of people could be found so utterly depraved and wicked.

But surprising as these statements may be, there is nothing in them but sober truth. Our acquaintance was formed amid the scenes which he describes. His tent was near to mine during those gloomy days and weeks which we spent, as far this side of the Mormon settlements as the snow capped mountains would permit us to get. We had left the settlements, with our wives and little ones, in the month of February, in that high region, and lived in our tents and wagons amid the howling blasts of winter, rather than to remain among that God provoking people. There with the snow drifting around us, our limbs benumbed with piercing cold, and those vile gestures of the High Council,[16] the blood thirsty Danites[17] prowling around, and an armed force repeatedly charging in upon us, threatening our property and our lives, we anxiously

---

15. *St. Louis Intelligencer,* 7 August 1851, Vol. 2, No. 186, 2/3, reprinted in full as Appendix B. While neither Goodell nor the St. Louis editor identify the writer, Singer's name was not difficult to discover.

16. A regional church ruling body comprised of twelve members whose duties during this period took in both religious and secular affairs.

17. The Danites, or Sons of Dan, was an oath-bound paramilitary organization that was organized in 1838 to execute judgment on apostates from the faith and take vengeance on Mormon enemies in Missouri. Many emigrants became convinced that it also existed as a secret instrument of church policy in Utah Territory, but there is little evidence to support this. At the same time, there also can be little doubt that outsiders were closely spied on.

waited, wishing and praying that heaven might be propitious and
open a way for us through the mountains, that we might find an
asylum among the Snake river savages. Never, sir, shall I forget
those days of suspense, anxiety and distress. It was there that the
emigrants made a solemn pledge, that if they were ever again permitted to breathe the air of freedom, they would to the utmost of
their power expose the corruption of that people. In fulfillment of
this pledge I have been urged by my brother emigrants to give to
the public through the press, a faithful history of that affair. But
since my arrival in Oregon, with a large and dependent family,
without means, I have found such a draught upon my time, as to
give me no leisure for the fulfillment of my promise.

Recent events, however, to my mind demand that such a history
should be written. When the Mormon delegate to Congress can
with brazen face stand up before Congress and before the world,
and solemnly deny facts set forth by the United States officers,
which hundreds of us know to be facts; when many in Oregon and
out of it believe that the Mormons are slandered, and that it was
not the Mormons but the emigrants themselves that were the cause
of the troubles of which they complain, is it not time for us to
speak? Will you then, Mr. Editor, allow me a small corner in your
paper for a few weeks for this purpose?

But as I have spun out this introduction to such a length, I will
close the present article by remarking that I know how to
appreciate the privilege of speaking and writing what I think
without the fear of losing my head. When imprisoned by the
mountains among that ungodly people, we dared not even to *speak
aloud*, much less to put a word on paper. So accustomed did we
become to expressing our thoughts in a *whisper*, whenever the
subject was Mormon outrage or superstition, that long after we had
scaled our prison walls, and were far on our road to this land of
promise, we would detect ourselves unconsciously *whispering*
when speaking upon those subjects. My fellow emigrants will call to
mind the hearty laughs we had on this account. Nor would I have

your readers infer that the emigrants, who wintered at Salt Lake were a cowardly set of old women; there were as brave men among us as ever found an enemy—men who had gathered laurels on the field of battle—men whom the Mormons had better never meet in the open field of conflict.

YOURS TRULY,
J. W. GODDELL

These members of Po-ca-ta-ro's band of Northern
Shoshoni were neighbors of Terikee's Weber band. This
posed image was probably taken about 1870.
— *Courtesy Special Collections, University of Utah.*

LETTER 2

"With Spartan Intrepidity"

Jotham Goodell addressed the issue of Mormon relations with the "Lamanites," their term for American
Indians, in the second letter about his winter in Utah
Territory. He described the 1850 Indian scare in Utah's
Weber County settlements that began the day after Goodell
camped for the winter on Ogden River. About midnight on
16 September, thirty-two-year-old Urban Van Stewart rushed
up to Goodell's wagon with alarming news. He had just shot
an Indian and begged the Oregon pioneer to help him
move out of his cabin before other members of the tribe
found the body and acted to impose tribal justice, which
virtually guaranteed the death of a white man. Stewart, an
1847 Utah pioneer, had a farm on Four Mile Creek, some
three miles to the north, in today's Harrisville. Hearing
noises in his garden, he had fired at the sound and killed
Terikee, the friendly chief of the Weber Shoshoni band,
who apparently had been trying to drive his horses out of

Lorin F. Farr,
founder of Farr's settlement, later first president of
Weber Stake of Zion and first mayor of Ogden City.
—*Courtesy Utah State Historical Society.*

Stewart's corn. A short time before the settler's thoughtless
shot, the Shoshoni chief and his son had visited Farr's
settlement to express their friendship.[1]

Now badly frightened, Stewart found few friends willing to
risk their own lives to help him. Lorin Farr, soon to become
first president of the Weber Stake of Zion, advised him to
leave the area while Farr prepared a defense and tried to
pacify the natives. In the meantime, angry Indians rode down
from Box Elder Creek and attacked a small party rounding up
cattle and horses near the mouth of Ogden Canyon. They
killed and mutilated one man and made off with some
animals. Goodell explains why he chose not to name the
victim of native vengeance, but other accounts identify him as
one of several Campbells at the settlement, allegedly a non-
Mormon emigrant, who had been hired as a millwright to
build Farr's gristmill. Goodell tells a different story.

At this atrocity, leaders of the two Weber County settle-
ments appeared to panic. At 2 P.M. on 17 September they sent
Kentuckian Daniel Burch with an urgent appeal to
Nauvoo Legion Col. John S. Fullmer at Great Salt Lake.
Signed by both Farr and James Brown, the message reflects
the fright that Goodell describes:

> Sir I wish you to Raise from one Hundred to one hundred &
> fifty men forth with and repare to this plase forth with [sic] the
> Indians has Commensed burning Houses Hay & wheat & have
> taken Broth[er] Camel [Campbell] prisone[r] and then shot &
> masse Crede [massacred] him[2] Our Lives and that of our

---

1. See Moore, Journal and Life History of David Moore, Items of History,
67–70, and L. H. Nichols, "Dictation of David Moore," Bancroft Library,
University of California at Berkeley.

wives & Children are exposed with all we have the word is our wheat & houses will be in ashes before to morrow morning nine o clock the Indians are geathering very fast be sertain to be hear by to morrow morning. Our Lives is Exposed.[3]

Late that day, Nauvoo Legion commander Maj. Gen. Daniel H. Wells ordered Brig. Gen. Horace S. Eldredge to select fifty additional men from his brigade and "act with promptitude in preserving the lives of our brethren and subduing the Indians."[4] Eldredge, a six-foot-plus New Yorker, took command of the combined mounted force now numbering about one hundred men. Without further bloodshed the military expedition soon subdued the Indians, whose sense of justice had been satisfied and who seemed as afraid of the Mormon soldiers as their new neighbors were of them. Eldredge ordered outlying families to move into Farr's settlement and Brownsville and build forts at both locations. Goodell's account of this episode adds some humor and new information to the story.[5]

---

2. This is the only Mormon source that seems to confirm Goodell's claim that Campbell was a converted member of the faith.

3. Lorin Farr and James Brown to Col. John S. Fullmer, 17 September 1850, Doc. No. 2, Territorial Militia Records, Series 82210, Reel 4, Utah State Archives.

4. Daniel H. Wells to H S. Eldredge, Special Orders 17 September 1850, Doc. 69, Ibid.

5. For one of the best of many accounts, see Carter, ed., *Our Pioneer Heritage*, 6:117–18.

THE OREGONIAN

PORTLAND, OREGON TERRITORY
SATURDAY, 1 MAY 1852, VOL. 2, NO. 22,
THE MORMONS – NO. 2.

EDITOR OF OREGONIAN

I will not detain your readers with a recital of the causes which led me to the alternative of either wintering among the Mormons or among the savages. Much to our regret afterwards we chose the former. It was in the month of September that we made our entry into this famous city. Long trains of Mormons were also arriving, and we were at first taken to be ourselves Mormons; and though when we disabused their minds on this point, we were treated at first with a good deal of civility, still we perceived that a wide distinction was made between them and the gentiles, as they term all who are not Mormons.[6] For instance, the price of flour, as regulated by the high council, was at that time $10 per hundred pounds, when sold to Mormons, but $25 when sold to the gentiles. It was only a few days after our arrival, that a lad came to our camp to inquire if we wished to purchase any flour, saying that there was a man in the city who had brought in some flour which he had not disposed of, and which I could buy at an advantage if I were disposed. I accordingly repaired to the place, and while attempting to make a bargain with the man, a woman living in the house opposite, came to the door and squalled out at the top of her voice: "that man is a gentile, you know that Brigham says we must not sell flour to the gentiles for less than $25 a hundred."

---

6. Brigham Young explained, "Nine tenths of those who come into this Church are the pure blood of Israel, the greater portion being purely of the blood of Ephraim." See Collier, ed., *The Teachings of President Brigham Young*, *Vol.3*, 191, and Discourse by Brigham Young, 6 April 1855, *The Deseret News*, 9, May 1855, 68. Considering themselves literally to be children of Israel, Mormons referred to outsiders as "gentiles."

To the credit of the Mormons, however, I will say, that this order from the high council, for some cause, became inoperative.[7] The Mormon farmers were mighty glad to sell us their wheat at $3 per bushel, or their flour at $10 per hundred. And the time is close upon their heels, even though they are the favored saints of the Most High, when they will be glad to get 25 cents a bushel for their wheat, or else I will relinquish my claim as being a better prophet than their prophet Brigham.

Subsequent events, however, convinced me that we owed no thanks to the high council for the fall in the prices of flour to the gentiles. In the early part of January Brigham Young, in company with several of the twelve apostles, visited that part of the church established on the Weber, about 40 miles north of the city, where many of the emigrants passed the winter, and while there, publicly declared it to be his will that we poor gentiles should not be supplied with provisions at all![8] It devolved upon one of the apostles, I think it was Amos Lyma [Amasa Lyman], to introduce this matter in public.[9] It was in an inflammatory speech against the emigrants. "Most of these gentiles now among you," said he, "are from Missouri," (as though that was in itself a crime), "many of

---

7. While notably obedient in many respects, most Utah settlers quietly ignored repeated attempts by Brigham Young to control prices and trade.

8. Brigham Young's company, including apostles Heber C. Kimball and Amasa M. Lyman, left Great Salt Lake on 20 January 1851 to visit settlements in Davis and Weber counties. On 26 January he organized at South Fort (James Brown's settlement) the Weber Stake of Zion, a church entity that conformed in coverage to Weber County, created one year before, and named Lorin Farr as its first president. On his return, Young on 28 January met a cavalcade with a band some fifteen miles north of the capital coming to inform him of his appointment as governor of Utah Territory.

9. Amasa Mason Lyman, then thirty-seven, was ordained an apostle in 1842 and arrived in Utah in 1847 as a member of Brigham Young's pioneer company. He and Apostle Charles C. Rich established the Mormon settlement at San Bernardino, California, in 1851. He was excommunicated from the L.D.S. Church in 1870 for preaching false doctrine.

them helped to mob us out of the State, and all sympathize with our enemies, and will you nourish them with the fruit of your toil?"[10] For his part he said, "he had rather that the wheat in the valley was piled up as high as the mountains which surrounded them, than a bushel of it should be consumed by the emigrants then in the valley."[11] To this inflammatory harangue, Brigham rose and gave his unqualified approval. "But," said he, "it will be asked what will become of our wheat if we do not sell it to the emigrants? Keep it to feed the saints who are coming here next fall by thousands."[12] But Brigham's counsel came too late, most of the emigrants had already secured their bread, and those who had not, found that when it came to the test, Mormon cupidity was stronger than Mormon credulity.

I remarked that upon our arrival we were treated with much civility. This was certainly the case so far as my own family was concerned, and so far as I have been able to learn, it was the case with the emigrants generally.[13] In all my intercourse with them, from the highest to the lowest, so much civility was manifested, that

---

10. At this point in their history, Mormons were deeply bitter over persecution they had suffered from 1833 to 1846 in Missouri and Illinois. Gold Rush emigrant Dr. Israel Shipman Pelton Lord noted in 1849 that a Mormon ferryman told him that "none of their persecutors would be safe in passing through [Great Salt Lake City], and while he told of their wrongs, he ground his teeth so as to be heard two or three yards. Yet he was not naturally a violent man, rather the reverse." See Liles, ed., *"At the Extremity of Civilization": A Meticulously Descriptive Diary of an Illinois Physician's Journey in 1849 Along the Oregon Trail to the Goldmines and Cholera of California, Thence in Two Years to Return by Boat Via Panama,* 158.

11. This policy may have prompted some emigrants to become what was known as "winter saints," described by Hosea Stout as "those Emigrants who stop here, join the Church & Marry wives and go to the mines in the Spring." See Brooks, ed., *On the Mormon Frontier: The Diary of Hosea Stout,* 19 January 1851, 2:388.

12. The editor has not found any other source of such alleged "inflammatory" remarks by Lyman and Young.

I thought to myself, surely this people cannot be as bad as represented. A people who can be so civil certainly must have some redeeming qualities. But this bright sunshine was of short duration. The sky of Mormon civility soon became overcast with lowering clouds, and the proscriptive edicts of the high council, gave notice of the gathering storm of wrath.

I will remark here, that I do not blame those persons who, having stopped a few days at Salt Lake, and been treated with civility, think that we very much exaggerate when we tell the story of our wrongs from that people. I will only say that were we to judge of the climate of the frigid zone by the very few sun shiny days of summer, we should make a woful [sic] mistake. The Jesuits of the 16th century were not more deceitful and cunning than are the leaders of the Mormons. With the most deadly hatred rankling in their bosoms against our republican institutions, predicting with the utmost certainty the downfall of our nation, and anxiously waiting to see the hour when our fair republic shall be shattered into a thousand atoms, they can, when the occasion suits them, speak of our institutions in the most glowing terms of commendation; and in the language of Brigham Young, in his letter to President of the United States, can say: "No people exist who are more friendly to the United States than the people of Utah."[14] Before I get through with these articles I will show how friendly this same Brigham Young and his servile followers are to the United States.

---

13. As Goodell indicates, most Gold Rush and Oregon-bound emigrants reacted favorably to what he and others called the Mormon "half-way house," especially if their visit was short. But emigrant opinions soured the longer they stayed beyond the average six or seven days, and many of those who wintered in Utah because they arrived too late to go on or ran out of money, afterward told stories similar to Goodell's.

14. Goodell apparently took this quote from Brigham Young's 29 September 1851 letter to President Fillmore. The exact quote is: "Now, sir, I will simply state what I know to be true—that no people exists who are more friendly to the government of the United States, than the people of this Territory." See House Exec. Doc. 25, 30; Appendix A, page 197.

MORMON COURAGE AND INTREPIDITY.

After entering the city, it immediately became a question of importance to be settled, in what part of the valley I should spend the winter. I finally decided that it would be best for me [to] come as far this way as their settlement extended. This was the settlement on the Ogden [River], some 42 or 43 miles north of the city. This settlement I reached on Saturday night, one of the last days in September.[15] On Sabbath night, about midnight, a man came to my wagon and informed me that he had just shot an Indian—the Indians for a few days previous had been very saucy and would steal his vegetables in the night. Determined to protect them he had watched that night, seeing an Indian approach shot him down.[16] His house was about three miles off, and he wanted to get help in the morning to go and move his effects, as he had no doubt but the Indians in the morning would come and destroy them. Being a stranger, I could of course know nothing of the number or disposition of the Indians, and of course felt some uneasiness for the safety of my family, as we were camped some distance from the settlement and alone. Early in the morning I went into the settlement to ascertain how matters stood. You may judge of my surprise when I found the inhabitants perfectly paralized [sic] with fear.—An express had been dispatched to the city for help. The inhabitants were driving in their cattle and preparing for defence [sic]. Most of the houses were built adjoining each other in a single row. Those who lived in houses a little distance off forsook them, and taking what effects they could into their wagons, came and camped by the side of this row of buildings. For my part, seeing the panic into which the community was thrown, and having no wish to expose my family to be butchered by savages, I concluded to return

---

15. If Goodell arrived at the Ogden River on the Saturday before Chief Terikee was shot, he must have come on 14 September 1850.

16. Stewart said he fired a shot at the sounds in his field to frighten intruders away.

to the city [Great Salt Lake]. But I finally yielded to the entreaties of the Mormons to stay and assist in their defense, and so rolled my wagon into line with theirs. In the meantime the Indians had gathered at the house where the Indian had been killed, and held a most terrible pow-wow over the body of their fallen chief—as chief he proved to be. This they continued till about noon, when discovering two men out hunting cattle, they gave chase. One man being well mounted made his escape, the other seeing the Indians were gaining upon him, and himself forsaken by his companion, surrendered and was immediately butchered and left in the road weltering in his blood.

And here a painful duty devolves upon me. I will not mention the name of the murdered man,[17] lest these lines might meet the eye, and wound feelings of loved friends in a distant land. I would also remember that we are to tread lightly on the ashes of the dead. But we have a duty to discharge to the living. The emigrants, among whom he had intimate friends, looked upon this event as the just and righteous visitation of Almighty God.

He was himself an emigrant on his way to California. He left, as I have been informed, an interesting and dependent family in the States—an amiable wife and several children. He was respected in the county where he lived, and had filled several important offices of trust and honor. But his financial affairs had become deranged, and he had torn himself away from the loved ones around the domestic hearth to endeavor to retrieve his fortune in the land of gold. How tender and painful the parting hour! Methinks I can almost see the wife and mother bathed in tears, gazing long after the vehicle which bears from her sight, for a season, perhaps forever, the husband and father! But she bows in submission,

17. John Q. Blaylock has identified him as John Campbell, but this is difficult to confirm since the 1850 Utah Census for Weber County was apparently taken after his death. See Blaylock, "History of North Ogden, An Economic and Social Study."

believing the sacrifice necessary to their future happiness. He arrives at Salt Lake—the season is far spent, and concludes to spend the winter there. In all honesty he tells the Mormons of the wife and children he has left behind. But alas! This is not enough to shield him from the powers of woman, in a country where the marriage tie is so slender. He is told that if he only joins the Mormons he may have as many wives as he pleases. The woman who is thus artfully contriving to catch him in her toils is a widow. Alas! She too well succeeds. The very day previous to his death he was baptised into the Mormon church, and that week was to have witnessed his marriage to that woman! This the Mormons and the woman herself openly avowed.—She appeared as chief mourner on the occasion. She received all the sympathy that was bestowed by the Mormons on the occasion. As I was assisting in washing the body and preparing it for burial, this woman, (her name was Geans—the widow GEANS,[18] I hope she will see it right here in print, and I want you to put it in capitals, and I would to God that I could condense into a single sentence, the indignation and abhorrence which the emigrants felt towards her, and she could be compelled to read it alone by herself and her God!) she having stepped out for a moment, a person present exclaimed—"poor Mrs. Geans! How she is to be pitied. This is a sore affliction to her!" Why? Exclaimed I in anger. "Oh," said he, "they were to be married this week."   Married! Married! Exclaimed I, why, has he not a family of his own? "Oh, yes, I suppose he has in the States,"

---

18. The "widow Geans" may have been forty-eight-year-old Esther Ann Peirce Gheen, a former Pennsylvania Quaker, whose husband, William, died in 1845 at Nauvoo, Illinois. Two of their eight children, Ann Alice and Amanda, at ages sixteen and fourteen, respectively, married Mormon Apostle Heber C. Kimball, then forty-three, on the same day in 1844 at Nauvoo. The 1850 Utah Census for Weber County, taken soon after Campbell's death, appears to show her as the wife of Canadian Lemuel Mallory, age fifty, whose first wife, Elizabeth, died in 1850 during their journey to Utah. Esther Gheen subsequently had at least two other husbands.

was the indifferent reply. Not the first syllable of sympathy was expressed for that truly widowed mother and her poor fatherless babes who were yet to hear of the deplorable blow.

But I am not prepared to leave this subject yet. It was at this point that my eyes began to be torn open to the abominations of that people. I want to mention in this connection their inhumanity. There were at the Ogden at that time but four male emigrants. One of these was a nephew of the deceased. Two of the others immediately set about making a coffin. The number of men who were Mormons amounted to over thirty. As the murdered man was a recent proselyte to their faith, I had no doubt but his remains would receive the utmost attention. But what was my surprise, after his body was brought in, it was suffered to lie in its gore, until his nephew went from one to another begging of them to lay his "uncle out." I went but found no one to assist in preparing the body but the widow of whom I have spoken and another woman. With some difficulty I got a man to help me, and with the assistance of the women, we got the body washed and prepared for the grave. The next day he was buried, and then the same difficulty occurred in getting men enough to carry him to the grave, although there were not less than 30 men within a stone's throw. Nothing like a funeral was had. I felt at the time, and so expressed to my family, that it was more like the burial of an ass than that of a human being.

Having died in the Mormon faith, the Mormons took possession of his property. The widow Geans keeping all she could, which was supposed by his nephew to be considerable.

But let us return to the narrative of our Indian war. The Mormon assembly in their memorial to Congress, relative to the U. States officers leaving their territory, speak of their people as possessed of "more than Spartan intrepidity and fortitude."[19] I have already spoken of the array which was made to repel an attack of the Indians should they venture to make one. There were in the fort at the Ogden [River] at least 30 men capable of bearing arms.[20] At the Weber [River], three miles from there, there were at least 70 more.[21] These were all under arms. They had sent to the city for help, and that night and the next morning there arrived in the neighborhood some 200 more. From this marshalling of forces I had formed the idea that the Indians must be very formidable in numbers. But what was my surprise when I learned that the whole band, all told, would not exceed 60 or 70 fighting men, and these the most despicable cowards on the face of the earth. After they had committed the murder above mentioned, they seem to have been in as great a panic as the Mormons; for hastily shooting a few cattle, burning a hay stack or two and loading their ponies with what wheat they could carry, they hastily decamped, taking with them 6 or 8 stolen horses. In the mean time the most masterly preparation was going forward in the Mormon camp for pursuit, and on the morning of the third day about 9 o'clock A.M., the grand army, 150 or 200 strong, well mounted, armed to the teeth, with great military display, moved out of camp in pursuit of the enemy. Their trail was easily followed, for they had fled in such a panic that they strewed their plunder all along the way. With "Spartan intrepidity," the army pressed on in pursuit, till the day was so far advanced that the officers deemed it prudent to halt for the night. In the morning as they supposed themselves near the enemy, a scouting party was sent forward to reconnoiter. In the meantime a strong guard was posted some distance in advance of the army to prevent any surprise. In due course of time, the scouting party, not having been able to find any enemy in all that region, returned, and as they came in sight of their companions in advance of the army, feeling somewhat frolicksome, they put their

---

19. The exact quote was "more than Spartan integrity and fortitude." See "Memorial signed by members of the Legislative Assembly of Utah to the President of the United States," 29 September 1851, House Exec. Doc. 25, Appendix A, page 202.

20. Farr's Settlement.

21. Brownsville or Brown's Settlement.

horses upon the charge, gave the Indian yell, and came dashing in upon their comrades, not doubting for a moment but their comrades knew them. But they mistook them for Indians and run [*sic*] for the main body, giving the alarm that the whole band of Indians were charging with fury into camp! Upon this the whole body broke and run like lightning, and it was not until they had retreated several miles that they learned their mistake. They then all returned to the fort, court martialed the men who gave the false alarm, and thus ended the famous Indian war; with "Spartan intrepidity" they had succeeded in effecting a most masterly escape from an imaginary foe.

J. W. GODDELL

LETTER 3

"The United States Would Be Overthrown"

Migrating Americans, who passed through Utah during the great population shift known as the Gold Rush, often accused Mormon leaders of disloyalty toward the United States. "[They] deny the authority of the United States, and gasconade around as if they were able to maintain themselves against any force that might be sent against them," one forty-niner said.[1] More than a hundred California emigrants agreed that Mormon leaders "often avow their aversion to any connection with the United States, and their preference for an independent government."[2]

In 1850 Franklin Langworthy from Illinois was among some two thousand or so emigrants who attended July 24th observances at Great Salt Lake City to commemorate the

---

1. Morgan, "Letters by Forty-Niners Written from Great Salt Lake City in 1849," 114.
2. Slater, *Fruits of Mormonism*, 82.

arrival in Salt Lake Valley of Brigham Young's pioneer company in 1847. He heard speakers "read a paper entitled 'Declaration of Independence of Deseret,' and another, 'The Constitution of Deseret.'" Orators said "many hard things against the Government and people of the United States, and heaped the most withering curses upon the States of Missouri and Illinois," he said. "They prophesied that the total over-throw of the United States was at hand, and that the whole nation would soon be at the feet of the Mormons, suing for mercy and protection."[3]

Another transient from Illinois, but not a member of Langworthy's company, also described the third Pioneer Day celebration that year at Great Salt Lake. Henry S. Bloom from Kankakee had stopped for two weeks in the Mormon "half-way house" to find work as a carpenter and restore his resources before going on to the California gold fields. "A great deal of ostentation and pomp was displayed," he said. "They bid open defience [sic] to the United States, her government and her people." To this, Bloom added: "They were also very insulting to the emigrants."[4]

At that time, Mormons believed God had inspired the framers of the U.S. Constitution to create a land of religious freedom where His Kingdom would be restored and super-sede, as it prevailed to universal dominion, the American republic and all other earthly realms. To them, the nation's charter was a stepping stone to a higher, millennial form of

---

3. Langworthy, *Scenery of the Plains, Mountains and Mines: or a Diary kept upon the Overland Route to California, by way of the Great Salt Lake*, 80.

4. Burroughs, ed., "Tales of the Pioneers of the Kankakee: Taken from the Diary of Henry S. Bloom," 24 July 1850.

government, not an end in itself. It was cherished as the founding document of the Kingdom of God, established as the State of Deseret, which they viewed as the true heir and champion of the Constitution, not the government that blocked the fulfillment of its divine purpose.

So it was that Brigham Young and other Mormon leaders without contradiction often vowed their devotion to the Constitution in one breath and excoriated the national government and its officials in the next. Their loyalty was first, last, and always to God's Kingdom on earth, but their outspoken opinions often offended other Americans. Jotham Goodell expressed this outrage in his third letter.

THE OREGONIAN

PORTLAND, OREGON TERRITORY
SATURDAY, 8 MAY 1852, VOL. 2, NO. 23, 1.
THE MORMONS, NO. 3.

Editor Oregonian—With much regret we had been compelled to turn aside from our journey, and spend the winter among the Mormons. Having been compelled to this decision, I resolved to pass the winter as quietly as possible. I could not hope to turn them from their delusions, and to attempt it would be to expose my family to their fury. I therefore resolved to tie my tongue, but to open my eyes and my ears, to learn all I could of their doctrines and their practices, and know for myself the truth or falsehood of the reports I had heard concerning them. The result of what I saw, and heard, and *know* to be truth, without exaggeration, I shall endeavor to lay before your readers. And first I will speak of

MORMON HOSTILITY TO OUR REPUBLICAN GOVERNMENT.

"No people exist," says Brigham Young, in his letter to President Fillmore, "who are more friendly to the United States than the people of Utah."[5] Well, if it is so, they have a strange way of showing it. I travelled the whole length of their valley, mingled among their people, spent the night in very many of their families, took the utmost pains to ascertain their feelings toward our government, but in all my intercourse with them I never heard the first syllable expressed of friendship for the United States. But on the contrary, whenever they spoke of the government or people of the United States, there was always a rancorous feeling exhibited; they always spoke of the United States as an *enemy*, with which, ere long, they were expecting a deadly struggle, and they were nerving for the conflict.[6] The predictions of their prophets, that the United States would be overthrown, were constantly repeated, expressing the conviction in tones of exultation, that the time was close at hand when such predictions would be verified. They are taught to believe that in the accomplishment of these predictions, they have an important part to act, and that when our government shall be dashed into a thousand atoms, the dominion will be given to them and they will possess the land.

Although the act of congress organizing their territory, passed that body in the month of September, not a Mormon was to be found, from the highest to the lowest, in public or in private, in the pulpit or on the bench, that would admit that they were in any way connected with the United States, or amenable to United States law.[7] In repeated instances did the emigrants in those unjust and cruel suits which were waged against them, appeal to the usages and laws, by which courts in the United States were governed. But in vain was the appeal. As late as in the month of March, 1851, I

---

5. Young to Fillmore, 29 September 1851, House Exec. Doc. 25; Appendix A, page 197.

6. One emigrant heard Brigham Young say from the stand that his followers would "meet any force sent from the United States, and bid them God speed with musket and grape shot." See Slater, *Fruits of Mormonism*, 83. True or not, the report appears to reflect Young's attitude in 1857 toward an approaching U.S. Army expedition.

heard the presiding judge of "the honorable the county court of Weber county," while on the bench, say that they had nothing to do with United States' law, and he would not allow it to be quoted in court.[8]

For reasons best known to themselves, they petitioned congress to be organized into a territory, yet that act of congress gave them the highest umbrage.[9] They were loud in their denunciation of that act, and their determination never to be the "territory of Utah." That they were the "state of Deseret," and they would be nothing else. That no governor sent there from the states would be received. And in more instances than one, I heard them say that if a governor was sent there *they would shoot him!*" In the early part of January, Brigham, in company with several of the twelve apostles made a visit to the Ogden and Weber [settlements].[10] While there, in his public addresses, he made frequent allusion to the act of congress constituting them into a territory, and always used the most denunciatory language possible; asserted positively that they were not the territory of Utah, and never would be; denounced the

---

7. As noted, Mormon leaders had already created the "free and independent" State of Deseret and desired either its admission to the Union as a state or no ties to the federal government. Congress under the Compromise of 1850 ignored the statehood petition and created Utah Territory. President Fillmore signed the bill on 9 September 1850.

8. The judge may have been forty-four-year-old Isaac Clark who became probate judge for Weber County in 1852 under the territorial government. A native of Kentucky, Clark settled in Weber County in 1849 where he became bishop of Ogden's South Ward in January 1851. He died at Ogden early in 1854.

9. After first preparing a petition for a territorial government, Mormon leaders in 1849 changed their mind and withdrew the request before it was ever presented to Congress. In its place they submitted a memorial for Deseret to enter the Union as a state.

10. Young visited the Weber County settlements on 24–26 January 1851. His traveling party included apostles Heber C. Kimball, Amasa Lyman, and firebrand Jedediah M. Grant.

government in no measured terms, and predicted its overthrow and downfall. "The United States," said he, "may send a governor here, and probably will send one," but said he, "we will send him back or send him *duck hunting.*" Said he, "I am the governor of the state of Deseret, I was elected for life, and no other person shall hold that office here while I live."[11] At another time he said, "If they send a governor here, he will be glad to black my boots for me." This is a specimen of his language, and as nearly in his own words as it is possible for me to repeat them. He had much more of the same kind. The emigrants all felt that his language was treasonable, and that he ought to be indicted for treason against the United States. Their indignation was intense, but they were obliged to suppress it, and only speak of it in the lowest whispers to their brethren. You may judge then, sir, what was our surprise, when shortly after this the news reached Salt Lake, that this same bloated, swaggering imposter had himself been appointed governor, by President Fillmore.[12] This changed the whole face of affairs, and the creatures of that vile man got together and passed a resolution, accepting the act of congress constituting the territory of Utah. Still let it be known that up to the very day we left, the 1st of April, all public business was performed in the name of the "state of Deseret." The receipts we received from the state marshal for taxes, were all dated "*State of Deseret.*"[13]

---

11. If inexact, this quote accurately reflects Young's point of view throughout his career. Alfred Cumming, Utah's second governor, when asked in 1861 how his successor would get along said, "well enough, if he will do nothing. There is nothing to do. Alfred Cumming is Governor of the Territory, but Brigham Young is Governor *of the people.*" See Stenhouse, *The Rocky Mountain Saints: A Full and Complete History of the Mormons, From the First Vision of Joseph Smith to the Last Courtship of Brigham Young,* 445.

12. Brigham Young learned of his appointment as governor on 27 January 1851 as he was returning to Great Salt Lake City after visiting Davis and Weber County settlements.

"No people in the world are more friendly to the United States than the people of Utah!" Why then, sir, are you cultivating so sedulously a military spirit among your deluded followers: Why such zeal in accumulating military stores: Why did you send one hundred of your most tried and choice followers, in the month of December, 1850, to Little Salt Lake, where it was known there was an abundance of coal and iron ore, to erect a foundry for the casting of cannon?[14] Why those deep plans laid for the destruction of an army approaching your country from the United States? Why did the general of your forces,[15] on a grand review of your trained bands, in an address to the officers and soldiers, in your hearing, urge the necessity of the most perfect organization, and of attaining to the highest state of military science and discipline, for they might yet have to measure swords with the United States?[16] Why, sir, was a little company of emigrants, citizens of the United States, who were so unfortunate as to be shut up in your dominion for a few months, warned by your people against peacefully memorializing

---

13. As if nothing had happened, the State of Deseret functioned as an independent government for seven months after President Fillmore on 9 September 1850 signed the law creating Utah Territory. Only after the General Assembly of Deseret on 5 April 1851 approved a resolution "cheerfully and cordially" accepting the federal act did anyone in Deseret or Utah Territory ostensibly recognize the latter as legitimate.

14. After an exploring party led by Apostle Parley P. Pratt discovered coal and iron ore deposits in southern Utah, Apostle George A. Smith on 7 December 1849 led a colonizing company of 167 men, women, and children, known as the Iron Mission, to establish an ironmaking industry at present Cedar City. The venture aimed to achieve economic independence, not simply to produce cannon. It eventually failed after repeated attempts and was finally abandoned in 1883. See MacDonald, *The Magnet: Iron Ore in Iron County Utah*.

15. An apparent reference to Major General Daniel Hanmer Wells, then thirty-six, commander of the Mormon forces known as the Nauvoo Legion. Wells became second counselor to Brigham Young in 1857 and later was named mayor of Salt Lake City.

[sic] congress upon the subject of those unjust and high handed measures they were made to feel? Why was it, that at the peril of their lives, they dared not draft such memorial? And why were a company of emigrants thus situated, when they had prepared a flag—an imitation of the banner of our glorious country, the simple *stars and stripes*—afraid to spread it to the breeze, till mountain barriers had placed them beyond the reach of your people? Why were they told by your people, that to raise that flag would be considered by them as an act of defiance?[17] Perhaps you will say these Mormons had no authority for such an assertion. Grant it. What other people in the world, most friendly to the United States, would consider the stars and stripes a *nuisance*, an *aggression*, an *act of defiance!* Ah, sir, if the world can produce no better friends to the United States than the people of Utah, then I have only to say, God save my beloved country!

---

16. While this statement cannot be independently verified, it should not be dismissed out of hand. For the destiny of God's Kingdom, as foretold by the Prophet Daniel, was universal dominion within the lifetimes of those who bore its banner. Mormon leaders no doubt hoped the millennial movement would prevail to world rule peacefully, but they also knew by that time that it might require a confrontation with the U.S.

17. The preferred flag in Utah during this period was the flag of the Kingdom of God, also known as the national flag of Deseret. Brigham Young said in 1846 at Nauvoo that Joseph Smith had instructed him on the design of a flag for the Kingdom of God, which Young meant to unfurl in the mountains. According to historian D. Michael Quinn, it was a blue and white banner with twelve white stars encircling one large star, with blue and white stripes. A replica of this banner can be seen today at the base of Ensign Peak in Salt Lake City where the Ensign Peak Foundation has erected a monument with three flagpoles to fly the American, Utah State, and "other" flags. Samuel Brannan reportedly bore an even earlier version of the Kingdom of God flag to California in 1846 on the ship *Brooklyn*. This one featured the figure of a young woman circled by twelve red stars on a white silk background. For more on this, see Quinn, *The Mormon Hierarchy: Extensions of Power*, 263; Bagley, ed., *Scoundrel's Tale: The Samuel Brannan Papers*, 154–56; and *Sacramento Daily Union*, Vol. 15, No. 2232, 22 May 1858, 2/3.

But further than this, the *institutions of the Mormons* are at antipodes with the *republican institutions* of the *United States.* Theirs are institutions of despotism. I venture the assertion that on the face of the whole earth there is not another people to be found, so completely under the control of one man, soul, body, and property, as are the Mormons to Brigham Young. No man is his own master. He cannot elect for himself the place of his residence even in Salt Lake. Brigham appoints the place and fixes the bounds of his habitation. He cannot hold the right to the soil he cultivates.[18] He may occupy the portion allotted him, till this modern Nabob orders him elsewhere, but he cannot sell[,] only his own improvement. And he is liable at any hour, at the bidding of the high council, to leave his improvements, however valuable, or sell them for what he can get, and go elsewhere to further their plans. A practical demonstration of this was witnessed while I was among them. The high council wanted to send a colony of 100 men to Little Salt Lake, to establish a foundry for the casting of cannon, &c. A list of the names of the persons who were to go was made out by the high council, and published in the Deseret News. Many of the persons thus designated, were among the first who removed to Salt Lake, and after enduring great privations, had just begun to gather the comforts of life around them; but they must pull up stakes and leave all. The decree was imperative. In conversation with one of the men on the subject, speaking of the

---

18. Land in early Utah was awarded under an earlier revelation on consecration and stewardship and was not privately owned. Settlers received parcels to keep as long as they were good stewards and faithful to the church. In 1848 Thomas Bullock, one of Young's clerks, described this system to friends in England, "We have found a place where the land is acknowledged to belong to the Lord, and the Saints, being His people, are entitled to as much as they can plant, take care of, and will sustain their families with food." Bullock to William, 4 January 1848, *Latter-day Saints' Millennial Star*, 15 April 1848, 118. Since this practice directly countered U.S. land laws, the issue of ownership became a primary source of conflict between the Mormon theocracy and the United States.

great sacrifice he had got to make, he said there was no help for it, go he must. For said he there are but three articles in the Mormon creed—*believe in the book of Mormon, pay tithing, and obey counsel.* About the same time, another expedition was fitted out of some 150 families, if I mistake not, to go to southern California to commence a colony there.[19] This company were ordered in the same name as the others, and thus a great number of the oldest and finest improvements in the valley were thrown into market, and disposed of at forced sales.[20]

No Mormon can leave the valley, even for a short time, without first getting counsel from Brigham. If he wants to go to California to dig gold, he must go to Brigham for counsel; if that functionary says go, he may go, but if he says stay, there is nothing more to be said. Indeed, neither a man nor woman can *marry* without first asking counsel. Several marriages occurred at the Ogden [River] during the winter I spent there, both of wives and of *spirituals*,[21] but in every case the parties had to post off down to Brigham, over forty miles, before the nuptials could be celebrated. This is republican, surely!

But it may be said, they have at least the semblance of liberty, they have a legislature. Ah, indeed! But we will presently show that it is only the semblance—a mere shadow of liberty. How is that

---

19. Apostles Amasa Lyman and Charles C. Rich in 1851 led a company of about five hundred men, women and children to southern California where they purchased the Rancho del San Bernardino and established a settlement on the one hundred thousand-acre spread. The colonizing party left Payson, Utah, on 24 March, about one week before Goodell's departure.

20. In authorizing apostles Charles C. Rich and Amasa Lyman to establish a colony in southern California, Brigham Young expected about twenty-five families to volunteer. When he arrived in Utah County to see the party off, he was angered that Rich and Lyman had enlisted so many Mormons who wanted to go to California. See Bagley, ed., *Frontiersman: Abner Blackburn's Narrative*, 196.

21. A reference to the practice of polygamy, which at this time was still publicly denied.

legislature elected?[22] Why, by the people to be sure. So Napoleon was elected Emperor of France by the people—every man having the right to vote for or against him; but it was well understood that if he voted against him he would lose his head! Why, Brigham *counsels* the people in Weber county to elect such and such a man, in another county such a man, and so on, and this counsel is omnipotent.[23] Of course there is no opposition. Thus all of their officers are elected; voting is a mere farce. The legislature are [sic] the mere creatures of Brigham Young. They get together, pass the laws and do the work he has prepared for them. They dare not move a hair beyond his *ipse dixit.*[24]

Allow me to give you a single instance of their way of doing things. In the spring of 1850, Brigham made a visit to the Ogden and Weber [settlements] and laid out a city about half way between the two places. The location was the most unsuitable that could possibly be conceived. The inhabitants ventured to remonstrate with him on the subject. But he told them it was *counsel,* and it was accordingly laid out into squares and streets and named Weber City.[25] But the houses were wanting. Not a shanty was there, nor likely to be. The settlements were all made on the Ogden and

---

22. Not until Congress forced the issue did the Utah legislature in 1878 finally approve an election law that allowed voters to cast their ballots in secret. See Bigler, *Forgotten Kingdom: The Mormon Theocracy in the American West, 1847–1896*, 50, 313.

23. Utah's first election law, which remained in force for more than a quarter century, set forth the following procedure: "Each elector shall provide himself with a vote containing the names of the persons he wishes elected, and the offices he would have them fill, and present it neatly folded to the judge of election, who shall number and deposit it in the ballot box; the clerk shall then write the name of the elector, and opposite it the number of his vote." The absence of a secret ballot resulted in such lop-sided wins as the one scored by John Bernhisel, territorial delegate to Congress, who won in 1851 by 1,259 to zero.

24. An assertion supported by the mere authority of the speaker but not proved; a dictum.

Weber [rivers]. What was to be done? It would not answer for him to say he was mistaken, for this would call in question his prophetic mission. What then was to be done? Why, that winter I was there, Brigham sends a petition to the Ogden and Weber for the inhabitants to sign, praying the legislature to extend the limits of this great city of Weber, not yet honored with a single hut, from Weber kanyon to the mouth of Ogden hole, *a distance of more than ten miles!* And this petition was meekly signed by the faithful. While it was circulating, I ventured to ask some of them the object of such a curious petition. The answer was, "we do not know, but Brigham has sent the form of the petition, counseling us to sign it, and that is all that concerns us." One old woman, however, who was shrewd enough to see through the trick, but not wit enough to keep his secret, answered my question in the following words as nearly as I can repeat them.

"Brigham is a cunning fellow—he knows he made a blunder when he laid out the Weber City; but it wont answer for him to acknowledge it. And now he gets us to petition to have it all a city for ten miles, and hereafter if any shall say 'your city was a failure'— he can say: 'you *would not obey counsel;* I *laid out the city in accordance with wisdom;* but you, who *are always rebelling against counsel, would not be satisfied, but petitioned me to change it,* and *to please you, I did so, and now if you all go to the devil it is not my fault—you should obey counsel..*'"26

In this connection, I will mention the *taxing* and *tithing.* The taxes are enormous—amounting to two and a half and three per cent., [sic] on all their property.27 But this is nothing in comparison to the other drafts made upon the purse. *One tenth of everything—*

25. There may have been some uncertainty over the initial location of today's Ogden City, but Goodell has the dates wrong. According to historian B. H. Roberts, Brigham Young chose the site between the two rivers on 3 September 1849. Other sources report that Young and Apostle Heber C. Kimball left Great Salt Lake on 28 August 1850 to locate a city on the Weber, returning on 31 August, shortly before Goodell arrived.

one tenth of the capital, and one tenth of the income. If a man has been to the mines, and made a raise of $1,000—$100 of it goes at once to the high council. Then of the remaining $900—one tenth of the income of that must be given. If a poor widow has *ten* hens, Brigham takes *one* of them—if the remaining *nine* lay *one hundred* eggs, he takes *ten* of them; if from the remaining *ninety* she raises *sixty* chickens, he takes *six* of them, and so on to the end of the chapter. *One tenth of every-thing* [sic]. One tenth of the cows, and then one tenth of the butter and cheese made from the balance. One tenth of the vegetables of the garden, and one tenth of the grain of the farm.

If I am asked—"what becomes of this immense income?"— perhaps I might as well answer in the sublime language of Brigham, himself. Said that distinguished personage in a public address, complaining that the brethren were not prompt in paying these dues, said:—"I am sometimes asked by the brethren, what is done with all the tithing of the Saints?" said he—'I TELL THEM IT IS NONE OF THEIR BUSINESS!'" Surely if it is *none of the business* of the Saints, who have these enormous sums to pay, *what becomes*

---

26. Goodell and the old woman may have underestimated Young. As a territory, Utah by this time came under U.S. land laws, which excluded claims on federal land within the limits of a city or town. To keep outsiders from acquiring land, Utah lawmakers made city limits large enough to control available water and timber resources and arable land. This was probably the reason the Deseret General Assembly, shortly after Young's Weber visit on 26 January 1851, passed a law to incorporate Ogden City. It expanded the city limits and gave the city council "control of the water and timber adjacent upon said streams, from the mouth of the Ogden and Weber river Kanyons [sic] to the western boundary of the city." See Morgan, *The State of Deseret*, 82, 183.

27. Under the law enacted by the Deseret General Assembly on 10 January 1850, property was taxed at the rate of two percent, not the higher amount Goodell indicates. Emigrants to California and Oregon who wintered in Utah bitterly protested this law as unjust and discriminatory. See Unruh, *The Plains Across: The Overland Emigrants and the Trans-Mississippi West, 1840—60*, 325, 326.

of it, it is not the business of us poor gentiles to inquire. A good Mormon woman, however, complaining in the hearing of Mrs. Goodell, that she could get nothing to clothe her children, for every thing they got went to Brigham—saying, it went to *support his wives!*

Respectfully, yours,
J. W. GODDELL

LETTER 4

"This System of Concubinage"

A sojourn of more than six months in Mormon settlements gave Jotham Goodell ample exposure to the practice of polygamy. As an "Old School" Presbyterian minister, the matrimonial system outraged him more than it did most members of the human flood who poured through Salt Lake Valley during the gold rush years with their eyes fixed on the placer diggings along the Sierra Nevada's west slope. The average emigrant stopover to rest, resupply, trade worn-out animals for fresh ones, or enjoy a homecooked meal usually lasted only six or seven days, hardly long enough to think about the number of wives some men appeared to have, even if one cared. Many rough-and-ready gold seekers, who found old rumors of polygamy confirmed by a short visit to Mormon settlements, poked fun at the practice rather than expressing indignation.

Allegedly divinely revealed in 1843 to the faith's first prophet, Joseph Smith, the doctrine of plural marriage was practiced openly in the West, but it was publicly denied for the next nine years, including the time Goodell spent in Utah. What they saw of it did offend some emigrants, especially women, who passed through Mormon settlements later in the gold rush period. Typical of those who disapproved the practice was Lucena Parsons, a twenty-eight-year-old schoolteacher from Wisconsin who viewed so-called "spiritual" wives as "a poor heart broken & deluded lot" who had "not as much liberty as common slaves in the south."[1] And to flaunt her own liberated status before the male-dominated Mormon society, Hannah Keziah Clapp, an early feminist from Michigan, brazenly wore her "bloomer dress" to a service in the Salt Lake City tabernacle. She also packed a pistol on her hip, presumably to discourage some polygamist from attempting to add her to his imagined harem.[2]

The invasion of curious sightseers in 1849 and publication in 1852 of a book about Mormon society in the Great Basin by a respected U.S. Army officer forced leaders of the faith that year publicly to admit and defend the doctrine. Said Lt. John W. Gunnison: "That many have a large number of wives in Deseret, is perfectly manifest to any one residing long among them, and, indeed, the subject begins to be more openly discussed than formerly, and it is announced that a treatise is in preparation, to prove by the scriptures the right of plurality by all Christians, if not to declare their own practice of the same."[3] But "celestial marriage" was less a source of

---

1. Holmes, ed., "Journal of Lucena Parsons," *Covered Wagon Women: Diaries & Letters from the Western Trails, 1840–1890*, 2:274.
2. Ibid., "A Salt Lake City Stopover, July 1859," 7:245–254.

conflict with other Americans at this time than it would become in later years when the enemies of the Mormon Kingdom used it as a moral weapon to destroy theocratic rule.

In the meantime, Goodell in his fourth letter does more than indignantly denounce the marriage custom. The observant New Englander also draws an irreverent and at times amusing picture of Mormon matrimony as engaged in by some of northern Utah's most respected early pioneers.

THE OREGONIAN

PORTLAND, OREGON TERRITORY
SATURDAY, 3 APRIL 1852, VOL. 2, NO. 18, 1.
THE MORMONS. [NO.4]

EDITOR OREGONIAN:

Sir:—I knew little about the Mormons previous to my arrival among them. Living at a great distance from the theatre of their operations, all my knowledge of them was derived from the testimony of others. I knew indeed that they were a *deluded*—but I thought them to be a *persecuted* people. I was disposed to censure the inhabitants of Missouri and Illinois, for the part they took in driving them out of their respective states. Some of the people in Vermillion [*sic*], Ohio, will bear me record, that during the time of the great excitement, consequent upon driving the Mormons from Nauvoo, I publicly declared my conviction, that those measures were both impolitic and unjust, and that Jo Smith was truly a

---

3. Gunnison, *The Mormons, or Latter-day Saints, in the Valley of the Great Salt Lake: A History of their rise and progress, peculiar doctrines, present condition and prospects, derived from personal observation during a residence among them,* 67–77. In announcing the practice, Brigham Young said, "[Polygamy] will be fostered and believed by the more intelligent portions of the world, as one of the best doctrines ever proclaimed to any people." See *Deseret News,* 14 September 1852.

murdered man.[4] I make this remark that the reader may understand that I did not go into the valley with my mind overcharged with prejudice against the Mormons—that I was neither an actor nor sympathizer with those who drove them from Jackson county or Nauvoo, or who imbued their hands in the blood of that prince of imposters—Jo Smith. A great deal had been said in our part of the country, about their abominable practices, but I believed there was much exaggeration, if not misrepresentation. That these leaders were licentious I had no doubt, for it is in accordance with history that such is the character of all imposters. But I also thought that to their followers and to the world they would put on a virtuous garb, and maintain outwardly the appearance of decency at least. Such a state of open, unblushing, beastly impurity and vileness as I found to actually exist among them, I had never dreamed of, and did not suppose could possibly exist among civilized beings. Although from my earliest infancy I had been taught the doctrine of human depravity, I had never expected to witness, on this earth, such glaring development of it.

I think, sir, the apostle Paul tells us in some of his epistles, speaking of certain works of darkness, that "it is a *shame to speak* of those things which are done of them in secret."[5] Had Paul lived in the 19th century, and visited Salt Lake valley, he would have omitted those words *"in secret."* Yes, sir, let it be known that here, in christian America—in a land of Sabbaths and bibles, there exists a large community practicing deeds, openly, in the face of the sun, which one cannot even speak of without shame. Sir, I know not how to pen this article. I cannot tell the truth without shocking the sensibilities of your readers. Were I to pen *all* which they unblushingly avow, you would never publish it in your paper; and if

---

4. Amid growing conflict in western Illinois, following the June 1844 murder of Joseph Smith, the Mormons began their move west from Nauvoo on 4 February 1846 when the first wagons crossed the Mississippi River.

5. Eph. 5:12.

you should, one half of the families to which your paper is a welcome visitor, would not permit it to be read. And yet the people of these United States should know something of the filth and slime of that community, who are wanting to shine amid the glorious constellation of sovereign states which compose this Union—something of that festering mass of disease and death which is issuing from that tomb of corruption, demanding a reception into the bosom of our virtuous republic. Suppose some things, and confining myself to generalities, I will try to give the reader a faint idea of their immoralities.

SUNDERING OF THE MARRIAGE RITES.

The marriage institution—an institution framed by Jehovah himself, and worthy his perfections—an institution fraught with infinite blessings to the human family—blessings which keep the moral world in being, and secures it from an untimely and terrible dissolution—the foundation of natural affections and domestic ties—an institution, which, when respected, elevates man and woman to the highest state of social relations, and when trampled in the dust, degrades them to all that is odious, brutal and savage. This institution the Mormons have trampled under foot, and in its place have reared a system of concubinage of as vile a character as ever debased a ruined man and woman, body and soul, for time and eternity. The marriage *contract*, in which the parties invoked as a witness the great and blessed God, is openly and shamefully violated. These concubines they call *spirituals*—not, I suppose, from any peculiar grace or purity which they possess above other females, but because that when they began to introduce this system of wickedness, it was pretended that this connexion [sic] was only of a *spiritual* character. But now they are prepared to throw off all disguise, and openly declare the true character of their relations. Still the old name of *spiritual* is retained, and used with as much freedom, and is as much a house-hold word among them, as the word *wife* is among decent folks. These *spirituals* are taken publicly, and when a new one is added to the harem, a ceremony is performed. What this ceremony is I did not learn. It binds, however, the man to provide food and raiment for the *spiritual*, and her children, as long as they shall remain *his* spirituals. The woman however can throw off the degrading condition if she can wheedle any one to take her for a wife. And the man can get rid of her, if he can get any one to take her off his hands, and assume her support. A case occurred in the immediate neighborhood of where I spent the winter, where a man of high standing, who had several spirituals, but one of them, a young woman of rather pleasing countenance, carried rather too many guns for her lord to manage, and he hired another man, who had already several spirituals, to take her off his hands, by giving property valued at $300.—These spirituals do not always all reside under the same roof. A man by the name of Brown,[6] living at the Weber, has a row of houses, somewhat resembling negro huts on the plantations in the southern states, where his are kept.—Brigham has, perhaps, some twenty,[7] which he keeps in his large house—the remainder are scattered about, two or three in a place, in his different houses in the city. I was informed by Mormons, who had the means of knowing, that he owned a house in every ward in the city, where he kept some of these women.

Of the number of *spirituals* kept by any one individual, Brigham goes far ahead of any of his followers. Of the exact

---

6. A former Baptist preacher, James Brown, age forty-nine, was the founder of Ogden, Utah. During the War with Mexico in 1846–47 he commanded the Mormon Battalion's detachments at Pueblo where he openly expounded the virtues of polygamy when it was supposed to be kept secret. According to a descendant, he had thirteen wives and at least twenty-four children before his death in 1863 from injuries suffered in a mill accident. See Bigler and Bagley, eds., *Army of Israel: Mormon Battalion Narratives*, 306, 307; and Hill, "Biography of James Brown."

7. Goodell's estimate of the number of Brigham Young's wives in 1850–51 is not far off, but is probably high. Young's biographer Leonard J. Arrington lists twelve in 1846. Before his death in 1877 the Mormon leader took from fifty-three to fifty-six wives, depending on which authority one accepts.

James Brown,
former Mormon Battalion captain and founder of
Brown's Settlement, today's Ogden, reportedly kept
wives in a row of houses on Weber River.
— *Courtesy Utah State Historical Society.*

number, no one knoweth. Indeed, a distinguished Mormon told me that he presumed Brigham did not know himself. The winter that I was there, they were computed by Mormons, who had the best opportunity of knowing, at *seventy* or *eighty*, and he was frequently adding to the number. I perceive that the returned officers from that territory, have set the number down at *ninety!* Others have as high as twenty and thirty—others nine and ten—others five and six, and others again two and three. The rule which Brigham advocates on this subject is, that every man should have as many as he can support!

As most of the inhabitants at the Ogden, where I wintered, had but recently came [sic] to the valley, the number of spirituals were [sic] less numerous. Yet there were enough in all conscience to render the place damnable in the sight of all decency. Why, there was Graham cohabiting with a mother and *her daughter!* as his wives, openly, without rebuke from any one, indeed by Brigham's sanction.[8] And there was Brown, a high Mormon, he had at least eight or ten spirituals. His old wife, (a poor disconsolate, wretched woman, according to the showing of the Mormons, I never saw her), he left in the city.[9] Although there were not many spirituals at the Ogden, I found there was getting a mighty itching among the men to have them, which caused no little fluttering among the wives. For however coolly a woman may look upon this system at a distance, as practiced by others, it cuts to the quick when it comes to her own door. Callous indeed must be that female heart, who

---

8. "Obeying the counsel of [Brigham] Young," forty-seven-year-old Irishman James Graham in 1849 married widow Christiana Gregory Reed, age fifty, and her daughter, Hannah Tucker Reed, twenty-nine, who had a son by a previous marriage. The mother's age suggests this union was not a customary husband-wife relationship. Her daughter bore two children by Graham. See Carter, ed., *Our Pioneer Heritage*, 3:568–69.

9. None of James Brown's known wives at this time appears to meet this description. His first wife, Martha Stephens Brown from North Carolina, who married him in 1823 and bore nine children, died in 1840.

can see without emotion, a stranger enthroned in her husband's affections—to witness those tender ties which bind the affectionate wife to the heart of her husband, sundered at a stroke. A man by the name of Moore, at the Ogden, who had lived several years with an amiable wife, early in the fall fell in love with a young woman, struck up a bargain—went down to Brigham—was married—returned, and duly installed his new bride in her appropriate place, under the domestic roof.[10] Of course his old wife dared not remonstrate—indeed she was compelled to be present and witness the celebration of the nuptials.—She even tried to be cheerful, but the most casual observer could see that a worm was gnawing at the heart. And though she appeared in company with the *new* Mrs. Moore, her haggard looks could not be mistaken, and the Mormon women were compelled to speak of her as "a poor broken hearted woman!"

And there was Lorain [Lorin] Farr, the president of that branch of the church—the father of several children, he became enamored of a pretty black-eyed Welch lass, just budding into womanhood, but his wife happened to be of the true blue. She floundered like a newly caught eel, and giving the reins to that unruly member—the tongue, she poured out such a torrent of burning lava from the pent up fires within, that the black-eyed beauty fled from the house as though the heaven and earth were coming together, and the poor love-sick Lorain had to give up the idea of a spiritual for that time.[11]

And there was a man by the name of Dana, (he might think himself slighted, if I did not give him my compliments.) He came into the valley the fall that I did. We were told by the Mormons

---

10. Canadian David Moore, age thirty-one, on 6 September 1850 married twenty-one-year-old Sarah Barker from England. Nine years before, he had married Susan Maria Vorce from Windsor, Vermont, who was nine years older than he. They had no children of their own but in 1843 adopted Louisa Catherine Smith, the infant daughter of Addison Smith, following the death of her mother at Nauvoo, Illinois. See Moore, Journal and Life History.

that he forsook a wife and family of children in the states.[12] Soon after he came into the valley he married a wife, and also took a spiritual, and was immediately elevated to a high position in the church.[13]

At the visit of Brigham, and the twelve, to the Ogden and Weber, to which I have more than once referred, a great deal was said in their public addresses, not only in defence of this system of concubinage, but by way of urging its extensive adoption. Brigham said—"he felt that the brethren were holding up his hands when they got a number of wives." I thought I could understand this. He knew it was safe to trust men who had married several wives, for they had too much at stake to betray his cause. For if Mormonism were to be blown to atoms, and they compelled to submit to United States law, the penitentiary would be their doom. It was safe to trust that scoundrel Dana, just as soon as he came into the valley and married a wife, with high offices; for now he must sink or swim with Brigham; for should he leave the valley and go to any state in

---

11. If so, he did not give up the idea for long. Four months after Goodell left for Oregon, Lorin Farr married Sarah Giles, his second wife. Nor did he stop there. Before his death in 1908, he had as many as five wives and at least thirty-six children.

12. Assuming Goodell referred to forty-eight-year-old New Yorker Charles Root Dana, his information is not precisely correct. Dana had been sealed to two women in 1846 at Nauvoo, who apparently did not join the Mormon migration, but his first wife, Margaret, died of cholera in 1850 during their journey west with seven of their eight children. In December 1850, Dana married Harriet Gibson, who left him for another man while he was on a mission to Europe. On returning to Utah, he told Brigham Young he wanted "to take me some wives." The very next day, 14 September 1857, Young married him to four English women, Mary Ann Cato, twenty-four; Ann Barlow, twenty-one; and sisters Elizabeth and Jane Culley, twenty-one and twenty-six, respectively, all on the same day. By three of them he fathered sixteen children. See Bitton, *Guide to Mormon Diaries & Autobiographies*, 84, 85.

13. In 1851 Dana was set apart as first counselor to Lorin Farr, first president of the Weber Stake. Later that year he also served in the first Legislative Assembly of Utah Territory and became a councilman in Ogden City.

the Union, the ghost of that forsaken, suffering, broken-hearted, murdered wife, would probably haunt him, and he might possibly get his deserts among many other infamous wretches in the penitentiary. It is with such tools that Brigham holds his sway over that kingdom.

There were other things in this connexion which I had thought to mention, but they are too polluting and I forbear. I will only say that as one abomination after another came to my knowledge, of the most filthy and incestuous character, it seemed to me as though the very earth must open her mouth and swallow them up; and I more than once involuntarily exclaimed to my family—"we must up and out of this place, for God will surely destroy it."

But lest this picture should be thought by some to be overdrawn, I will quote a passage from the communication of an officer—a Major in the United States' army—which was published in the St. Louis Intelligencer, and referred to in my first number: "Truly" he says, "were an angel from heaven to tell you of the wicked practices, and the base unprovoked crimes of this people, you would discredit the report. Such is the enormity of their conduct, that in a series of resolutions drawn up by a Presbyterian clergyman," (that clergyman was the Re. M. Slater, from Tennessee),[14] "and signed by the emigrants, 'the truth and the whole truth' was designedly avoided, lest it should be too shocking for belief." "With them, human feeling has been debased to worse than beastly passion and instinct, and all sympathy is consumed by, or absorbed in lust, while sentiment there finds its lowest degree of degradation."[15]

Nor will I pain your readers with a recital of the disgusting argument, by which they seek to justify this course of conduct.

---

14. This was Nelson Slater, author of *Fruits of Mormonism, A Fair and Candid Statement of Facts Illustrative of Mormon Principles, Mormon Policy, and Mormon Character.*

15. Goodell refers again to Major William Singer's letter in the *St. Louis Intelligencer* on 7 August 1851, Vol. 2, No. 186, 2/3. See Appendix B.

Much of it is too blasphemous for repetition. They even say that the great and blessed Redeemer had no less than three wives— Mary, Martha, and Mary Magdalene.[16] Brigham urges its expediency in order to raise up a "holy seed;" but judging from what I saw, I should take their "seed" to be the seed of devils; for of all the blasphemous wretches out of hell, the children of Salt Lake valley are the chief.[17]

MORMON PROFANITY

This leads me to notice that the Mormons—young and old, high and low, male and female, are by far the most profane people I ever met with. In a life of more than forty years, I never heard so much profane swearing as during the few months I spent in that wretched, mountain-walled prison. Whether Brigham in his private conversation uses profane language, I am not advised, but both he and the twelve are not slow in using it in their public addresses. Such language as "the damned Missourians"—"the damned mobocrats"—"the accursed gentiles," are refined flourishes in their pulpit eloquence. However, it should be said that they do not consider such language as profane. I heard Brigham say in public, that they did not consider any language as profane, unless it was blaspheming the name of Deity.

And here I must notice a curious reformation which took place among them. I had traveled up and down the valley—stopped at their houses—mingled with them in conversation, and every where I went it was the same—profanity!—profanity!!—taking the name of God in vain. But all at once, in the month of February, a wonderful

16. For another report of this teaching, see Gunnison, *The Mormons, or, Latter-day Saints, in The Valley of The Great Salt Lake,* 68.

17. Lt. John W. Gunnison, who came to Utah in 1849–50 as second in command of the Stansbury Expedition to survey Great Salt Lake, said: "Of all the children that have come under our observation, we must, in candor, say, that those of the Mormons are the most lawless and profane." See Gunnison, *The Mormons, or, Latter-day Saints, in the Valley of The Great Salt Lake,* 160.

reformation took place. The high council issued their edict that if any one was guilty of profane swearing, he should be fined and punished.[18] In less than a week, many *emigrants*—how many I do not know, as I was far from the city—were at work on the public buildings, with a ball and chain attached to their limbs. The amount of fines thus collected must have amounted to a considerable sum. I did not in this instance pity the emigrants much; and was sorry that they should have degraded themselves so low as to use the dialect of the Mormons; but I was amused at this lucid demonstration of that quaint idea—the devil punishing sin! And as there were not Mormons fined, it looked for all the world just like a trap, set purposely, to catch emigrants, and I regretted that any were foolish enough to be caught in it.

RESPECTFULLY, YOURS,

J. W. GOODELL

Polk county, O. T

---

18. Goodell apparently refers to Section 19, Criminal Laws of the State of Deseret, enacted on 16 January 1851, which provided that "if any person or persons shall swear by the name of God, or Jesus Christ, in any manner using their names profanely, [he] shall, for each offence, pay the sum of not less than five dollars, or be imprisoned at the discretion of the court." See Morgan, *The State of Deseret*, 178.

Farr's Grist Mill on Ogden River,
near the Goodell family camp, still stands as one of the
oldest buildings in Utah. Painting by David Sawyer.
— *Courtesy Weber State University.*

LETTER 5

"This Infamous Pack of Blood-Hounds"

Over the seemingly endless winter of 1850–1851, Jotham Goodell came to believe that members of a secret body of enforcers known as the Danites kept watch on him around the clock. Nor was he alone in thinking he was being spied on. One hundred fifteen other emigrants who spent the same winter in Utah later signed a memorial to Congress alleging the territory harbored "a class of persons called 'Danites,' appointed for the express purpose of pursuing obnoxious individuals, not only throughout their own dominion, but to other countries, in order to privately dispatch them, in murderous, and in imitation of the savage who, with relentless hate, pursues his victim to death."[1]

The Danites were actually the legacy of an earlier period in Mormon history. Recruited during the 1838 Mormon War in Missouri, this paramilitary society, also known as Sons of

---

1. See Slater, *Fruits of Mormonism*, 91.

Dan, was created to punish dissenters and apostates within the religious movement and intimidate unfriendly outsiders.[2] So secret were its operations that members were sworn to silence under penalty of death. All available evidence shows the order was disbanded when the Mormons moved from Missouri to Illinois. Its legacy cast a dark shadow over the faith's nineteenth-century history, and its legend continued to strike fear in the hearts of Mormon neighbors for years to come.

So it was with Goodell and fellow emigrants. While they were probably mistaken in thinking the eyes of the feared Danites were on them, there can also be little doubt that they were kept under close surveillance by agents of local Mormon authorities, some of whom were former members of the order. The latter included Porter Rockwell, to whom Goodell gave prominent mention in several letters.

The Presbyterian minister also protested the murder that winter of Dr. John M. Vaughn at Manti, which spread fear among wintering emigrants because it went unpunished. There was no doubt about who killed him. Madison Hambleton shot the self-styled "Physician and Oculist"[3] on 9 February 1851 in broad daylight right after church in front of

---

2. The organization took its name from Gen. 49:16, 17: "Dan shall judge his people, as one of the tribes of Israel. Dan shall be a serpent by the way, an adder in the path, that biteth the horse heels, so that his rider shall fall backward." It was first known as the Daughters of Zion (see Mic. 4:13) but this name seemed oddly out of tune with its aims. For more on this order and the evolution of its name, see LeSueur, *The 1838 Mormon War in Missouri*, 40–53; Schindler, *Orrin Porter Rockwell: Man of God, Son of Thunder*, 28–36; and Quinn, *The Mormon Hierarchy: Origins of Power*, 93–99.

3. See advertisement in *Deseret News*, 13 July 1850.

everybody in town, allegedly for seducing his wife.[4] Since Hambleton said later his four children "was all that saved his wife,"[5] the object of the alleged seduction was apparently his first wife, Chelnicia, age thirty-three, not his new second wife, Maria Jane, nineteen.[6] At a March hearing before the Supreme Court of Deseret (a bench of uncertain standing since Utah was by now a territory), Brigham Young showed up and pronounced Hambleton justified. His word was almost always final, but this time not quite.

More than two years after Goodell had gone, Andrew Love at Nephi settlement added a noteworthy Old Testament touch to the affair. Said he: "Saw Brother Madison Hamilton of Sanpete which it appears has forfeited his life & Priesthood by taking back his Wife after Killing Vaughn for seducing her."[7] For reasons unknown, Hambleton was able to escape such dire consequences at a church trial in Great Salt Lake.

In the meantime, Jotham Goodell described Vaughn's murder and other alleged offenses against the lives, property

---

4. Timothy B. Foote at Great Salt Lake had accused Vaughn earlier of the same offence, but the case was apparently dropped. See Brooks, ed., *On the Mormon Frontier: The Diary of Hosea Stout*, 2:380, 381.

5. Journal of Azariah Smith, 11 February 1851.

6. Seduction was a broadly defined offence in Utah during this period. In 1853 an armed posse arrested one Edward Potter, a member of the train of William Hollister (after whom Hollister, California, is now named) for this crime after the emigrant to California offered to assist two girls at Fillmore who reportedly wanted to go back to Ohio rather than become the wives of Bishop Noah Bartholomew. The posse released Potter only after he gave them his horse and Hollister paid an additional $150 fine in cash. See Flint, "Diary of Dr. Thomas Flint," 107, 108.

7. Journal of Andrew Love, 1852–1880, 8 May 1853. For the Old Testament nature of Hambleton's offense, see Lev. 20:10 and Deut. 22:22.

and privacy of the American emigrants, who stopped in Utah for a season on their way to California and Oregon, in his fifth epistle.

THE OREGONIAN

PORTLAND, OREGON TERRITORY
SATURDAY, [15] MAY 1852, VOL. 2, NO. 24, 1.
THE MORMONS, NO. 5.

For No. 4 of this series of articles, see Oregonian of April 3d, which on account of some mistake was received previous to the first three numbers.

EDITOR OREGONIAN—In my last [No.4.] I spoke of the immorality and profaneness of the Mormons. There were several other things which I wanted to say in that connexion, but want of room compelled me to omit them.—There are various *little* items which combine to exhibit the character of a people. Some of these little items I wanted to mention—such as their *disregard of the* BIBLE. This book is seldom read among them; indeed in all my travels among them, I never saw it read, nor did I ever see a copy in any of their houses.

The *Sabbath is disregarded.* So far as I could judge, a large proportion of the inhabitants pursue [sic] their avocations on this as other days. True they have a meeting every Sabbath in the city, and in the other branches of the church; but these meetings, so far as I could learn, were occupied in giving counsel about building mills, herding cattle, paying tithing, raising grain, and a thousand things about temporal matters; the whole interspersed with liberal denunciations of the United States and predictions of the overthrow of its government.

Two meeting houses were built while I was there, one at Utah, and the other at the Ogden, and both were dedicated with a ball! Utah settlement is situated near the lake of that name, in the Utah valley, some fifty miles south of the city. When the new sanctuary at this place was dedicated, it was graced with the presence of Brigham. I happened to be at Utah on that pompous occasion.[8] Brigham made his triumphant entry amid the roaring of cannon, escorted by a company of cavalry. He was riding in a large carriage capable of accommodating some 20 persons, in which I noticed some dozen women, most of whom I was informed were his spirituals. I noticed three or four babies in the arms of the women, but whether they were the legitimate descendants of the prophet, it did not become a poor gentile like myself to inquire. But this, however, does not come up to the story which some of the government party tell, who saw Brigham riding in this same carriage, with *sixteen of his women, fourteen of whom* had babies in their laps![9]

Several other carriages were also in the company containing numbers of the apostles and other big dignitaries, with a large representation from the fold of their wives, and the cradles of their nurseries. That night their new temple was duly consecrated by the merry dance, accompanied with the enchanting sound of the viol, and the bewitching smiles of beauty. So entertaining were the performances of the sanctuary, that the day dawned ere the dedication exercises closed, or the worshipers were weary. As for Brigham, he was so enraptured with the performances, that his heart exploded like a keg of powder, when ignited by a coal of fire; and he actually fell in love with a pretty damsel, and the next day, for he could wait no longer, the nuptials were celebrated, and thus another was added to his already crowded harem!

But, sir, there are matters of a much graver character to which I must call the attention of your readers. And I will notice first,

---

8. Goodell gives no reason for his visit to Fort Utah or the new site of Provo City, some eighty miles south of his winter camp on Willow Creek at present Willard, Utah. He was probably recruiting members of his company that left for Oregon on 27 March. Brigham Young visited Utah Valley on 17–26 March 1851.

9. Apparently another reference to the federal appointees who fled from the territory in 1851.

THE BASE SYSTEM OF ESPIONAGE PRACTICED THERE.

I know this is a grave charge, but I fear it is too true. I received my first convictions of its truth from what the Mormons told me themselves. I was told by Mormons in the city, whose names I am prepared to give at any time under oath, that *no letters deposited in the post office, by either gentiles or Mormons, ever left the valley without its contents being known!* If it contained nothing prejudicial to the Mormons, it was suffered to fulfil its mission, but if it did, it was destroyed.[10] Perhaps my informants were mistaken, but one thing is certain, they honestly believed themselves that such was the fact, and for their life, were their dissatisfaction ever so great, would they dare to communicate a lisp of it to their friends out of the valley. Some of the emigrants tried the experiment while they were there, by writing something which they knew about the Mormons, but we never could learn that any such letters crossed the Rocky mountains. For my part I wrote several letters while in the valley, in some of them I alluded to the vile practices of that people, while in others I purposely avoided all allusion to them. The latter reached their destination in safety, the others my friends never received.—One young man belonging to our company deposited a letter at the post-office. A day or two after, he was passing in the rear of some out houses near to the post-office, and his attention was arrested by observing a large pile of waste paper, and

---

10. Many federal officials and emigrants believed the Salt Lake post office routinely opened their letters and destroyed those that made unflattering remarks about their Mormon hosts. Major William Singer posted his mail from Carson Valley because he had earlier been "constrained by the practice of the Mormons to destroy letters containing anything against themselves." See Appendix B. David H. Burr, non-Mormon surveyor general of Utah, reported Mormon agents waved a letter he had written to the General Land Office in his face and threatened him. For this and other examples, see House Exec. Doc. 71, "The Utah Expedition," 118–21, 124, 125, 138; Slater, *Fruits of Mormonism,* 92; and *The Daily Union,* Sacramento, 28 June 1851, Vol. 1, No. 88, 1/4. See also Appendix C.

actually fished from that pile, *pieces of the identical letter he had mailed*, one of which, if I mistake not contained his signature.[11] Some of these fragments he took into the office and showed to the post master, but obtained no satisfaction. To this statement the young man has expressed his willingness to be qualified to at any time. The next thing to which I will allude is the

MURDER OF AMERICAN CITIZENS.

But here I need to proceed with caution. I would not for my life accuse the Mormons of a single crime of which they are not guilty, and especially of a crime of so high a magnitude as that of murder. But if citizens of the United States, while passing through that Territory, have not been murdered in cold blood, then the Mormons themselves are the most atrocious liars on God's footstool. I was repeatedly told, and so were many other emigrants, all of whom are ready to testify to it under oath, by Mormons of as respectable standing as any in their community, that individuals (some of them only told me of *one*, others told me of two), who had passed through the city on their way to California, and had been recognized as having been associated with the mob in Missouri, and that Brigham had only to say: "*mark that man!*" it was enough—*he never passed the Weber!*[12]

And this was told, not as a secret, but as an act in which they gloried—as one of the ways in which the Almighty was delivering into their hands those who had oppressed them, that they might be

---

11. It is not clear whether the contents of this letter or a shortage of paper in the territory decided its ultimate destination.

12. Whether such stories were true or intended only to frighten former enemies, many emigrants took them seriously. On being told of their danger, two alleged Illinois persecutors took off so fast they forgot to fill their canteens. According to one, "They crossed the Great [Salt Lake] Desert 83 miles without water, and lost their horse; saving their own lives by eating or drinking, perhaps, the blood of a dead creature." See Liles, ed., "*At the Extremity of Civilization*": *An Illinois Physician's Journey to California in 1849*, 158.

avenged. But, mark, the *name* of those executioners so ready to do the bidding of their prophet, was never mentioned. No, the names of those blood-hounds who are sworn to obey all *orders* from the high council, the *Danites*, is [sic] never lisped by Mormons. Nor did the emigrants know much about them till about the time we left the valley, though, as we afterwards learned, they had dogged our steps the whole winter.

And perhaps I may as well speak of this infamous pack of blood-hounds now as ever.—They are the spies—the informers and executioners of that Mormon inquisition, the high council. They are men of desperate character; men who will not flinch at the execution of any order, however bloody. Some of them were leaders in the most notorious band of robbers ever known in the United States. They are sworn to the utmost secrecy and to the prompt execution of any order of their master. Their commission refers not alone to the gentiles, but to their own brethren the Mormons. Acting in the infamous character of spies, they report to the high council every thing transpiring in the valley. The Mormons stand in the utmost awe of them, and well they may. They are frequently sent a great distance to fulfil their mission. One of them went all the way to California last year to "stop a man's breath," as they express it. This the Mormons told me themselves. They did not tell me he was a Danite, for this is a term they never use. But he returned from his mission while I was in the valley, and he was repeatedly pointed out to me with exultation; as being the man who shot Governor Boggs, of Missouri; and, said they, "he went to California this spring on purpose to stop a man's breath, and took an oath before starting, that he would neither cut his hair nor shave his beard while that man breathed!" He returned with his hair cut and his face shaved, and when rallied on the subject said—"the Almighty saved him the trouble of stopping his breath, as the man died a natural death before his arrival."[13] I state things just as I received them from the Mormons. But let the reader understand me, I never heard the term *Danite* mentioned by the Mormons. I learned their character from other sources—from observation, and from the testimony of those Mormons who made their escape with us from the valley. In a future number I will tell the reader the *personal acquaintance* we formed with some of these Danites. A lady, who had been a Mormon,[14] and who had made her escape with us from the valley, informed Mrs. Goodell that the wife of one of these men had told her that she had set up many a night to wash her *husband's bloody shirt* when he came home.

These were the men, if any who were employed to assassinate the emigrants above referred to; a transaction frequently alluded to in that sarcastic phrase: *"pickled down in Salt Lake!"*[15]

Said one of their leaders, in a public discourse at the Bowery: "I saw a man the past week pass through the city, whom I knew as one who assisted in the Mob at Nauvoo, and let him go in peace. But if the Almighty will spare me this time, may he wither my arm if I am guilty of the like again!"[16]

Brigham, too, publicly threatened the lives of the emigrants who wintered in the valley—I will give his language. He was at the

---

13. The renowned Mormon gunman Orrin Porter Rockwell went to California in 1849, ostensibly to escort Apostle Amasa Lyman in delivering Brigham Young's request for tithing money to Samuel Brannan. His main purpose may have been to execute a warrant issued by "judge" Heber C. Kimball for the arrest of Hyrum Gates. In a remarkable display of courage, the forty-seven-year-old Canadian, already married three times before, had eloped to California with Rockwell's daughter, Emily Amanda, age sixteen. He died of unknown causes on 5 September 1850 at Greenwood in El Dorado County. Rockwell was probably not clean-shaven when Goodell may have seen him, since Mormon Prophet Joseph Smith had promised seven years before that if he stayed faithful and let his hair grow, no enemy bullet or blade would ever harm him. For more on this episode, see Schindler, *Orrin Porter Rockwell: Man of God, Son of Thunder,* 184.

14. The editor has been unable to determine this woman's identity.

15. The expression Brigham Young applied in 1847 to anyone who dared to "blaspheme the God of Israel or damn old Jo Smith" was that "we will salt him down in the lake." See Morgan, *The Great Salt Lake,* 202.

Weber,[17] holding forth against the emigrants, many of whom were present. He had just quoted his favorite passage of scripture, the only passage I remember having heard quoted while I was in the valley, and this passage I heard Brigham quote on several occasions. The reader will find it in Ezekiel 9:5,6. He quoted just what follows, and no more: "He said in my hearing, go through the city, and *smite*, let not your eyes spare, neither have ye pity; slay utterly old and young, both maids and little children, and women." He said to his brethren, that the time had come when they had got to fulfil that command, and he had felt it strongly impressed upon him for some time to take up the sword and go forth to slay the wicked!—That they were the people who had got to slay the wicked from the face of the earth. Then turning to the emigrants, he exclaimed: "Hear it ye emigrants! If any of you say ought against the Mormons or their practices we will take off your heads!" Then pausing for a moment, his countenance flushed with rage, he repeated with vehemence: "Yes! We will take off your heads! By the eternal God we will do it, in spite of all the emigrants! And all the United States!! And all hell!!!"

MURDER OF DR. VAUGHN.

From what I have written, it will appear to the reader that there is a strong probability at least, that United States' citizens, while passing through Brigham's territory have been assassinated. But I will not stop at probabilities, I am compelled to relate an event of bloodshed, *done in open day*, if not by Brigham's order, at least by his connivance—the murder of Dr. Vaughn. This occurred while we were in the valley; I think it was in the month of January. I had

---

16. Dr. Thomas Flint of Maine, who drove sheep and cattle over the southern route to California in 1853, said emigrant trains were harassed "in most every conceivable manner, particularly if they were from Illinois or Missouri." See Flint, "Diary of Dr. Thomas Flint," 91–110.

17. This was Brigham Young's visit to the Weber County settlements in January 1851 when he organized the Weber Stake of Zion.

no acquaintance with the Doctor. The murder occurred in the settlement farthest south, while I was in the settlement farthest north. The circumstances, according to the best information I could get from the Mormons, were these: A Mormon suspected that he was too intimate with some of his spirituals, and as Vaughn came out of the meeting house, at the close of a public meeting, surrounded with a multitude of men and women, at mid-day, the murderer stepped up behind him, and with a revolver shot him in the back. The Dr. staggered, turned round, and seeing his murderer, exclaimed: "For God's sake! Why have you shot me?" The murderer damned him and repeated his fire till the Dr. fell dead, only a few rods from the door of the building where the meeting was held.[18] Some said, Mormons I mean, for all my information was from them, that he was struck several times on his head after he fell; but as the matter never underwent a legal investigation, I could get nothing certain with regard to the details. No form of trial was even had. The murderer never was arrested. I happened to be in the city the week following, and was told that he had just come to the city, and Brigham, after hearing his story, had blessed him and told him he served him right![19] I am not aware that the Dr. had any friends in the valley. He was on his way to California. Where he was from I was not able to learn. The Mormons said he had $2000 on his person. What disposition was made of his effects I was

18. According to settler Azariah Smith, Madison Hambleton shot Vaughn once in the left side; otherwise Goodell's account is essentially accurate. Smith said that "after the me[e]ting was dismissed I started for home, but after get[t]ing about 20 foot from the door I stop[p]ed to look around and just as I turned around I heard the report of a pistol about four foot [away] which was loaded very heavy; I instantly looked around and saw brother Hamilton [sic] just taking his pistol from his face, haveing shot doctor Vaughan through his left arm, and in to his body, and it is supposed that the ball struck his heart. he ran about two rod[s] in a short circle and fell right in the path, partly on his side; he did not speak but groaned a lit[t]le, and did not live but a short time." Smith went on to rehearse some town gossip about Vaughn and Hambleton's wife. See Journal of Azariah Smith, 11 February 1851.

never advised. I am not aware that any other emigrants wintered in that part of Mormon territory.

OTHER ACTS OF INJUSTICE TOWARDS THE EMIGRANTS

In the month of December [1850] a large number of emigrants left the valley by the way of the southern route for California. They had proceeded, however, but a few days on their journey, before they were pursued by an armed force and searched, under the pretence that they might have stolen property. Many of them had exchanged cattle in the valley, as the cattle they had brought over the plains were too poor to prosecute the journey. These had been nearly all branded by their Mormon owners, and as the brand had not been changed, they were claimed as stolen property, and bro't back to the city. They, however, in every instance proved themselves innocent and were discharged, after paying a heap of expense.—I was not present at any of these trials, but a gentleman who was, and whose veracity I have no right to question, related the following circumstance: One young man was charged with having a stolen horse; but he proved that he brought the horse through with him from the States; that the horse was branded in the States; that on the day of his arrival in the valley, he put the horse, with the same brand on him, into a herd kept by a Mormon; that the horse remained there till the day he left the valley; proved as clear as day that he was the lawful owner of the horse, and of course they had to honorably acquit him. But *they kept the horse to pay the costs!*[20]

---

19. Young on 17 March 1851 appeared before the Supreme Court of Deseret and "spoke on the part of Hambleton," Hosea Stout said. "[Vaughn's] seduction & illicit conversation with Mrs Hambleton was sufficiently proven insomuch that I was well satisfied of his justification as well as all who were present and plead[ed] to the case to that effect. He was acquitted by the Court and also by the Voice of the people present. The court was not a trial but a Court of Inquiry." Young's justification ended the matter. See Brooks, ed., *On the Mormon Frontier*, 2:396.

There were many instances of unjust and cruel suits instituted against the emigrants, which I might relate, but lest I should prove tedious to the reader, I will confine myself to only a few cases. There was an emigrant by the name of Rider.[21] He spent the winter at the Weber. He was a man of warm temperament, and could not very well submit to be continually bored [sic] by the Mormons without saying something in defence.—One day an old hypocrite fell upon him rough shod for not being a Mormon. Rider endured his browbeating and abuse of the gentiles till he thought endurance ceased to be a virtue, and turning short on his heel he told his tormentor that "if a man in the States should get as many wives as Brigham had, he would be called a notorious libertine." (This was not exactly the word he used, it was of similar import, but a little more offensive.) This was too much for Mormon endurance. Rider was arrested and dragged before the court. I was present at the trial. He was terribly frightened, and well he might be, for what would his shoulders be worth minus the head! He was somewhat in the predicament of the son of Erin who was about to stretch the rope: he said he did not mind hanging at all if they would only adjust the rope to some other part of the body, but he was naturally very *ticklish about the neck*.—He set up his defence—did not deny using the offensive words, but plead in extenuation of his offence, that they were uttered without premeditation, in the heat of excitement, and that upon reflection he was sorry that he had used them; and inasmuch as this was the first offence of the kind he had been guilty of since he had been in the valley, he hoped they would forgive him.—The court, therefore, said that in consideration of the palliating circumstances, his previous good conduct, and his apparent penitence, they would put the fine as low as possible, but

---

20. Nelson Slater, who reported these cases in his own book, may have told Goodell about them. See Slater, *Fruits of Mormonism*, 93.

21. Fifty-four-year-old Aaron, or Ansel, Rider was a millwright from New York who had no other members of his family with him. See 1850 Census for Weber County and Slater, *Fruits of Mormonism*, 93.

warned all other emigrants against presuming too much on account of their great lenity to him. The fine was only $50 and costs; amounting in all to over $80.

One thing was a little curious. This Rider had put up a saw mill for the presiding and associate judges of the court.[22] They were owing him for his labor about $85. His bill against them overbalanced the fine and costs about $150. This small balance, to the credit of the Mormons be it said, he received in cash, and thus this hard labor was paid for his winter's toil! I will, however, take this occasion to congratulate friend Rider for his good success. Other emigrants toiled all winter and were compelled to leave in the spring without a cent, and without the privilege of breathing a lisp in Mormon ear of the infinite contempt they felt for their licentious prophet. Could they have done this—could they have been allowed just two minutes in which they might have given vent to the pent up fires of their deep indignation, and told the Mormons to their faces what they thought of them and their leaders, they would have said: "Keep our wages in welcome. We cheerfully relinquish the whole." Ah, friend Rider, I hope your lines are now fallen to you in pleasant places.[23] Should I ever meet with you again in this world, I hope it will be in very different circumstances, than when you stood trembling at a Mormon tribunal.

Respectfully yours,
J. W. GOODELL

22. Isaac Clark and Lorin Farr.
23. Rider did not go to Oregon with Goodell's company, but went to California where he signed the petition to replace Utah's territorial government with military rule.

LETTER 6

"A Struggle of Life and Death"

By February 1851 the wintering emigrants in Utah were becoming desperate. Without the protection of traditional American law, they viewed with growing alarm an apparent increase in intolerance and discrimination toward them. They also feared they would be punished for the crimes of a few lawless young men among the transients who stayed in Salt Lake Valley that winter before going to the gold fields. Most fearful were those with families moving to make permanent new homes in Oregon and California.

That month, as Goodell tells in his sixth letter, twenty-five or thirty men who had little in common before arriving in Utah came together in secret, or so they thought, and pledged themselves to act as one in protecting their families. They promised to share their resources to the last crumb, if need be, to ensure that all got away safely. They further decided to report to the rest of the country on conditions in the new territory and named Goodell to serve as chairman of a committee of three, apparently chosen on the basis of literacy, to prepare a memorial to Congress. Other panel members were New York schoolteacher Nelson Slater, referred to earlier, and twenty-five-year-old Gold Rush emigrant Asa C. Call, who had studied at Oberlin College in his home state of Ohio.[1]

In the meantime, to avoid giving any offense, real or imagined, to their Mormon neighbors they decided to move away from the settlements and live in their wagons and tents until the arrival of spring allowed them to escape from Utah. As emigrants headed north with their families to locate on Willow Creek and points beyond, Goodell traveled across Salt Lake and Utah valleys to round up Northwest pioneers in a single company.

"Mister Goodal came around hunting up the emagrants that were going to Oregon," recalled forty-three-year-old Solomon Zumwalt, who was wintering on Dry Cottonwood Creek in southern Salt Lake Valley with his wife, Nancy, forty, and their nine children, ranging in age from one to eighteen.[2] Their nearest Mormon neighbors resided on Little Cottonwood Creek, some six miles to the north, on a mile-square plot known as the Amasa Lyman Survey. "There was a settlement of Mississippians there that had some black people," Zumwalt said.[3] These families formed the first

---

1. Ironically Call was a relative of Mormons Cyril and Anson Call. As he left to join a party to California in 1851, he wrote, "I started for their encampment in company with Mr. Slater of whom I have before spoken as being on the committee with Mr. Goodell and myself to draw up a memorial to Congress." Regrettably Call's diary for most of the time he spent in Utah is missing. See John and Vanessa Call, eds., *The Diaries of Asa Cyrus Call: March 28th, 1850 – December 26th, 1853,* April 1851, 81. For Call's letter on 28 June 1851 to *The Daily Union* at Sacramento, see Appendix C.

2. See the 1850–51 Utah Census.

Asa Cyrus Call,
Gold Rush emigrant, was named to serve with Jotham
Goodell and Nelson Slater as a committee to draft a
memorial to Congress on conditions in Utah.
— *Courtesy John R. Call of Derby, Kansas.*

Cottonwood Ward under Bishop William Crosby, a convert
from Mississipi, whose slave, Oscar Crosby, had been one of
three black members of Brigham Young's 1847 pioneer
company.

Unlike Goodell, Zumwalt kept out of trouble with local
settlers, a wise policy for a Missourian, and "got a long well
with the Mormons generally I thought," he said. One day his
son, Andrew Jackson, age eighteen, and an emigrant friend,
William Crow, twenty, visited a camp of Californians near his
cabin. Not knowing they belonged to the faith, Zumwalt said,
the "boys bore down hard on the Mormons." A few days later,
"some emigrants from Utah told me the Mormons talked of
running my cattle off," Zumwalt went on. "I went over to
Little Cottonwood and gave the case just as it was," he said.
"They made light of it, said there were as bad people in the
Mormon Church as there were anywhere. So I was all right
again."4

Even so, Zumwalt decided to join Goodell's company and
pursue his journey to Oregon. He said: "We selected a stream
called Boxelder. It is between Ogden and Bear River. We was
to collect about the 20th of March. I got my herd off of my
hands and started for our rendezvous. I had to pass through
the city [Great Salt Lake]. They levied a tax on me of $19.80. I

---

3. Mulder and Mortensen, eds., "An Oregon Emigrant," in *Among the Mormons: Historic Accounts by Contemporary Observers*, 239–41, using their corrections of Zumwalt's "impossible spelling." Mulder and Mortensen noted, "For want of better evidence to the contrary, Zumwalt's experiences as a winter 'guest' among the Mormons must be accepted as typical of the treatment any law-abiding Gentile received during his sojourn in Zion." For a sample of Zumwalt's original journal, see the Epilogue.
4. Ibid, 240–41.

got to Boxelder. I found a goodly number collected there bound for Oregon. We made a raise of 24 wagons."[5]

How closely outsiders were watched in the controlled society became apparent soon after Goodell agreed to serve as chairman of the committee to draft a memorial to Congress. The dubious honor would have dire consequences for the Presbyterian minister and his family. He now became the target of nuisance lawsuits that for many transients proved more life-threatening than annoying. A frequent outcome was that the emigrant paid all court costs, including those of arresting officers or posse members and often highly inflated, whether he was found guilty or not. If he could not pay, the court attached his possessions, starting with horses and oxen, the animals needed for survival.[6]

Over the next six weeks, such proceedings would impoverish Goodell, whose possessions were modest to start with. To move his family to its final destination in Willamette Valley, he would be forced to depend on the charity of another, ironically a Mormon. In the meantime he vowed to go to Oregon with packs and children on his back if that was what it would take to get away.

---

5. Ibid, 240.

6. In one example, emigrant William Fuller and twenty-three others in 1852 forded Weber and Ogden rivers rather than use the toll bridges operated by the same James Brown mentioned by Goodell. Even so, Brown imposed the toll anyway. An officer and "twelve or fifteen men armed to the teeth" arrested them on Bear River. With the posse rode the judge who imposed fines and costs totaling $120, no small sum at that time. "Many of us had no money," Fuller said, so the officer took a horse, guns and other property "at about a third of their actual value." One posse member told him that Brown had a similar dispute with emigrants almost every day. See Fuller to Young, 23 July 1852, Brigham Young Collection, MS 1234, LDS Archives; and Marriott Library, University of Utah.

THE OREGONIAN

PORTLAND, OREGON TERRITORY
SATURDAY, 22 MAY 1852, VOL. 2, NO. 25, 1.
THE MORMONS, NO. 6.

EDITOR OREGONIAN—Slowly did the days and weeks of our imprisonment among the Mormons wear away. It seemed as though the winter would never be gone. February came at last, but as we looked upon the towering mountains around us, it seemed as though it would require an age of warm sunshine to thaw away the snow sufficiently to permit us to escape to a land of morality and religion. Every day, too, seemed to come loaded with some new foreboding of evil. The gathering clouds of Mormon intolerance were seen in the distance, rolling up in blackening volumes, and the muttering thunder of inquisitorial wrath, warned us that a storm was nigh. Every messenger from other parts of the valley confirmed our suspicions that "evil was determined against us." Numbers had been arrested in the city, as we were informed, and without trial, and in some instances without knowing their accusation, had been loaded with irons. Many for the most trivial offences, or rather for that which in any other lands would be no offence at all, had been amerced in heavy fines.[7] We were told that the emigrants were all to be taxed before they left the valley.[8] Our property, and even our lives, had been threatened by the high council. A strong guard was secretly stationed every night, for some purpose, on all the thoroughfares leading from the city. What this purpose was, I never could

---

7. To punish by a pecuniary penalty the amount of which is not fixed by law but is left to the discretion of the court.

8. Emigrants often complained about the 2 percent tax levied on their property by the General Assembly of Deseret. They protested that property was arbitrarily assessed at inflated values and the tax imposed the same day with no opportunity to appeal. See Unruh, *The Plains Across*, 325–27.

divine, and should have doubted the truth of the report if it had not been confirmed in the following way:

THE MORMONS CAUGHT IN THEIR OWN TRAP

Brigham had stationed this guard about the city[9] so privately that very few Mormons were aware of its existence. A bridge west of the city had been thus guarded. Brigham's brother had occasion to cross this bridge in the night. Perhaps he was making a pious visit to one of his spirituals out of the city, and his thoughts were so absorbed with *spiritual* contemplations, he had forgotten his illustrious brother had guarded the bridge against the approach of ungodly gentiles.[10] He approaches the bridge—the night is dark and gloomy—a voice from the bridge breaks upon his ear: 'Who goes there!' Not dreaming of a guard, and suspecting robbers, he turned his horse to fly—a stream of fire issues from the bridge, followed with the crack of the deadly rifle, and the brother of the prophet was rolling in the mud! Thanks, however, to the guardian spirits about him, he was not killed—a ball had broken his arm, which was the only injury he received.[11]

---

9. Great Salt Lake City.

10. Forty-three-year-old Lorenzo Dow Young had but two wives at this time, neither of whom lived west of the Jordan River. Earlier that day, 1 March 1851, the gentle younger brother of Brigham Young, a devoted horticulturist, had visited his land on that side of the stream to tend his garden and sheep.

11. Guards on the bridge, where North Temple Street now crosses the Jordan River, shot Young when he ignored their challenge and spurred his horse to get away, fearing they were outlaws. One ball just missed his head, but another struck his upper left arm allegedly severing the artery, but not breaking the bone. He rode to a nearby house and asked the owner and another Mormon to "lay hands on me, and ask the Lord to stop this blood." They did so and "the blood stopped flowing while their hands were still on my head," Young said. See Little, "Biography of Lorenzo Dow Young," winter 1850–51.

THE EMIGRANT MEETING.

One event of thrilling interest following another in rapid succession, the open threats of Brigham and the twelve apostles, filled the emigrants with alarm. There were many emigrants in the valley—some for Oregon, the great mass for California. Among these we had no doubt would be found some as bad as the Mormons, and who, perhaps, had left the States to escape the penitentiary. We were afraid they might commit some act of wickedness that would give the Mormons a pretext for injustice and robbery. We were afraid, too, that men of warm temperament might be provoked to say something which might endanger our safety.—Up to this time there had been no concert among the emigrants. They were scarcely known to each other. But now they began to whisper to each other and ask—"What is to be done?" One said—"I am here with my wife and children; my means are all expended; I have barely team enough to take me out of the valley; if they should fine me, as they did Rider, they would take my team, and then what should I do?"[12] We felt the need of consultation, and resolved to have it. But how? Though American citizens, and on American soil, we dared not meet publicly to peaceably inquire what we should do. If we met at all, it must be by stealth. An emigrant had built his shanty far from the settlement, here, on a certain day, 25 or 30 emigrants *accidentally* met. We were by ourselves. No Mormon near us, we fully discussed the course we were to pursue under existing circumstances. We exhorted one another to prudence in all our intercourse with the Mormons; to say nothing and do nothing that could give them the least occasion against us. We pledged ourselves to stand by each other in case of difficulty, and to divide our last morsel with the unfortunate, to enable them to leave the valley. Fearful some one might be provoked to say something against the Mormons, we concluded to move out from the settlements, and proceed as far north as the mountains would permit,

---

12. For Rider's case see Letter 5.

and spend the rest of the winter in our wagons. A day was fixed upon for moving, and a committee appointed to go forward and select a camping ground. A committee was also appointed to draft a memorial to Congress on the subject of our unjust and cruel treatment. Of this committee, unfortunately for me, I was made the chairman. The meeting closed, and the emigrants, most of them, retired in better spirits than they had been in for a long time. Alas! We little knew what the future was to reveal! Before 12 o'clock that night the high council were in possession of all that was done at that meeting! Does the reader ask—"How was this?" I can only answer by referring him to what I said in my last number about the *Danites.* Our subsequent acquaintance with some of these gentlemen unraveled the mystery.

Personal Troubles.

Up to this time I had managed to avoid all difficulty myself with the Mormons. Having at the first formed the resolution to quietly pass away the winter without any controversy with them, I had been enabled thus far to carry it out. True, I had been compelled to submit to a great deal of browbeating and abuse, of extortion and robbery, yet so quietly had I submitted to it, that many thought I was almost a Mormon! But now the scene was to change. A morning or two after the meeting above referred to, an old Mormon elder came into my shanty in a perfect rage. He fairly foamed at the mouth. Smiting his fists together, with great vehemence, he pronounced me a damned mobocrat! "Here," said he, "the Mormons have taken you in, and protected you, and if they had not done it, you would have been dead and in hell!" I tried, in a cool way, to tell the old man that we had protected the Mormons as much as they had protected us, and to remind him how earnestly he had himself besought me to stop there and help defend them against the Indians. But it was of no use, I might as well have reasoned with the tornado. I was a mobocrat! That was what I was, and if I was suffered to leave the valley, the first thing they would hear of me I would be writing against the Mormons, and he was going right down to the city and inform of me to the high council. This was in the presence of my family, who were much alarmed at his closing threat. But as I had a good understanding with all the Mormons with whom I had formed any acquaintance, and as the time was near when we were to leave their settlements, I flattered myself that I should get off without difficulty.

The day at length came when we were to form our encampment at Willow creek, 20 miles this side [of] the Weber.[13] I was nearly ready to start when I was waited upon by an officer of the law, who very politely informed me I was his prisoner. A prisoner? For what? Why, here is a demand against you—the price of 3 bushels of wheat at $3 per bushel, $9.00; and the costs, making in all a bill of about $16.00. Well, what about this wheat? And how came you to owe for it? The reader will be apt to inquire.

When I went into the valley, my first care was to secure bread for my family. I bought at once all the wheat I thought I should need during my stay, paying at the rate of $3 per bushel. Nearly one half of this wheat was stolen from me, and went to feed the families of the "saints." Eight bushels went at one time—three at another, and so on. I had good reason to believe where the eight bushels went to, but I thought prudence the better part of valor, and so held my tongue. Unfortunately I had positive proof who took the three bushels. He acknowledged he took it, and paid me for it. But now he sued to recover back the money! So I was a prisoner, and as such, was brought before their honors, Esq. Brown and Esq. Dona.[14] I demanded a jury trial. It was granted, and a jury of 6 men, all Mormons, was summoned. The case came on. The plaintiff admitted he took the wheat—took it without my knowledge

---

13. Willow Creek is the site of present Willard, Utah. The mileage suggests that Goodell may have confused Willow Creek with nearby Box Elder Creek, location of today's Brigham City.

14. James Brown and Charles Root Dana.

or consent, but said he was going to mill for brother McGary, and brother McGary wanted more wheat, and sent him to *borrow* this wheat of me, and as I was not at home, he took it without my leave, intending brother McGary should return it.—Brother McGary swore that he never sent the plaintiff to borrow any wheat of me, and never received any to his knowledge.[15] This was the substance of the whole matter as it came before the court, as every emigrant who was present will testify. The two magistrates, however, told the jury there was no doubt but brother McGary had the wheat—that the plaintiff was acting as his agent, and therefore I must look, not to the plaintiff, but to brother McGary for my pay! The jury, under this charge, retired, and I had no doubt but would return a verdict against me. But to my surprise, and to their credit, they returned a verdict of "No cause of action." I was free, and returned to my family with a light heart. The next day we started for our encampment, and had got about half way there, when along came the sheriff and made me his prisoner. They had appealed the case to the county court, and the judges had ordered a special session of the court to be held the next day, to try that important case of $9.00! I had to leave my family and teams right in the road. The snow was then about 6 inches deep, and falling very fast, fuel was scarce, and the cold was intense. To add to our misery, the two young men who were with me, were both taken back by the sheriff at the same time,[16] and my wife and oldest daughter, and six little children, were left alone in the storm, with no other protection

---

15. This may have been forty-two-year-old Canadian Charles Aron McGary, a blacksmith, who arrived in Utah in 1850 and settled at Ogden. In 1855 McGary was called to serve as an Indian missionary at Fort Limhi, near present Salmon, Idaho.

16. Goodell no doubt refers to his two sons in-law, Holden A. Judson, age twenty-four, who was going to California while his wife, Phoebe Goodell, remained in Ohio, and twenty-five-year-old emigrant Nathan H. Melory from Pennsylvania, who married Phoebe's twin sister, Mary Goodell, at the Ogden River emigrant camp in December 1850.

than the   wagons. That night and the next day will be remembered by my family, while they have a being, as one of fear and suffering. The storm increased all night and the next day. Having no fire, they remained in their wagons all day, wrapped in their blankets, in the deepest anxiety as to what was to be our fate. One of the young men succeeded in reaching them that night about midnight, built a fire, and made them comparatively comfortable.

But let us return to the narrative. When I reached the fort, I was met by one of the emigrants in great terror, who assured me I was a doomed man, "for," said he, "I heard President Farr say this morning in conversation with a brother Mormon, that it would be no use now for you to get a jury, for if you should, and the jury should return a verdict in your favor, the judge would at once set it aside." At this stage of the proceedings, situated as I was, I should have submitted to the outrage, and went forward and paid the whole sum, costs and all, amounting to about $50, if I had had the money. But I had it not, and knew not where to get it, without sacrificing my team, and hence it had become with me a struggle of life and death.

Depending, therefore, upon the justice of my cause, I went into court and demanded a jury. The jury was impanneled, [sic] and the case came on. No new feature was introduced, save that wheat was now, in the month of February, worth but $2.50 per bushel, and so they demand, at least, a verdict of $1.50 against me. The jury retired, but could not agree. They all agreed that I ought not to pay back to the man the price of the wheat which he had taken from me without leave, but two of them thought that as wheat had fell [sic] since I purchased it, I ought to pay $1.50 and the costs! The jury could not agree, so we had to have a third trial.

The third and last trial came. The jury returned a verdict of "No cause of action."—For once, I will assure the reader, my heart beat quick. Surely, thought I, I am free! I am free! But judge of my surprise, when the judge on the bench began to inquire: "Who shall pay the costs?" "*No cause of action,* is not a verdict for either party," said the learned judge. My counsel informed his honor, that when a man in the States commenced a suit without cause, he must pay his own costs. The judge would not allow him to proceed. Said they had nothing to do with United States law, nor with the usages of courts in the United States.[17]

But I will not detain the reader longer with personal matters. Suffice it to say, two days after this the sheriff came and attached all my team and wagons for the costs, and had it not been for a Mormon who left the valley with us, who advanced the money, waiting on me till we got to Oregon for his pay, I know not but we should have been compelled to have taken our packs and our little ones on our backs and come through on foot; for I will assure the whole Mormon fraternity we should have done this, sooner than we would have staid in that den of pollution. One thing is certain, if a Mormon were ever to take any of my property again without leave, I should pay him whatever he should ask for his trouble in carrying it off, and then hold my peace. This three bushels of stolen wheat cost me about $75.

Respectfully yours,
J. W. GOODELL.

---

17. One emigrant that winter said he heard Apostle Willard Richards say, "what was law one day, was not law another day; that they [the Mormons] were governed by the Holy Ghost." In what may have been the same case, Mormon attorney Hosea Stout noted on 23 January 1851 that Richards warned the officers of the court "never to admit a foul spirit [apparently referring to non-Mormon lawyer James McCabe from Michigan] where the Holy spirit should rule and direct either the affairs of State or Church." See Slater, *Fruits of Mormonism*, 12; and Brooks, ed., *On the Mormon Frontier*, 2:389.

LETTER 7

"How the Dogs Howled"

About the time Jotham Goodell moved north to distance his family from Ogden settlements, the State Attorney of Deseret at Great Salt Lake made an ominous prediction of things to come for the Oregon pioneer and his fellow sojourners. "The emegrants [*sic*] are commencing to move off," wrote the forty-year-old Hosea Stout, the former police chief of Nauvoo. "Several of our people are now out after them which I expect will result in quite a number of emegrants being arrested & brought back for trial," the Kentuckian went on. "The appearance now is that we will have an uncommon full docket at the next term of Court in March."[1]

The move away from Mormon settlements to Willow Creek not only took the emigrants to a more secure location. It also placed them on the main road from Salt Lake to California and Oregon, known as Hensley's Salt Lake Cutoff,

---

1. Brooks, ed., *On the Mormon Frontier,* 20 February 1851, 2:393.

opened in 1848 by California pioneer Samuel J. Hensley and a ten-man pack party. Bypassing Fort Hall, this short cut ran on the line of present Interstate 84 and Utah Highways 30 and 42 to Raft River in southern Idaho. At that point, Oregon pioneers followed this stream to meet the Oregon Trail on Snake River, while California pioneers struck the California Trail in the Silent City of Rocks, near present Almo, Idaho. Either way, the emigrants at Willow Creek were well placed to take off as soon as the weather allowed.

How Deseret Attorney Stout found out about the move on about the same day it occurred is suggested in Goodell's seventh letter. In it, he describes an apparent spy who joined the emigrant encampment claiming he was a disaffected Mormon who was fed up with the theocratic system and wanted to leave. This infiltrator's appearance and story fooled no one, and if he deliberately tried to lay a snare for emigrants by leading them to commit a criminal act, as Goodell suggests, he failed in his clumsy attempt at entrapment.

The one who followed this mysterious interloper to the emigrant encampment, however, did not fail to do what he came for. This visitor held the combined offices of marshal, assessor and collector of taxes, and brigadier general of the Nauvoo Legion for the State of Deseret. In his letter, Goodell pours out his feelings over the treatment he and others suffered at the hands of this authoritarian figure. His anger and indignation were as fresh a year after as they were the day it happened.

THE OREGONIAN

PORTLAND, OREGON TERRITORY
SATURDAY, 12 JUNE 1852, VOL. 2, NO.28, 1.
THE MORMONS, NO. 7.

EDITOR OREGONIAN:

It was about the 20th of February that we bade adieu to Mormon settlements, and formed our encampment on Willow Creek. We had hoped that here, unmolested, we should have been permitted quietly to wait till the snow should thaw in the mountains sufficiently, to permit us to leave a valley, which to many of us, had emphatically been a *vale of tears.* We soon found, however, that our hope in this respect was a delusive one; that the place of promised security was the scene of our greatest trials.

A DANITE DISCOVERED IN CAMP.

While I was a prisoner at the Weber for daring to take pay for three bushels of wheat that had been stolen from me, I was introduced by some emigrants, in whose prudence I had great confidence, to a Mormon, who pretended to be terribly disgusted with the whole system, and anxious to leave the valley. In no measured terms he denounced Brigham and the twelve, as the vilest imposters that ever cursed the earth. I was surprised at the boldness of his denunciations, but the circumstances under which he had been introduced to me, disarmed suspicion. At that time I had but very little knowledge of the Danites, and was disposed to be incredulous with regard to them. There was something, however, in the appearance of this man, which struck me as singular. He was armed to the teeth; a superb Spanish dirk reposed in a scabbard, stuck in his leggins; his belt secured a brace of Colt's revolvers. I rallied him on his being so well armed.[2] "Yes," he said, "he meant to be ready for Brigham's boys, should they come after him."

---

2. Goodell's clues provide insufficient evidence to identity this man.

The day following he requested an interview with me, at which he informed me he meant to leave the valley, and should like to join our company—gave me a history of his connexion with the Mormons. At first he thought they were a good people, till he came to the valley and learned some of their abominations; had been disgusted with them for a long time, and should have left them before, but for his wife, who was a Mormon, and determined to stay among them; that he had now made up his mind to leave at any rate, whether she would or not; that he loved his wife, and wanted to take her with him, but he knew she would not go—said he should have to sacrifice all his property, &c., &c. I told him we could promise him no assistance; that we were scarcely able to help ourselves, and if we got out, we should be thankful. He said he knew we had been most shamefully treated, and if he was in our places he would have revenge before he left the valley; said he could put us in a way of indemnifying ourselves for all the robberies the Mormons had committed upon us; said if we would admit him into our company, he would take it upon himself to drive off large herds of horses and cattle, which would not be missed, till we had got well on our way to Oregon—too far for the Mormons to pursue; said he knew every inch of the road to the Pacific; that he would not compromise the company; that he would travel on a parallel line with the company, and occasionally come into camp to get provisions, &c.

From these remarks, I at once inferred that he was a consummate villain, and held no further conversation with him. A few hours afterwards he started for the encampment.—Shortly after he left, a good Mormon lady, who left the valley with us, and who had witnessed my interview with him, whispered in my ear—*that man is a Danite,* BEWARE! I was instantly alarmed for my friends at the encampment. I knew he had been sent by his master to lay a snare for our feet. What that snare might be, God only knew. I had no means of putting them on their guard, and was obliged to wait the issue.

MORMON CHIVALRY.

Late in the afternoon of the next day, I observed an uncommon stir at the fort.[3] Armed men were gathering in the streets—officers, fully equipped, were riding back and forward, and something of great moment seemed to be on foot. What it could be, I could not divine; but from the profound secrecy of the affair, I inferred that evil was determined against my friends at the encampment. But what could it be? Why should they send an armed force against an inoffensive company, composed chiefly of women and children? I knew there was a Danite in the camp, and I feared his presence, in some way, had a connection with this movement of troops. But what are they going to do with soldiers? Are they going to exterminate us?—A storm, I was certain, was about to burst upon my friends—among whom was my own unprotected family. But what could I do? A prisoner myself, I could not fly to their relief, or even inform them of the threatening storm. After dark, the stir of preparation seemed to increase. A young man, an emigrant, who had been left at the fort sick, and was still quite ill, volunteered to take a message to the encampment. He mounted a horse, but had scarcely left the fort before he was stopped by a guard, and warned to remain quiet at the fort until morning. This information increased my alarm. A guard on the road that leads to the encampment! What does this mean? The young man, however, resolutely determined not to be foiled; so leaving his horse, and under cover of darkness stole past the guard, and though very ill, make [sic] his way on foot, wading through snow up to his knees, and delivered his message, a short time before the arrival of the armed force.

You may judge, sir, that this night was to me a sleepless one. About midnight, the bustle ceased, and all was quiet till about an hour before day, when a great tramp of horses was heard in the streets, and looking out of the door, I could discern a line of cavalry, drawn up in martial order, numbering forty or fifty men.—

3. Brown's Settlement.

After calling the roll, I heard the order given—"MOUNT!" and they passed rapidly out of the fort, and then all was quiet.

What was done at the encampment I learned from my friends.

They reached the encampment just as the emigrants were peacefully finishing their morning repast. Passing round a bluff, that they might not be discovered till they were close upon the camp, they made a full charge and took the whole camp—men, women and children! It was, sir, a glorious achievement, such as the annals of war present but few examples! If Brigham does not engrave the name of the commanding officer, and of every private under his command, in the walls of the Temple of the City of the Saints, may he be henpecked by his wives as long as [he] lives! Why, sir, of all the men, women and children, cattle and horses, dogs and cats of that whole encampment, not one escaped! So intrepid and gallant a charge of cavalry has not been known in modern days. I regret that I have not the name of the distinguished chief in command, that I could do him honor in this narrative. No doubt his bosom swelled with glorious emotion, as he informed his illustrious master of the panic into which he threw the enemy—how the dogs howled—the children shrieked and clung to their mothers—the women cried, and the men swore! And all accomplished by a single charge of cavalry! A few more such intrepid charges, and the world will be annihilated—the Gentiles will be slain, (that is the *male* portion,) and the "Saints" and *the women* will possess the earth! I have no doubt but Brigham's legislature had this feat in their eye, when they assured congress that they were "a people possessed of more than Spartan intrepidity and fortitude."[4]

But, sir, to be serious, and return to the narrative: Having taken possession of our camp, their first business was to secure their spy, the Danite, to which I have already referred; this they did with considerable flourish—pretending that he was guilty of enormous crimes, and that the company were knowing to it, and of course equally guilty; and that there were others of similar character

---

4. See House Exec. Doc. 25, Appendix A, page 202.

among them, and unless they were given up they were to be all marched back to the city. A guard was placed at each tent and wagon, to prevent the emigrants from holding any correspondence with each other. In this position they were kept that day and night and the next day till about noon, when they were released, and the gallant troop, taking with them their *famous prisoner*, fell back to head quarters. I witnessed their return to the fort. Their prisoner had been liberated, and was riding with the commanding officer, at the head of the company, and was received by President Farr, and the other Mormon officials with marked respect. His arrest was all a farce—a piece of Mormon jesuitism—to blind the eyes of the emigrants. He was sent there by the order of Brigham, to lay a snare for the emigrants. The plot was a cunning one, which Brigham had no doubt would certainly succeed. This Danite was to represent himself as a disaffected Mormon—anxious to leave the valley. Having obtained the sympathies of the emigrants, he was to propose to drive off a band of cattle, as some compensation for the robberies he had suffered from the Mormons. He would not compromise the company—would not travel with the company, but occasionally come into camp to get provisions. This was all he would ask of the company—occasionally to furnish him with provisions. This plan, Brigham had no doubt the emigrants, some of them at least, would countenance. The Danite would then come in as a witness—fines of course would follow, and then we should have lost our teams if not our lives. There is not a particle of doubt but that if the emigrants had shown that wretched Danite the least favor, the whole company would have been marched down to the city, and where the matter would have ended God only knows. Thanks to a kind Providence that shielded us from this snare! This cut-throat failed in his mission. The emigrants were on their guard. They had no secrets to divulge, and they were generally too high-minded, and possessed too much principle, to listen to dishonest plans.

The next visit we received from the servants of Brigham, was in the shape of the State Marshal and his posse to collect taxes from us.[5]—The season of the year for assessing property in the valley had not yet arrived. This usually was done in the month of May, and the taxes were collected in the months of November and December. But the emigrants must be taxed. Brigham had decreed it—his servants were ready to enforce it. Accordingly the State Marshal, armed to the teeth, pursued us to our encampment, between 60 and 70 miles this side of the city, and nearly 20 miles this side of any of their settlements, with authority to assess our property, and if the taxes were not paid on the spot, to drive off our teams. He also informed us that his instructions were, "to make diligent search after we had given in our property, and if he found any which we had not given in, *he was to consider it as forfeited and to take it into his immediate possession.*"

Our property was valued at Salt Lake prices, and the amount of taxes to each emigrant who had a team, ranged from $15 to $60. I know of none in our company who paid less than $15. My own taxes on 4 yoke of oxen, 4 cows, two wagons, a silver watch, and what few rags we had left to keep us warm, amounted to $18.80. Mr. Harlow,[6] a worthy emigrant from Missouri, who had 5 wagons, and teams to draw them, had to pay between $50 and $60 tax. Aware of Brigham's impudence, and that it would be just like him to deny the statements of the emigrants, we were careful to demand receipts for our money, which was reluctantly complied with.

The Marshal was one of the twelve apostles, and as he approached my tent, with his huge knife stuck in his leggins, and his pistols by his side, I could not help drawing a contrast between

---

5. Although Utah was by now a territory, the 2 percent tax was imposed under the ordinances of the State of Deseret. This makes it probable that this official was thirty-five-year-old Horace S. Eldredge, a native of upstate New York, who was Deseret's marshal and tax assessor and collector, as well as brigadier general, not Joseph L. Heywood, appointed U.S. marshal for the territory by President Fillmore.

6. The 1850 Utah Census for Weber County lists M. H. Harlow, age forty, and his wife, Frances, thirty-six, as natives of Kentucky, but their four children, ages eight, ten, twelve and fourteen, were born in Missouri.

Marshal Horace S. Eldredge,
Deseret tax assessor and collector, probably imposed
the 2 percent tax on fleeing emigrants in 1851.
— *Courtesy Utah State Historical Society.*

him and the apostle Paul![7] However, when I came to hear his language, I could not doubt his title to the apostleship, for who but an apostle would tell a man he was "a d—d fool," for asking for a proper receipt for taxes!

This tax was not only unjust but *cruel* to the last extreme. We were traveling the vast desert which separates the Pacific from the Atlantic States. We had been compelled by distress to stop at this, which should be, half way house, during the winter months. This was an item of expense in the journey which few had made provision for. Many of the emigrants had already expended their last cent, and were now living on coarse bread, without meat or vegetables. A thousand miles of dreary waste still lay between them and the end of their journey. At the closest calculation they had barely bread enough to last them to Oregon, if they could come directly through. But they were confined by snowy peaks, and how long it might be before they could commence their journey, none could tell. To pay this tax, some families were compelled to sacrifice the cow which they had hoped would afford nourishment to the little ones on the way. Others had to part with a portion of the team already too weak for the journey.

I remember how forcibly the injustice and cruelty of this measure was impressed on my mind, by a remark which a gentleman sympathizingly expressed, soon after I arrived in the valley. He hoped that Congress would make them refund the money. Refund the money! and what compensation would that be? I confess that the very thought of their making reparation for this robbery, by refunding the paltry dimes they took from us, chilled my blood.

---

7. Whether the marshal was Horace S. Eldredge, as is likely (see note 5 above), or U.S. Marshal for Utah Territory, Joseph L. Heywood, he was not an L.D.S. apostle as Goodell claimed. At this time, however, both were members of the ultra-secret Council of Fifty, ruling body of the Kingdom of God and, as such, powerful figures in the Mormon theocracy.

Would the mariner, whose ship had foundered at sea a thousand miles from land, who had taken his desperate chance in an open boat, with a morsel of bread, not knowing but weeks might intervene before he would be picked up by any ship, and a pirate had fell upon him in his helplessness and robbed him of one-half of his morsel—would he consider it any atonement for such robbery, if, after he had reached the shore in safety and was basking at the table of sympathizing friends, were the pirate to enter and profer [sic] back the stolen morsel?

Were Brigham to come in person and tender back the money he robbed us of, there is not a man among us but would exclaim: "*Your money perish with you! In our distress and anguish of soul, you robbed us of our all, and exposed our wives and little ones to the danger of perishing with famine, amid the wastes of the desert!* When we had but a morsel, and long long miles intervened between us and civilized man, you robbed us of that, and now, when we are full, do you hope to wipe out the blot from your polluted soul, by coming and offering back to us the morsel? Never, *never,* NEVER!"

J. W. GOODELL

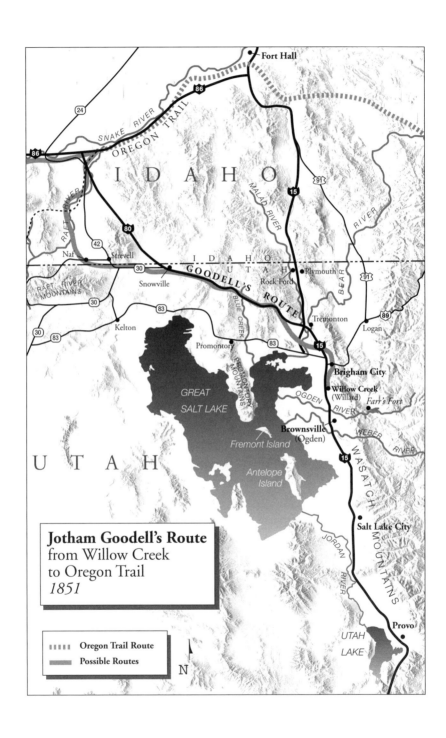

Jotham Goodell's Route
from Willow Creek
to Oregon Trail
1851

LETTER 8

"Some Wept With Joy"

Like a gift from "a kind providence," spring in 1851 came
early to open the way for Jotham Goodell and his growing
company of emigrants on Willow Creek to escape from Utah
a full month earlier than they had hoped. Before the snows
melted on the northern rim of the Great Basin, however, they
would undergo new trials that made their departure all the
sweeter. In reporting them in his eighth letter, he became an
early voice in a rising chorus of allegations during the mid-
1850s that Mormon agents, intentionally or not, encouraged
Indian depredations against emigrants on the overland trails.[1]

---

1. For examples see "The Utah Expedition," House Exec. Doc. 71, 139–44,
150–54, 175–82, 186–205; *Alta California,* 10 September 1854; *Sacramento Daily
Union,* 10 September 1857; *Daily Alta California,* 18 October 1857; *San
Francisco Evening Bulletin,* 28 October and 2 November 1857; and *San
Francisco Herald,* 2, 9, 12 November 1857.

Even before the Mountain Meadows Massacre in 1857,[2] other Americans had taken alarm at Mormon beliefs that the Indians, or Lamanites, were the descendants of Joseph, a remnant of Jacob in the New World and the Mormons' own Israelite cousins by blood. Hardly a source of comfort for settlers on the frontier or emigrants on the overland trails were *The Book of Mormon* promises that in the Last Days this remnant of Israel, meaning America's Indian nations, would sweep through the midst of unrepentant gentiles "as a young lion among the flocks of sheep."[3]

In 1857 President James Buchanan submitted nearly sixty documents to Congress to justify his decision to dispatch American troops to Utah to enforce federal sovereignty over the recalcitrant territory. Of this number, three-fourths came from files of the Office of Indian Affairs.[4] Written by U.S. Indian agents over a six-year period, these reports and emigrant claims indicate that the Presbyterian minister's accusations cannot be dismissed out of hand.

Goodell's eighth letter also describes how the emigrants, in the interest of their own survival, became vigilantes and took part in the great manhunt for one G. L. Turner. On the mountainous Fort Hall road,[5] they arrested the accused robber who had managed to elude everyone else in the territory. A Nauvoo Legion command, billed as "The White Indian

---

2. In September 1857 Mormon militiamen and Southern Paiute warriors massacred some 120 Arkansas emigrants to California, men, women, and children, at a resting place on the Spanish Trail to Los Angeles, known as Mountain Meadows, near present Cedar City, Utah.

3. *The Book of Mormon,* 3rd Nephi 20:16. Also see Micah 5:8.

4. See "The Utah Expedition," House Exec. Doc. 71.

Expedition,"[6] had closed in on the wanted man at Tooele, but caught only his dog, apparently left as a decoy. The alleged thief had not gone west over the Salt Desert trail, but headed north toward Fort Hall instead. Guards stationed at the Jordan River bridge to intercept him apparently mistook Lorenzo Dow Young for the fugitive and shot Brigham Young's brother by mistake.[7] Turner had slipped past the Jordan crossing without being seen, but his route led directly to the emigrant encampment on Willow Creek, implicating them in his escape.

Deseret Attorney General Hosea Stout wrote at Great Salt Lake on 8 March 1851, "to day O. P. Rockwell brought Turner in."[8] Fortunately for Turner, his was one arrest the notorious Mormon deputy sheriff did not make. If Rockwell had caught up with the wanted man on the road to Fort Hall, the chances were that "Port" would have brought his quarry's body back loosely tied across a packsaddle. It was Turner's

---

5. The original road to Fort Hall paralleled today's I–15 to Malad City, Idaho, then followed the Little Malad River to intersect on Wright Creek the California Trail's Hudspeth Cutoff, which ran between Soda Springs and Raft River. Crossing the divide between the Great Basin and Snake River, it followed Rattlesnake and Bannock creeks to reach the Portneuf River some five miles from the trading post, near present Pocatello.

6. For Nauvoo Legion reports on expeditions to arrest Turner and Harvey Whitlock, see Ferguson to Wells and Grant to Wells, 21 February 1851, Docs. 103 and 104, Utah Militia Records, Utah State Archives. Harvey G. Whitlock was an early Mormon who left the faith in 1838 and moved in 1850 to Utah where he practiced medicine. He later went to California and became a member of the Reorganized L.D.S. Church.

7. See Letter 6.

8. Brooks, ed., "On the Mormon Frontier," 2:394–95.

Lorenzo Dow Young,
brother of Brigham Young, was shot by guards at the Jordan
River Bridge when he was mistaken for fugitive G. L. Turner.
— *Courtesy Utah State Historical Society.*

good fortune that a self-appointed posse of emigrants made the arrest instead and turned him over to Rockwell.

In the end it all came to nothing. Turner reached an undisclosed accommodation with his main accuser, Brigham Young, who allowed him to go unmolested to California. Turner later claimed he had contracted with Brigham Young to open roads and cut timber in a "certain canyon," probably City Creek,[9] but had ceased operations after Young failed to keep his payments current.[10] Asa Call, another emigrant to California, told Turner's side of the story in a letter published on 28 June 1851 in *The Daily Union* at Sacramento and presented in this volume as Appendix C. Both Call and Turner signed the emigrant memorial that year asking Congress to replace Utah's territorial government with military rule.

By then Jotham Goodell and his company had arrived in Oregon, "the days of their bondage" at an end.

---

9. On 4 December 1850 the General Assembly of Deseret approved Brigham Young's request for "exclusive control over the timber, rocks, minerals and water" in City Creek Canyon for a payment "into the Public Treasury" of $500. Governor Young himself signed the measure on 9 December. See Morgan, *The State of Deseret*, 160, 161.

10. To stem the flow of money out of the territory, Mormon authorities that winter told their followers to stop paying emigrants in cash for the work they performed, according to Nelson Slater. Utah settlers profited in trades with passing emigrants, but then spent their gains on items provided by outside merchants, resulting in a decline in the money supply. See Slater, *Fruits of Mormonism*, 10, 11.

THE OREGONIAN

PORTLAND, OREGON TERRITORY
SATURDAY, 26 JUNE 1852, VOL. 2, NO. 30, 1.
THE MORMONS, NO. 8.

EDITOR OREGONIAN:

Having been honored by a visit from Brigham's spy, and Brigham's military, and having paid the taxes unjustly imposed upon us, we hoped we should now be suffered to depart the valley without further molestation; but we soon found that to the victims of Mormon hate, hope had lost its meaning, or at least it must always be followed by that little word "but." A storm had passed, but the sky was not serene. From the dark, portentous clouds the forked lightning still continued to stream, while the incessant roll of distant thunder warned us that another storm, perhaps more fearful than the first, was yet to burst upon our defenceless heads.

Our little encampment at Willow creek now numbered about twenty families, and accessions were being made by arrivals from more distant parts of the valley. From these new-comers we learned what was transpiring among the Mormons. We learned that the high council were offended at the military for not having dragged us all back to the city. That the most fearful threatenings were breathed out against us—that the Mormons believed, or pretended to believe, that many of us were concerned in driving them from Missouri, and now they were determined to have revenge. Whether any of our number were concerned in any of those mobs is more than I know. But the Mormons presumed there were, and henceforth *revenge* was to be the watch word.

The subordinate council at the Ogden, of which love sick [Lorin] Farr was the head, held its meetings nightly to discuss matters relative to us. Of some of their deliberations, though veiled in the profoundest secrecy we accidentally became informed. An emigrant, of unimpeachable character, who had built a mill for Farr, and had not succeeded in getting his pay, was remaining at the

Ogden trying to obtain it.[11] The hut where he stopped adjoined the one where the council met. These huts were built of logs, and this emigrant found that by removing some of the wood and mortar between the logs, he could not only see into the room where the council met, but could hear some part of their conversation. Information thus obtained was forwarded to us as opportunity permitted. From what he could learn he was sure another military expedition was on foot against us.—What was to be done with us, or what charge was preferred against us, he could not learn.—He heard several of our names mentioned as being peculiarly obnoxious to their displeasure—heard frequent allusion to the information that had [been] obtained from the Danite mentioned in my last number. What this information might be, none could tell. We knew that a man of his character would not be slow to testify to any thin g that would please his master.

Tidings like these came pouring in upon us from different parts of the valley, creating no little uneasiness in our camp. Nor was this uneasiness allayed by the sudden appearance of that murderous band of vagabond Indians referred to in my 2d article. The reader will call to mind what I there stated, that after the Indians had killed the man referred to, burned considerable property, killed and drove off much stock,—been pursued by the Mormons, who, in their turn, had made a hasty retreat, having been frightened by some of their own men—after this the Indians came back, and with their hands red with the unavenged blood they had shed, and retaining the property they had stolen, were suffered to live in the neighborhood during the winter, subsisting by begging and pilfering. They were the most despicable set of beings, taken together, I ever saw. This band of Indians, whom the Mormons dared not compell to restore the property they had stolen, nor to atone for the blood they had shed, left their *Wick-ey-ups* at the Ogden and came and camped right by the side of us.[12]

---

11. Apparently another reference to New Yorker Aaron (or Ansel) Rider. See Letter 5, page 85.

This movement of the Indians appeared a little singular, and there were other things connected with it still more singular. They were in possession of new blankets and new rifles, and an abundance of amunition [sic]. To *purchase* these was utterly out of their power. They must have received them as *presents* from some persons and for some purpose. The chief was possessed of a splendid rifle which was recognized by some of the company as having been, at the time we left the fort, the property of a distinguished Mormon, supposed to be a leader of the tribe of Danites. The military eye of Major S.[13] was quick to notice these things, who assured the emigrants these Indians had come there for no good. For my part, the idea that the Mormons could possibly be cold hearted enough to employ the Indians to watch our movements, or to hang on our camp when we should commence our journey, to rob or injure us in any way, seemed preposterous, and I would not for a moment admit it. The gentleman above referred to, and other emigrants, will bear me witness that I treated the idea at the time as most absurd. Subsequent events, and a mature reflection, I must confess have changed my mind in this respect, and I am now prepared to declare my conviction to the world, *that the movement of that savage band of robbers and cut-throats to Willow creek, at that time, was in accordance with the knowledge and counsel of the Mormons.* I should like to ask Brigham Young and the twelve, how it was, that when a body of emigrants, encumbered with helpless women and children, were about to leave the valley to perform a long journey thro' regions uninhabited by civilized man, and infested by savage hordes, lying in wait to rob us of our property, and our blood—that a special order was issued to the brethren not to sell these emigrants either powder or lead, and thus expose them, their wives and little ones, upon this hazardous

12. Goodell probably refers to Chief Little Soldier's mixed band of Utahs and Shoshonis.

13. Identified in the introduction to Letter 1 as Major William Singer, an additional paymaster at Santa Fe during the War with Mexico.

journey without the means of defence? How was this, when at the same time a band of the most villainous savages, who are to prowl along their track, are supplied with an abundance of amunition? How was it that when your high officials visited our encampment, they treated us as enemies, while at the same time they would repair to the camp of these savages and hold long and familiar intercourse with their villainous chief, whose hands, were yet reeking with the blood of one of your number? From whence, sir, did these loathsome, indigent wretches get these new blankets and rifles just at this juncture? Ah, sir, some of them were not *new*, we had seen them before, they had graced the backs of some of your "saints." Will you please to inform the world how they came to change owners?

This band of Indians remained encamped by our side as long as we remained at Willow creek. When we broke up our encampment they broke up theirs, and went in advance of us four or five days' drive from there, and attacked, in the night, the company who went to California, who were one day in advance of us, and succeeded in *stampeding* their cattle and capturing the finest American mare in the company.[14]

This attack would have resulted in serious disaster to the company if they had not been watchfully prepared for it. Fortunately none of the company were injured, but one Indian was killed in the encounter. The same Indians reconnoitered our camp in the night, and dogged our train for several days, but they found we were too well prepared to receive them to venture an attack. Had they done so, some of those fine blankets would have been rent in spite of any charm they had received by having graced the backs of the "saints."

But to return to the narrative. Rumors of evil were rife. A blow was suspended over our heads, but where it would fall none could tell. Some thought that the Danite who had visited our camp,

---

14. Possibly the horse lost by Major William Singer. See Appendix B.

would pretend that some of us had countenanced his nefarious plans, and that we should be arrested on that ground.—But we were not long kept in suspense. On a fine afternoon, a few days after the events above narrated, I was standing on a small eminence a few hundred yards from camp, with a brother emigrant, [when] we discovered a company of armed men emerging from behind a bluff, and moving at a full charge upon the camp. The scene was ludicrous in the extreme, and I could hardly refrain from laughing, to witness such a display of military skill and valor against an inoffensive company composed chiefly of women and children!—a company of peaceful emigrants who had never raised a finger of opposition, even to the most unrighteous exactions of the Mormons.

But there was no time for laughter, so I hastened down with my friend to face the storm. As we reached the camp I found the Mormon officers were pouring out upon the emigrants a perfect torrent of abuse—applying to them every vile epithet which the English language contained. It would be impossible for me to report their language. Suffice it to say, that if you were to connect the word *damned* with mobocrats, villains, scoundrels, rascals, thieves, robbers, yankees, Missourians, knaves, &c, you might have some faint idea of the very polite, elegant, and refined language bestowed upon us by leaders in this host of "saints." In the same polite and gentlemanly manner we were informed that they were clothed with authority from the high council to take us all back to the city—men, women, children, oxen, horses, mules, dogs and cats! This they well knew, though what might be sport to them was death to us. Our teams were our salvation—as every one realizes who has ever crossed the plains. To move them down to the city, 70 miles, in the heart of winter, when our cattle were unable to subsist in the fall, the feed had been so consumed, and where the snow was at this time 18 inches or 2 feet deep, we considered the same as to kill them outright.

But the reader will be anxious to know the crime charged against us—for surely such an array of power would not be made unless some offence had been committed. I will try to afford the information.

Early the preceding fall an emigrant went into the valley by the name of Turner, and it is said joined the Mormons—took a large contract of the church, and either failed on his part or they on theirs, I do not know which, neither do I care, (and perhaps the whole was a sham, merely to bring the emigrants into trouble.) He concluded to leave the valley, and passed through our camp on his way to fort Hall—he was an entire stranger to us—we knew nothing about him, nor his relation to the Mormons. He called on some of the emigrants, I think it was at Mr. Harlow's tent,[15] and they gave him his dinner, just as they would any other hungry man, and he went on his way. This was the head and front of our offending. He was now accused of being a horse thief and robber, and by this assistance rendered him, we were all accessory and must be dragged down to the city. I ventured to ask the commanding officer what robbery had been committed? Whose horse had been stolen? And will you, reader, believe it, it was not in his power to tell us? I inquired if any advertisement had been circulated describing this thief and robber? and he answered, no. I begged him not to take our teams to the city, as they would surely die if he did—to leave them, our wives and children, and if he must take the men, take us, and let us have an impartial trial, and we had no fears for the result. No, his orders were to take us *all* back; said he was censured for his lenity to us on a previous occasion.

So then back to the city we must go—our teams must perish of cold and hunger, and if they persist, we must perish with them. That night was a gloomy one, I will assure the reader, to our camp. Some of the company were for resistance; but this of course was futile, for though we might have scattered that band like the leaves

---

15. For more on Harlow, see Letter 7, note 6.

of the forest, we could not escape from the valley, and they could soon annihilate us. A strong guard was stationed around us during the night, not permitting us to hold communications with each other, and thus each family was left to brood over their misfortune alone. In the morning I resumed my efforts with the officers, and begged for the sake of our wives and children, for humanity's sake, for God's sake, not to remove us to the city—proposed to furnish a company of volunteers to pursue Turner, and if he could possibly be found, to bring him back—submitted to the most insulting language and behavior without a word, hoping I might yet find some spark of humanity in his breast. I however got no encouragement that any of us should be spared.

We were thus kept in suspense till about two o'clock that afternoon, when they finally contented themselves with taking 3 of the company prisoners, and released the remainder—Of the three taken, Mr. Harlow had the honor of being one. As soon as the soldiers had retired, we began to look about us, and to inquire who were left? Visiting Mr. Harlow's tent, I found his wife and aged mother-in-law in much anxiety and distress. What the Mormons would do with him they could not conjecture—the husband and father had been torn from them by ruthless hands, and they were left alone on the wide plains, not knowing what was yet to be their fate. All the consolation I could afford them was to cast their care on "Him who rules in the armies above, and upon the earth beneath"—who has "all hosts in his hands and can turn them as the rivers of waters."

Our first business, as soon as we were at liberty, was to secure Turner. For this purpose a company of volunteers set out in pursuit, overtook him in the mountains, brought him back, and delivered him up to the Mormon authorities.

And what think you, gentle reader, was done with this awful robber, on whose account our very lives had been put in jeopardy? Was he loaded with irons? Was he tried for his life? Not by any means. He was not even put under arrest! He rode down to the city.—had an interview with Brigham, is said to have walked arm in arm with him in the streets, and before we left the valley, he rode through our camp on his way to California! Will you believe it?—there had been no robbery committed, nor any property stolen![16]

But let us return to friend Harlow and his comrades, who had been torn from their families and friends under the most trying circumstances.

Dragged down to the Ogden like felons, they were put upon their trial! Trial for being accessory to theft and robbery which never had existence! He demanded a jury trial, and as they had not a shadow of evidence against him—could not prove that he had ever seen Turner—they were obliged to acquit him.

But I will not detain the reader longer with this narrative. A kind providence favored us. A way was opened for us through the mountains a month earlier than any teams had been known to pass through before. Unable so early to take the direct route by the way of fort Hall, we followed the California road to Raft river, and then followed down that river till we struck the Oregon road.[17] About the 10th of April we crossed the dividing ridge between Bear and Snake rivers, and soon struck the waters of the Columbia. The first stream we came to this side the dividing ridge is called Stony Creek.[18] Here we encamped at noon.—The company were in high spirits. We had scaled the mountain walls of our prison. Before us, to the north-west, lay the beautiful valley of

---

16. The 1851 Sacramento City Assessor's Rolls list a George Turner with personal property valued at $1,000. He apparently left the city in 1852 for the gold diggings.

17. Bypassing Fort Hall, Goodell's company followed Hensley's Salt Lake Cutoff, the shortest and easiest avenue from Utah to the Oregon Trail on Snake River. For more on this route, see DeLafosse, ed., *Trailing the Pioneers: A Guide to Utah's Emigrant Trails, 1829–1869*, 93–109; and Korns and Morgan, eds., *West from Fort Bridger: The Pioneering of Immigrant Trails across Utah, 1846–1850*, revised and updated by Bagley and Schindler, 277–306.

18. Today named Clear Creek on the Utah-Idaho border, near Naf, Idaho.

Snake river, stretching out as far as the eye could reach. At our feet we beheld the pure waters of the Columbia. All drank of it and pronounced it the best they had ever tasted! We were free, and we resolved to stop and hold a *jubilee!* We had prepared a banner at Willow creek—our nation's emblem, the glorious stars and stripes. The only motto it contained was the word LIBERTY on one side, and OREGON on the other. This simple flag we had been warned against raising while in the valley, but it was now brought forth and spread to the breeze. A large rock at the foot of the mountain served for a pulpit, from which speeches were delivered—guns were fired, and a shout went up from a hundred voices which made the mountains quake. It was an exciting hour. Some wept for joy—all felt that the days of their bondage was [sic] at an end.

J. W. GOODELL

LETTER 9

"To Stop My Breath"

Jotham Goodell's final letter delivered two depositions in support of the picture he had drawn of society in Utah. The first by Thomas McF. Patton is the most significant not only because it was legally sworn before the clerk of a U.S. district court in Oregon, but also because Patton was an eyewitness to the start of the confrontation that prompted Goodell to write his series. Moreover the twenty-two-year-old pioneer would become one of Oregon's most respected citizens. Of him it was said that scarcely a man in Oregon "held a greater measure of esteem, both in his own community and abroad."[1] In 1851, four months after Goodell had left Utah, the young Ohioan stopped in Salt Lake Valley where he attended the July 24th Pioneer Day observance. His account of what happened that day supports the accusations of the runaway officials and complements Goodell's letters. It cannot be easily squared with the report of Utah's delegate to Congress, John M. Bernhisel, who was also present.[2]

Since there was no authorized magistrate at Fort Hall to administer an oath, the professed attorney James McCabe questionably certified the second affidavit under his alleged prior office as Judge Advocate General of the Michigan Militia. The deponent, John Joseph Galvin of Boston, was no stranger in the courts of Deseret. He came before Justice of the Peace Aaron F. Farr at Great Salt Lake City in November 1850 on the charge of assaulting Joseph Egbert, a member of Brigham Young's 1847 pioneer company. He was found guilty and fined "five dollars & costs, in all Eighteen dollars."[3] Nelson Slater in another account said Galvin appeared before Justice of the Peace Willard Snow on the charge of "striking a Mormon." According to Slater, Snow told him, "If you ever lay your hands on another saint I will have your head cut off before you leave the city" and levied fines and costs of over $100.[4]

---

1. Born in Carrollton, Ohio, Patton was educated at Ohio Wesleyan University and admitted to the bar in 1850. He moved to Oregon in 1851, where he was elected judge of Jackson County in 1853, named chief clerk of the State House of Representatives in 1860, and elected to the House from Marion County in 1872. In 1884 he was appointed U.S. consul to Kobe, Japan. He died in 1892. See Hines, *Illustrated History of the State of Oregon*, 1893, 552–54; *History of the Pacific Northwest*, 2:516–17; Lang, *History of the Willamette Valley*, 743; Hodgkin and Galvin, *Pen Pictures of Representative Men of Oregon*, 103; and *Weekly Oregon Statesman*, 2 December 1892. Patton was also indicted in 1855 for "falsely representing or impersonating himself to be the person authorized to receive money intended to be delivered to the treasurer of Jackson County, Oregon Territory." The charge was dropped when his accuser could not be found. See Scrapbook No. 112, 122, Oregon Hist. Soc.

2. See House Exec. Doc. 25; Appendix A, page 152.

3. Brooks, ed., *On the Mormon Frontier*, 2:383.

James McCabe practiced law in Great Salt Lake during the winter of 1850–1851, representing other emigrants before the courts of Deseret.[5] His unsuccessful defense of twenty-two-year-old Washington Loomis of New York against the charge of stealing a pair of pants led the untrained Deseret State Attorney Stout to rail against "the low chicanery of the opposite attorney."[6] McCabe's legal tactics also touched off a courtroom outburst that prompted Apostle Willard Richards to warn officers of the court "never to admit a foul spirit where the Holy Spirit should rule and direct either the affairs of State or Church."[7] Not long after, Brigham Young told his Sunday congregation that McCabe was "going to report us to Washington."[8] At this, the troublesome lawyer prudently

---

4. Slater, *Fruits of Mormonism*, 80. Unless these were different cases, Stout's version is no doubt the most accurate if only because it was recorded on the day the trial occurred. Slater also apparently confused Judge Willard Snow, the brother of Mormon Apostle Erastus Snow, with Utah associate justice Zerubbabel Snow, also a Mormon, named in 1850 by President Fillmore as one of Utah Territory's three federal judges.

5. Oddly there were two emigrants named James McCabe who wintered in Utah in 1850–1851. A Virginian by this name, age twenty-four, was the son-in-law of Solomon Zumwalt, quoted in this work, but he was not a lawyer. He later lived in Lane County, Ore. A more likely candidate as the James McCabe in question was a twenty-nine year-old practicing lawyer from New York and former member of the Michigan legislature who was also on his way to Oregon. He later practiced law in San Francisco. See *Evening Daily Bulletin*, 22 May 1890, 3/7.

6. Brooks, ed., *On the Mormon Frontier*, 2:389, 390. The 1850 Census for Utah County listed Loomis as having no occupation. He was found guilty on two counts and sentenced to two years hard labor with ball and chain. Emigrant George Love who testified on his behalf was found guilty of "willful and corrupt perjury" and sentenced to five years hard labor "with the ball and chain."

7. Ibid. For more on the Loomis case, also see House Exec. Doc. 25; Appendix A, page 182.

decided to head for Fort Hall, where he later took Galvin's deposition.

Goodell finished his letters on a defiant note, holding himself not worth the time or trouble it would take to visit vengeance on him for what he had written. The God who made him, he said, would "stop my breath"[9] soon enough without any help from Brigham Young. When he said that, he was forty-three years of age and had just seven more years to live.

THE OREGONIAN

PORTLAND, OREGON TERRITORY
SATURDAY, 26 JUNE 1852, VOL. 2, NO. 30, 1.
[THE MORMONS,] NO. 9.

SIR:—When I closed my last number I did not intend to obtrude myself further upon your readers. But the following affidavits having been voluntarily furnished me, with a request from many of my friends that they should be published. I herewith send you true copies of the same;—the originals are now in my possession, but will soon be forwarded with others to Washington.[10] A word with reference to them: The deposition of Galvin, you will perceive, is informal, in consequence of its being taken in a region where there was no authorized officer to administer an oath. Mr. Patton's testimony is the more important from the fact that it comes from one who had no participation in our troubles. He fully fastens the charge of felony upon the Mormons in violating the sanctity of the United States Post Office. I shall have other depositions equally emphatic.[11]

---

8. Brooks, ed., *On the Mormon Frontier.*, 2:394.

9. For the source of this expression, see Letter 5, page 80.

10. The location or disposition of such documents, if they still exist, has not been discovered.

Peter [Porter] Rockwell, the mormon referred to in Galvin's deposition, is the man whom the Mormons pointed out to me as being the man who attempted to assassinate Gov. Boggs of Missouri.[12] He is a distinguished Danite.

By the way, some of my friends have expressed considerable anxiety lest I might receive a visit of ceremony from some of these gentlemanly cut-throats. I will therefore take occasion to say in advance, to his Hon., Brigham Young, that I most respectfully decline such a visit. I am, sir, too insignificant to receive such an honor, and of so little worth it would not pay the expense you would incur in such a mission. Make yourself quite easy, honored sir, we have no "Salt Lakes" in Oregon, suitable for "pickling" people in, and if we had I should not be worth pursuing. In due time, I doubt not, the God who gave us our being, will send his own messenger to stop my breath without your interference; in the mean time, I have a small duty to discharge with reference to yourself, and the people you have blinded by your delusions, and with the assistance of His Grace I shall do it.

Respectfully Yours,
J. W. GOODELL.

———

TERRITORY OF OREGON,
MARION COUNTY.

THOMAS MCF. PATTON, of Salem, in said county, formerly of Findley [Findlay], Hancock county, Ohio, being duly sworn, doth depose and say that in crossing the plains from the states in the summer of 1851, he stayed about one month in the vicinity of

———

11. The editor has been unable to locate any other depositions.

12. Orrin Porter Rockwell allegedly shot former Governor Lilburn W. Boggs through his study window on 6 May 1842 at Independence, Missouri, for his role in driving the Mormons from the state in 1838–39. Not expected to live, Boggs eventually survived the buckshot blast. See Schindler, *Orrin Porter Rockwell: Man of God, Son of Thunder*, 67–75.

Great Salt Lake City, in the territory of Utah. That he attended the Mormon celebration of the 24th July, that being the anniversary of their arrival in Salt Lake Valley. That he was present when his Honor, Judge Brandebury, made or attempted to make an address to the people, and was interrupted by Brigham Young and other of the leading Mormons. That he has read carefully the account of what took place on that occasion, as given by said Brandebury and others, and knows that the same is literally true. That Brigham Young then and there said, among other things, that the "gentiles were now coming into the Lord's valley, and that *if they said anything derogatory of them,* (the Mormons,) *or their religion, it was better to behead them at once;"—*and thereupon called for a vote of the people upon that proposition; a vote of the same was taken, and was *unanimous in the affirmative, not a solitary vote being given in the negative.*

And this deponent further says, that shortly after said celebration he wrote several letters to send home to the states, in some of which he detailed the proceedings as they occurred—that he deposited said letters in the United States post office, at the city aforesaid, that after so depositing said letters he was told by several individuals that said letters would not be sent on but would be destroyed. This induced deponent to go back to the said post office the next day, to see if he could learn anything in reference thereto; and there *under the table in said office, he discovered several of the envelopes in which his letters had been enclosed.* As to those envelopes, deponent could not well be mistaken; he is positive *that it was his own hand writing; he distinctly saw the names and places* to which they were severally directed, and is positive that they are the envelopes which his letters were in when deposited in said post office. That after learning the above, deponent wrote other letters in which he said nothing about the Mormons—these letters reached their point of destination, and have been answered, but in said answers no mention was made of the receipt of the other letters, (the envelopes of which he saw under the table,) from all of which deponent has no doubt that said letters were destroyed.

(Signed,) T. McF. PATTON.

Sworn and subscribed before me, this 7th day of June, 1852.

(Signed,) L. F. GROVER,

Clerk of the United States District Court within and for the county of Marion, in the territory of Oregon.

TERRITORY OF OREGON, *Fort Hall*.

I, JOHN JOSEPH GALVIN, of Boston, Mass., now sojourning at Fort Hall, which is not within the body of any organized county, as deponent believes, being duly sworn, doth depose and say, that he spent the winter of 1850–'51, in and about Great Salt Lake City, in the territory of Utah, and has recently left there.—That about the first of May, 1851, a volunteer company was raised there, consisting of sixteen men, to go against the Indians, who, it was thought, had stolen and driven off some cattle and horses from a herd in Toolie [Tooele] valley; that this deponent, Leonard D. Custer,[13] of Akron, Ohio, Robert Gregs, of Columbus [sic], Boone co., Missouri, Orr Truland, of Michican, Reuben Soltmorst, of Illinois, and John Hubbard, of Ohio—all of whom were "emigrants"—volunteered, and went in said company; that the other ten were "Mormons;" that after organizing said company, proceeded to said Toolie valley, in which, about forty miles from said city, a party of ten Indians were discovered and that said company immediately charged upon them; whereupon, said Indians seized their arms, and assumed a defensive attitude; that when said company approached quite near to said Indians, Porter Rockwell, the captain of said company—a "Mormon"—talked to said Indians in Indian dialect—which deponent could not understand, for some

---

13. Custer's first name was Lorenzo. He had been hired by Apostle Ezra T. Benson to build a dam for a sawmill in the Tooele area. The Ohioan was waiting for his last payment of $500 when the Indian trouble occurred.

fifteen or twenty minutes—and said to them, among other things, as he afterwards informed me, "that they, (said company), did not want to kill any of them, but only wanted them to show said company where the Indians were who stole the cattle and horses; that thereupon the Indians desisted from warlike operations; that some of the men then dismounted, and wanted to take the guns from said Indians; the said Rockwell said—'no d—n them, we will make them pack their own guns;'[14] that he, (Rockwell), then ordered said Indians to be divided, and five put in charge of said Custer, and five in charge of Augustus Sevire, with each of whom he sent three men; that said company then started for the settlements, a distance of four or five miles—the eight men not so detailed to guard the prisoners, going ahead; that by some means or other, Custer's party fell considerably in the rear—the three men with him apparently lagging, whilst the said Sevire and his company pressed rapidly ahead, and got far in advance of Custer's company, though in the rear of the aforesaid eight; that the names of the men with Custer, were Ocar Hamlin [Oscar Hamblin],[15] John Gilbert Taft, and Henry Jackson[16]—all 'Mormons'—that after proceeding some distance towards the settlement, and when Custer's division had fallen considerably in the rear, the three men with Custer, left him, (as they since say), and went ahead on their horses at full speed, leaving Custer alone with the Indians, who were on foot; that

---

14. In reporting the incident Rockwell failed to mention that he allowed the Indians to keep their weapons, which proved an unfortunate mistake.

15. Eighteen-year-old Oscar Hamblin was a native of Bainbridge, Ohio, and a younger brother of renowned Mormon Indian emissary Jacob Hamblin. In September 1857 he was with John D. Lee at the massacre of some 120 emigrants to California from Arkansas at Mountain Meadows.

16. This may have been Henry Wells Jackson, age twenty-four, who served as a musician in the Mormon Battalion's Company D, as a member of Nauvoo Legion Major Lot Smith's command during the 1857 Utah War, and as a Pony Express rider in 1860. A native of New York, he died in 1863 at Washington, D.C. in a Civil War hospital.

Custer, about this time, was shot through the heart, and fell from his horse dead; that said Hamblin among other statements, has since said, that he was near at the time Custer was shot, only about a rod from him, and says that an Indian did the deed, and that before Custer was shot, the Indians were talking in broken Spanish, and said—'*Mormons wano—Americanoes no wano*' —signifying that the Mormons were good, and the Americans not good. How they ascertained that Custer was not a Mormon, deponent does not know, unless said Rockwell in said speech so informed them; which is by no means [im]probable, and it was impossible for them to obtain such information in any other manner; that Hamblin is the only man of said company who pretends to have been near at the time Custer was shot. Four or five days after the death of Custer, the five Indians in charge of Sevire were shot in cold blood by said Rockwell, Lot Smith[17] and Ed. Walker[18]—all 'Mormons'—who gave no reason for shooting them; nor was there any evidence whatever against the Indians, of their having committed any offence.[19] That two days after the murder of said Indians, and six or seven after Custer was killed, in the evening, after the Mormons had got through their prayers, said Porter Rockwell,

---

17. Twenty-one-year-old Lot Smith was a native of New York. In 1846 he joined the Mormon Battalion at age sixteen and became one of Mormonism's most renowned frontiersmen, Indian fighters, and military leaders. His mounted command during the 1857 Utah War burned three U.S. Army supply trains on the Big Sandy and Green rivers in present Wyoming. Smith was an early pioneer of Arizona, where Navaho Indians killed him in 1892.

18. This may have been Edwin Walker, age twenty-two, a native of Vermont and former Company D private in the Mormon Battalion. He reenlisted in 1847 as a corporal in the volunteer company at San Diego under Capt. Daniel C. Davis. He died at Salt Lake City in 1873.

19. The number of Indians killed was four. Rockwell said they "were sacrificed to the natural instincts of self defense." For more on this episode, see Schindler, *Orrin Porter Rockwell: Man of God, Son of Thunder*, 193–96; Brooks, ed., *On the Mormon Frontier*, 2:398; and Gottfredson, *History of Indian Depredations in Utah*, 39.

James Ferguson,[20] (Sheriff of Great Salt Lake county,) and ——
Mukely,[21] (one of the Bishops,) each made speeches. Said Ferguson, in his speech, said, among other things, THAT WHILE THEIR
HANDS WERE IN, THEY MIGHT AS WELL KILL ALL THE EMI-
GRANTS THAT WERE LEFT IN THE VALLEY—THAT IT WAS THE
EASIEST WAY TO GET RID OF THEM, AND STOP THEIR COMING
THERE. Said Mukely expressed himself in favor of Ferguson's proposition, to KILL THE EMIGRANTS. Rockwell made some reply to it,
but deponent being some distance from him, did not understand
what it was.—Some of the Mormons in the company, took ground
against said proposition, and here it ended, so far as deponent
knows.

And the deponent further says, that he is well acquainted with
the affairs of the said Custer, in said Utah territory, and knows that
he was worth enough to pay all his debts, and leave him at least
$1000. That administration of the estate of said Custer, was granted
to said James Ferguson; that things have been fixed up in favor of
the "*brethren*," who were indebted to Custer, so as to screen them
from the payment, and the said estate brought *insolvent* about *two
thousand dollars*. That John Huntsman was a partner of said
Custer, in his business there, and after Custer's death, paid several
of the workmen their due, or a part thereof, in flour, and other
chattles [sic], that said administrator seized upon every article
thereof—took them from said men, and now has them in his custody, and the workmen remain unpaid.

---

20. A sergeant in the Mormon Battalion's Company A, twenty-three-year-
old James Ferguson was a native of Belfast, Ireland, and one of early Utah's most
colorful figures. He was adjutant general of the Nauvoo Legion, a leading man
for the Deseret Dramatic Association, and a gifted writer. L.D.S. historian
Andrew Jenson has described him as "handsome, dashing, eloquent . . . equally
brilliant as soldier, lawyer, actor and orator." As this reference suggests, he also
possessed a volatile temperament. He died in 1863. See Bagley, "*A Bright,
Rising Star*": *A Brief Life of James Ferguson, Sergeant Major, Mormon
Battalion; Adjutant General, Nauvoo Legion*.
21. This may have been Canadian Christopher Merkley.

And this deponent further says, that it is the general opinion, that said Custer was murdered for his money and property.[22] And further this deponent saith not.

[SIGNED:] J. J. GALVIN.

Sworn and subscribed before me, at Fort Hall, aforesaid, this 14th day of June, A.D., 1851.

JAMES MCCABE,
Judge Advocate General,
of the Militia of the State of Michigan.

---

22. While some made this charge, the evidence to support it is unconvincing.

EPILOGUE

As if to atone for a hard winter, the mild if unpredictable spring of 1851 invited Goodell and the wintering emigrants to leave weeks before they expected to get out. "We cold [called] a meting electid the Rev Mr Goodal a Prisbetrian minister from Mishagun," Solomon Zumwalt said.[1] "He mad[e] a very good captain." They "rold out on the 27 of March" from their camps on Willow and Box Elder creeks and "crost Bar river on the first day of April," the Missourian continued. "We had three snow storms on us," he said, but no one seemed to complain.[2] Rejoicing as they went, they traveled northwest from the Bear River crossing on the line of present I-84,

---

1. Goodell came from Ohio, not Michigan.
2. Above quotes are from The Biographa [sic] of Adam Zumwalt by His Son, Solomon Zumwalt, who came to Oregon in 1850. The editor is indebted to Dr. Jim Tompkins of Beavercreek, Ore., for a copy of this document. Also see James and McClarty, eds., "Three Generations in the Span of a Continent: The Zumwalt Family," 346–47.

fording Deep Creek at present Snowville, Utah, on Hensley's Salt Lake Cutoff.

Not until they had crossed the rim of the Great Basin, near present Naf on today's Utah–Idaho border, did they stop to drink from the headwaters of the Columbia River and celebrate their regained freedom. On about 10 April they "lade by thar a fiew dais [days] [and] had a silabracion [celebration] thar," exulted the happy, if barely literate Zumwalt. "We war out of the Morman country." A Methodist preacher "deliverd an adres" and the men with muskets "formed a line fired a platoon," he went on. They felt happy indeed they "war out of Mormindam," he wrote.[3] "A shout went up from a hundred voices which made the mountains quake," the better-educated Goodell said. "Some wept for joy—all felt that the days of their bondage was [sic] at an end."[4]

After the celebration, they traveled on the line of Utah Route 42 and Idaho 81, to Raft River, where the parade of wagons divided. Those headed for California, including Goodell's son-in-law, Holden Judson, and the Singer family, continued west on the Salt Lake Cutoff to its junction with the California Trail in the Silent City of Rocks, near present Almo, Idaho. As captain, Goodell led the Oregon company north down the river to meet the Oregon Trail on Snake River, near today's junction of I-84 and I-86, east of present Burley, Idaho, and follow the nation's longest emigrant road.

---

3. Ibid.

4. *The Oregonian,* Portland, Oregon Territory, 26 June 1852, Vol. 2, No. 30, 1.

At Three Island Crossing, near Glenns Ferry, the Oregon company found the river too high to ford and was forced to follow the trail's more difficult South Alternate Route, which at least avoided two river crossings. But the route along the south bank of the river did not offer any escape from the Western Shoshonis who often attacked emigrant trains on this stretch of the Oregon Trail in present southern Idaho. From the north side of the river these troublesome natives opened a harassing fire which was returned by Goodell's party, whose members "swore the[y] wood kill every Indian the[y] sede," Zumwalt said. But Goodell stopped such indiscriminate killing. "Cpt Goodall com to me [and] sade he wood see that the stock was drive[n] [and] for me to ride with thes[e] men and to not let them kill frendly indians."[5]

Goodell's party finished a journey of two months when it reached the Dalles on 29 May and became the first wagon train of 1851 to reach the Columbia River. The Barlow Road, a toll route over the Cascade Mountains to Oregon City, which ran to the south of Mt. Hood, was still blocked by snow and not yet open for travel.[6] The only alternative was to board boats or rafts for the dangerous journey down the swollen river to Portland, where *The Oregonian* reported their arrival on 7 June.

In Oregon, the impoverished Goodell first settled his family in the Willamette Valley in Polk County where he

---

5. Zumwalt, The Biographa [sic] of Adam Zumwalt by His Son, Solomon Zumwalt, who Came to Oregon in 1850.

6. Oregon immigrants Samuel K. Barlow and Joel Palmer in 1845–46 opened the ninety-mile Barlow Road, which ran to the south of Mt. Hood and avoided the dangerous Columbia River passage.

worked nearly a year to recover his Utah losses before ful-
filling his charge to tell the story of the Oregon pioneers. His
letters show how little the passage of time had cooled his
indignation. In his 1852 letter to Anna Maria Pelton in Ohio,
he reported Holden Judson's arrival from California and
added, "It has been a little over a year since we parted in that
land of abominations—the Salt Lake Valley."[7]

At the request of Presbyterian missionary Henry Harmon
Spalding, he joined the Congregational Association of
Oregon.[8] (Spalding's wife, Elizabeth, and Narcissa Whitman
in 1836 had been the first white women to cross the conti-
nental divide at South Pass.) He also served as Polk County
representative on the Standing Temperance Committee,
which met in Salem across the river in Marion County.[9] But
his stay in Oregon was short.

In 1853, when Washington became a territory, Goodell
crossed the Columbia River and moved north to Thurston
County, south of Olympia, where he filed a donation land
claim on 640 acres and delivered the territory's first
Independence Day oration.[10] At the spot still known as

7. J. W. Goodell to Anna Maria Pelton, 15 June 1852. After failing to find a
fortune in the California gold fields, Holden Judson went back to Ohio in 1852
and took his family west the following year. See Judson, *A Pioneer's Search for
an Ideal Home.*

8. See Eels, *History of the Congregational Association of Oregon and
Washington Territory,* 76. Narcissa Whitman and her husband, Presbyterian
missionary Marcus Whitman, were killed in 1847 at their mission to the Cayuse
Indians at Walla Walla.

9. For this information, the editor is indebted to Robert Marsh of Dallas,
Oregon.

10. Hargrave, *Goodale–Goodell Forebears,* 91.

Oregon pioneer Melancthon Z. Goodell was fifteen when he spent the winter of 1850–1851 in the Mormon settlements.
— *Courtesy Oregon Historical Society, 100124.*

Goodell's Point, east of Grand Mound, he built a large cedar shake house with floors of milled lumber, which served as an inn called the Washington Hotel for travelers between Olympia and Monticello on the Columbia River. As advertised on 18 June 1853 in the *Olympia Columbian*: "The table will always be spread with a view to please the taste and satisfy the hungry, good beds, clean sheets where the weary can rest without fear of Leshi, nightmares or bedbugs."[11]

Eighteen fifty-three also brought the arrival of his other twin daughter, Phoebe and her husband, Holden Judson. The following year, Goodell rode out to the numerous trail crossings of the Naches River on 24 September to welcome his son, William Bird, and his wife, Anna Maria Pelton Goodell, as they neared the end of their long journey from Vermilion, Ohio, to Grand Mound, Washington Territory.[12]

With the start of the 1855 Northwest Indian war, thirty families at Grand Mound, including the Goodells, built Fort Henness, a log stockade on high ground near Centralia, where they lived for sixteen months until peace returned. During this period, Goodell's son Melancthon, now nineteen, enlisted in the First Regiment of Washington Territorial Volunteers and rose to become a sergeant in Company B.

---

11. Clark, *My Goodell Family in America, 1634–1978*, 14. Leschi was an Indian leader from the Nisqually tribe who attempted to forge native alliances in opposing white settlement in the Northwest. A tragic figure, he was hanged in 1858 for his part in the 1855 uprising that terrorized settlers in the Puget Sound area.

12. For the story of this journey, see Anna Maria Godell [sic] and Elizabeth Austin, "The Vermillion Wagon Train Diaries, 1854" in Holmes, ed., *Covered Wagon Women: Diaries & Letters from the Western Trails, 1840–1890*, 7:78–130.

Anna Glenning Bacheler Goodell in about 1858.
— *Courtesy Naomi B. Baker.*

That year Jotham Goodell became the postmaster at Grand Mound, which he operated out of his home, and assisted in organizing the first Presbytery in Washington Territory.[13]

In 1859 Anna Maria Goodell wrote her parents in Ohio that Jotham Goodell had suffered a stroke after which he lived only a few days. Knowing that he was dying, she said, he called the members of his family into his room, one at a time, and asked God to bless them. His wife, Annie, then asked him, "if he could put his trust in his Savior and he said yes."[14]

This proudly independent man is survived today by a large posterity across both the western and eastern United States and nine letters that vividly highlight the earliest sources of controversy between a new theocratic form of government in the American West and its parent republic.

13. Clark, *My Goodell Family in America*, 14–17.
14. Margene Goodell to David Bigler, 1 March 1999.

APPENDIX A

*The Condition of Affairs
in the
Territory of Utah*

The following report to Congress provides a rich source of information on the first conflict between Mormon officials of Utah Territory, led by Brigham Young, and so-called "Gentile" appointees of President Millard Fillmore. It consists of original documents, described briefly in the introduction to Letter 1. Jotham Goodell's letters refer often to these documents. Their publication in January 1852 motivated him to write his series to support non-Mormon territorial officials and rebut countercharges emanating from the territory.

To keep the public informed on the affairs of government, the House of Representatives in 1813 ordered the printing of all communications between executive and legislative branches, motions and resolutions considered by the House, reports of House committees, and all other papers produced "in the usual course of proceeding or by special order of the House." Over the years, subsequent orders of House and Senate created what is known as the Serial Set, a composite of documents from Congress and the executive branch. Now filling a vast and growing library, these papers represent visible evidence of the American government's commitment to inform a free citizenry on the work of its elected representatives. Susan L. Fales and Chad J. Flake have pointed out the importance of government publications in providing a matchless, if at times underused, source of information on the controversial history of the Mormons during the nineteenth century.[1]

In keeping with the Serial Set's purpose, the House of Representatives on 15 December 1851 passed a resolution asking President Fillmore to provide all the information available from the executive branch relating to the controversy that erupted that year in Utah Territory. The president referred the request to Secretary of State Daniel Webster, whose department's Home Bureau took care of such domestic matters as correspondence with governors of states and territories and letters and reports to Congress. The resulting compilation was published in January 1852 as House Exec. Doc. 25, 32nd Congress, 1st Sess., Serial Set 640, which follows.

---

1. Fales and Flake, *Mormons and Mormonism in U.S. Government Documents.*

UTAH

MESSAGE

FROM THE

PRESIDENT OF THE UNITED STATES

TRANSMITTING

Information in reference to the condition of affairs in the Territory of Utah.

JANUARY 9, 1852

Referred to the Committee on Territories, and ordered to be printed.

To the House of Representatives:

In answer to the resolution of the House of Representatives of the 15th ultimo, requesting information in regard to the Territory of Utah, I transmit a report from the Secretary of State, to whom the resolution was referred.

MILLARD FILLMORE.

WASHINGTON, *January 9, 1851.*

DEPARTMENT OF STATE,
Washington, January 8, 1852.

The Secretary of State, to whom has been referred the resolution of the House of Representatives of the 15th ultimo, requesting the President to communicate to that House all such information as "may be in his possession, calculated to show the actual condition of things in the Territory of Utah, and especially to enable the House to ascertain whether the due execution of the laws of the United States has been resisted or obstructed; whether there has been any misapplication of the public funds; and whether the personal rights of our citizens have been interfered with in any manner,"—has the honor to lay before the President the papers mentioned in the subjoined list, which contain all the information in this department called for by the resolution.

Respectfullysubmitted:

DAN. WEBSTER.

TO THE PRESIDENT OF THE UNITED STATES.

LIST OF PAPERS

Accompanying the report of the Secretary of State to the President, of the 8th of January, 1852.

———

Mr. Bernhisel to the President of the United States, with enclosures, December 1, 1851.

Mr. Snow to the President of the United States, September 22, 1851.

Governor Young to the President of the United States, October 20, 1851.

Report of Messrs. Brandebury, Brocchus, and Harris, to the President of the United States, December 19, 1851.

Mr. Harris to Mr. Webster, January 2, 1852.

Mr. Harris to the President, with enclosures, January 2, 1852.

Mr. Bernhisel to the President of the United States, December 30, 1851.

Governor Young to the President of the United States, September 29, 1851.

Memorial signed by members of the Legislative Assembly of Utah to the President of the United States, September 29, 1851.

From John M Bernhisel, esq., Delegate from Utah Territory, to the President.

UNITED STATES HOTEL,
December 1, 1851.

Sir: Agreeably to your request, I have the honor to inform you that the news of the organization of the Territory of Utah was most gratefully received by its inhabitants. The news of the passage of the bill establishing the government, and the appointment under it of officers, executive and judicial, reached Great Salt Lake City about Christmas or New Year last, and was greeted by the firing of cannon and every other demonstration of enthusiastic joy. The governor took the oath of office soon afterwards, but the Territory was not fully organized until the beginning of August. The 4th of July, the last glorious anniversary of our independence, was celebrated at Great Salt Lake City with considerable eclat. The officers not residents of the Territory reached the scene of their duties a fortnight after, on the 19th of July, with the exception of Judge Perry C. Brocchus.

The officers were all respectfully and hospitably received. They showed themselves pleased with the condition of the Salt Lake settlement, and the comforts which the industry of its inhabitants had gathered around them in their Alpine home; although they found the California prices which prevail there, and the expenses of living under them, incommensurate with the rate of salary granted them by the United States. At their request, therefore, I am the bearer of a petition, of which I enclose you a copy, praying Congress for an increased remuneration. And though as yet, owing to the pacific character of our people, no case is known to have occurred which may invoke the action of the court or its officers, this request will not, perhaps, be deemed unreasonable. I left Utah Territory upon the first of September last. Up to that date the harmony and peace prevailing between the different officers of the Government and the people continued undisturbed. The only statements that I have seen to the contrary appear to be based upon a letter enclosed, which has appeared in some of the public prints, purporting to have been written by a judicial officer of the Government, and dating from Salt Lake City, September 20, 1851. As I have as yet received no mail from the Territory, nor any information of any kind about its affairs since my departure, I am left to the letter alone for the evidence which it contains, and to this I beg to refer you with some attention. It declares that "not only were the officers sent here treated with coldness and disrespect, but that the Government of the United States, on all public occasions, whether festive or religious, was denounced in the most disrespectful terms, and often with invectives of great bitterness;" and proceeds to mention two instances to substantiate this statement.

At the occasion first named, the celebration of the 24th of July, the *putative* writer (If I may employ the expression) was not present. Judge Brocchus did not arrive in the Territory till the 17th of August. But I was present. I had the privilege of listening to Governor Young's remarks attentively, and therefore *know* that he made no reflections injurious to the public services or private character of the late lamented President Taylor, or in fact any allusions to him whatever, that I can remember. The writer's statement, therefore, is so far untrue.

The second *"instance"* also is open to correction. Its statement is, that the writer being commissioned by the Washington Monument Society to procure for them a block of marble, apprized Governor Young of the trust committed to his hands, and expressed a desire to address the people *on the subject,* when assembled in their greatest number; that the governor, in order to accede to his request, upon the Monday following, *"respectfully and honorably introduced"* him for the purpose to a meeting of at least three thousand people; that he spoke for two hours, during which he was favored with the unwavering attention of his audience; but that he then, by his own statement, "incidentally thereto (as the Mormons supposed") attacked the governor and people, and concluded by what they cannot but have taken as a most wanton insult, "that if they would not offer a block of marble in full fellowship with the people of the United States, as brethren and fellow-citizens, they had better not offer it [at] all, but leave it unquarried in the bosom of its native mountain." I do not remark upon this strange mode of springing an insult upon a public meeting, after its patience had been tried by a *two hours'* oration; impolitic, one would think, in a judicial officer, desirous to keep the peace, or an agent of the Washington Monument Society, wishing to obtain a tribute to the memory of the Father of his Country, but merely ask you to observe that the public attack of the "judicial officer" upon the governor of the   Territory, appears also to have been based upon Mr. Young's alleged expressions upon the memory of General Taylor, which certainly were not cast upon the occasion to which I have already adverted.

The letter-writer states, moreover, that at the celebration of the 24th of July, "the orator of the day spoke bitterly of the course of the United States towards the Church of Latter Day Saints, in taking a battalion of men from them for the war with Mexico, while on the banks of the Missouri river, in their flight from the mob at Nauvoo; that the government had devised the most wanton, cruel, and dastardly means for the accomplishment of their ruin, overthrow, and utter extermination; at which time also Governor Young denounced, in the most sacrilegious terms, President Taylor." I again repeat, the writer of the preceding extract was not present at the celebration to which he refers. There were some ten or twelve orators on that occasion, and the whole day was occupied by their speeches; but I heard no such language as I have quoted, nor any other which could be construed into the slightest disrespect towards the Government of the United States. All the officers of the government who were then in the Territory dined with the governor on that day. I am not aware that a single incident occurred to mar its gaiety and good fellowship.

The government *did not* TAKE from us a battalion of men, but one of its most gallant officers made a call for volunteers, and Mr. Young said in reply; "You shall have your battalion at once, if it has to be a class of our elders." More than five hundred able-bodied men promptly responded to the call, leaving their wives and children on the plains, and five hundred teams without drivers, and rendered efficient service in the war with the Mexican republic.

When I took my departure from Utah, the architect of the contemplated capitol was busily employed in preparing the plans and drawings for the building, and the governor was very desirous that they should be completed, and a daguerreotype of them taken to be exhibited by me to the President and members of Congress, in order that they might see what kind of building it was proposed to erect. But it was not designed to commence the erection of the building until the ensuing spring.

I have the honor to be, very respectfully and truly, your most obedient servant,

JOHN M. BERNHISEL,
Delegate from Utah.

To the President of the United States.

————

[Printed slip enclosed with Mr. Bernhisel's communication to the President.]

Extract of a letter from a judicial officer of the government, at Great Salt Lake City, dated September 20, 1851.[2]

I shall leave for the States on the 1st October; and most gladly will I go, for I am sick and tired of this place, of the fanaticism of the people, followed by their violence of feeling towards the "*gentiles,*" as they style all persons not belonging to their church. I have had a feeling and personal proof of their fanatical intolerance within the last few days. I will give you a cursory view of the circumstances and the scene.

———————————

2. As Bernhisel indicates, the apparent writer of this letter, Associate Justice Perry E. Brocchus of Alabama, was not present at the July 24th celebration he describes. Brocchus based his story on information provided by the other federal officials who did attend.

As soon after my arrival here as my illness would permit, I heard from Judge B. and Mr. Secretary H. accounts of the intolerant sentiments of the community towards government officers and the government itself, which filled me with surprise. I learned that not only were the officers sent here treated with coolness and disrespect, but that the Government of the United States, on all public occasions, whether festive or religious, was denounced in the most disrespectful terms, and often with invectives of great bitterness. I will mention a few instances. The 24th July is the anniversary of the arrival of the Mormons in this valley. It was on that day of this year that they assembled to commemorate that interesting event. The orator of the day, on that occasion, spoke bitterly of the course of the United States towards the church of *"Latter Day Saints,"* in taking a battalion [sic] of their men from them for the war with Mexico, while on the banks of the Missouri river, in their flight from the mob at Nauvoo. He said the Government of the United States had devised the most wanton, cruel, and dastardly means for the accomplishment of their ruin, overthrow, and utter extermination.

His Excellency Governor Young, on the same occasion, denounced, in the most sacrilegious terms, the memory of the illustrious and lamented general and President of the United States, who has lately gone to the grave, and over whose tomb a nation's tears have scarcely ceased to flow. He exclaimed, *"Zachary Taylor is dead and gone to hell, and I am glad of it!"* and his sentiments were echoed by a loud amen from all parts of the assembly. Then, rising in the excess of his passion to his tiptoes, he vociferated, *"I prophesy, in the name of Jesus Christ, by the power of the priesthood that is upon me, that any other President of the United States, who shall lift his finger against this people, will die an untimely death and go to hell."* This kind of feeling I found pervading the whole community, in some individuals more marked than in others.

You may remember that I was authorized by the managers of the Washington National Monument Society to say to the people of the Territory of Utah, that they would be pleased to receive from them a block of marble or other stone, to be deposited in the monument *"as an offering at the shrine of patriotism."* I accordingly called on Governor Young, and apprized him of the trust committed to my hands, and expressed a desire to address the people upon the subject, when assembled in their greatest number. He replied that on the following Monday the very best opportunity would be presented. Monday came, and I found myself at their Bowery, in the midst of at least three thousand people. I was respectfully and honorably introduced by *"His Excellency"* to the vast assemblage. I made a speech, though so feeble that I could scarcely stand, and staggered in my debility several times on the platform.

I spoke for two hours, during which time I was favored with the unwavering attentions of my audience. Having made some remarks in reference to the judiciary, I presented the subject of the National Monument, and *incidentally thereto* (as the Mormons supposed) I expressed my opinions in a full, free, unreserved, yet respectful and dignified manner, in regard to the defection of the people here from the Government of the United States. I endeavored to show the injustice of their feelings towards the Government, and alluded boldly and feelingly to the sacrilegious [sic] remarks of Governor Young towards the memory of the lamented Taylor. I defended, as well as my feeble powers would allow, the name and character of the departed hero, from the unjust aspersions cast upon them, and remarked that, in the latter part of the assailant's bitter exclamation that he *"was glad that Gen. Taylor was in hell,"* he did not exhibit a Christian spirit, and that if the author did not early repent of the cruel declaration, he *would perform that task with keen remorse upon his dying pillow.* I then alluded to my nativity; to my citizenship; to my love of country; to my duty to defend my country from unjust aspersions wherever I met them; and trusted that when I failed to defend her, my tongue, then employed in her advocacy and praise, might cling to the roof of my mouth; and that my arm, ever ready to be raised in her defence, might fall palsied at my side. I then told the audience if they could not offer a block of marble in a feeling of full fellowship with the people of the United States, as brethren and fellow-citizens, they had better not offer it at all, but leave it unquarried in the bosom of its native mountain. At the close of my speech the governor arose and denounced me and the Government in the most brutal and unmeasured terms.

The ferment created by his remarks was truly fearful. It seemed as if the people (I mean a large portion of them) were ready to spring upon me like hyenas and destroy me. The governor, while speaking, said that some persons might get their hair pulled or *their throats cut on that occasion.* His manner was boisterous, passionate, infuriated in the extreme; and if he had not been afraid of final vengeance, he would have pointed his finger at me, and I should *in an instant* have been a dead man. Ever since then the community has been in a state of intense excitement, and murmurs of personal violence and assassination towards me have been freely uttered by the lower order of the populace. How it will end I do not know. I have just learned that I have been denounced, together with the Government and officers, in the Bowery again to-day, by Governor Young. I hope I shall get off safely. God only knows. I am in the power of a desperate and murderous set. I however feel no great fear. So much for defending my country.

I expect all the officers of the Territory, at least Chief Justice B., Secretary Harris, and Captain Day, Indian agent, will return with me, *to return here no more.*

———

GREAT SALT LAKE CITY,
September 22, 1851.

Sir: For reasons satisfactory to themselves, Judges Brandebury and Brocchus, and Secretary Harris, leave this Territory for the States next week.

But I, for reasons satisfactory to myself, have thought best to write you a line, stating that after the causes which led to this unhappy event occurred, I used all my influence to bring about a reconciliation, but failed.

Did my sense of duty require me to return without consulting you, the duties I owe to my little family would forbid my undertaking the journey so late in the season. Should you, or Congress, on inquiry into the facts, be of the opinion that I also ought to return, that opinion can be made known to me, and it shall then be done according to your wishes.

I forbear to state the facts for the reason that Judges Branderbury [sic] and Brocchus, and Secretary Harris, will see you in person, and also Doctor Bernhisel, delegate from Utah, who will be able to inform you much better than I can by letter.

It is proper to state that Doctor Bernhisel left here before the main facts occurred which led to this event; he, therefore, will have to be informed of them by the people here.

I have the honor to subscribe myself your obedient servant,

Z. SNOW

To his Excellency MILLARD FILLMORE,
President of the United States.

———

GREAT SALT LAKE CITY,
October 20, 1851.

Sir: Owing to the peculiar situation of our Territory in relation to public officers, I presume again to address you a few lines. You will please to recollect, that at the close of my last communication the Legislative Assembly was still in session. It so continued until the third instant, at which time they adjourned until the first Monday in January next, when they will resume their sitting.

Upon the departure of Mr. Secretary Harris, and the two judges, Messrs. Brandebury and Brocchus, the Legislative Assembly proceeded to re-district the Territory, and assigned the remaining judge, the honorable Zerubabel Snow, to perform the duty of holding all the district courts in the Territory until other judges shall be appointed and enter upon the discharge of their duties.

Being extremely inconvenienced by the want of a secretary, and apprehending some considerable delay might occur before another would appear, I took the liberty of appointing one, to act in that office pro tem., until the disability should cease to exist, or the vacancy be filled by the President. Dr. Willard Richards is the gentleman I have so appointed, who would be a good selection for that office, if the President and Senate should feel inclined to favor him.[3] The proceedings of the legislature will be forwarded as soon as they can be arranged in proper form.

I also beg leave to add, that upon Indian affairs I have never received any instructions; the Indian agent, Mr. Holeman, came here, but immediately left to attend a treaty at Laramie, which he had pre-engaged to do. He has not returned to this place since. Mr. Day accompanied the officers, and it is presumed that upon meeting with Mr. Holeman they all returned to the States together; no report has been received from any of them as yet, except Mr. Rose, who is now in this city.[4] I shall report to the proper department, to which I refer you for further particulars. My object in mentioning this subject in this letter, is to keep you authenticated, in order that the proper instructions may be had in this superintendency.

The Indians are generally peaceable, with the exception of those on Mary's river,[5] where it has become very unsafe to travel. Those Indians have never been under the influence of the

------

3. Apostle Willard Richards was a native of Massachusetts, born in 1804, an herb doctor, and cousin and second counselor to Brigham Young.

4. Non-Mormon U.S. Indian agent Jacob Holeman stuck to his post and did not return to the states with the other federal officials. President James Buchanan later listed Holeman's 1851–53 reports of Mormon tampering with the Indians among his reasons for ordering a U.S. Army expedition to Utah in 1857 to assert federal authority. See "The Utah Expedition," House Exec. Doc. 71 (35–1), 1858, Serial 956, 128–65. Stephen B. Rose was a Mormon sub-agent who arrived in Utah with Secretary Harris on 19 July 1851.

5. Today the Humboldt River, which generally follows the line of I-80 to Humboldt Sink, about seventeen miles southwest of Lovelock, Nevada.

settlers of this Territory. It is proposed by some of the citizens to make a settlement, and establish a trading post in the vicinity. If the heretofore favorable influence of such a proceeding shall in like manner be successful and prevail in that region, the desired security will be obtained, and the traveller, with the usual and necessary caution, can go in safety.

With sentiments of high esteem, I remain, sir, most truly, your humble servant,

BRIGHAM YOUNG,
Governor of Utah Territory.

To his Excellency MILLARD FILLMORE,
President of the United States.

———

Report of Messrs. Brandebury, Brocchus, and Harris, to the President of the United States.

WASHINGTON, *December* 19, 1851.

Sir: It becomes our duty, as officers of the United States for the Territory of Utah, to inform the President that we have been compelled to withdraw from the Territory, and our official duties, in consequence of an extraordinary state of affairs existing there, which rendered the performance of those duties not only dangerous, but impracticable, and a longer residence in the Territory, in our judgment, incompatible with a proper sense of self-respect, and the high regard due to the United States. We have been driven to this course by the lawless acts and the hostile and seditious feelings and sentiments of Brigham Young, the Executive of the Territory, and the great body of the residents there, manifested towards the Government and officers of the United States in aspersions and denunciations so violent and offensive as to set at defiance, not only a just administration of the laws, but the rights and feelings of citizens and officers of the United States residing there.

To enable the Government to understand more fully the unfortunate position of affairs in that Territory, it will be necessary to explain the extraordinary religious organization existing there—its unlimited pretensions, influence, and power; and to enter into a disagreeable detail of facts, and the language and sentiments of the governor and others high in authority, towards the Government, people, and officers of the United States.

We found upon our arrival that almost the entire populations consisted of a people called Mormons; and the Mormon church overshadowing and controlling the opinions, the actions, the property, and even the lives of its members; usurping and exercising the functions of legislation and the judicial business of the Territory; organizing and commanding the military; disposing of the public lands upon its own terms; coining money, stamped "Holiness to the Lord," and forcing its circulation at a standard fifteen or twenty per centum above its real value; openly sanctioning and defending the practice of polygamy, or plurality of wives; exacting the tenth part of every thing from its members, under the name of tithing, and enormous taxes, from citizens, not members; penetrating and supervising the social and business circles; and inculcating, and requiring, as an article of religious faith, implicit obedience to the counsels of "the Church," as paramount to all the obligations of morality, society, allegiance, and of law.

At the head of this formidable organization, styled "The Church of Jesus Christ of Latter Day Saints," stood Brigham Young, the governor, claiming, and represented to be, the Prophet of God, and his sayings as direct revelations from Heaven, commanding thereby unlimited sway over the ignorant and credulous. *His* opinions and wishes were *their* opinions and wishes. He was consulted by them, upon almost every subject, as an oracle. No man pretended to embark in any kind of business without his permission, or conciliating him by a deferential consultation. In a word, he ruled as he pleased, without a rival or opposition, for no man dared question his authority.

Congress having established a territorial government for this people, and extended the constitution and laws of the United

States over them, we were not only anxious for a cordial cooperation of all the officers and people in the organization of the Territory and a faithful administration of the laws, but equally anxious to avoid everything in the execution of our duties that would be likely to exhibit a conflict between the government and the church. Our main reliance was upon Brigham Young, the governor, for no man else could govern them against his influence, without a military force. As he had sought, and been honored with the office of Executive of the Territory, we presumed he was well disposed towards the government, and would wield his unbounded influence to secure respect and obedience to the government and the laws.

But in this we were disappointed. He made us feel, upon our arrival in the Territory, in a manner that could not be mistaken, that he was jealous of his power as head of the church, and hostile to the government of the United States and its officers, coming there to perform this duty, under the organic act.

One of the undersigned (Chief Justice Brandebury) arrived in the Territory on the 7th of June, a month and more before any of the other officers from the States. He availed himself of the earliest day after his arrival not only to pay his respects to Governor Young, as Executive of the Territory, but to inform him that he was there ready to enter upon his official duties, and for that purpose invited the United States attorney, Mr. Blair, (a Mormon,) to accompany and introduce him.[6] Before the hour arrived, however, on the day appointed, Mr. Blair called to say that the governor's engagement would prevent an interview that day, and proposed another time to call upon his Excellency. At the appointed time, another effort was made, in company with Mr. Blair, who led the way to the office occupied by the governor. The chief justice was requested to tarry

---

6. Mormon lawyer Seth M. Blair was thirty-one when President Fillmore appointed him U.S. attorney for Utah Territory. A native of Missouri and a former Texas ranger, he became editor of *The Mountaineer*, a Mormon newspaper at Great Salt Lake and an officer in the Nauvoo Legion.

upon the stairway until Mr. Blair advanced to open the door and make inquiry if the governor could be seen. He was anticipated, however, by the governor's clerk (an Englishman) meeting him at the door, and after a few words between them in an undertone, returned with the information that the governor was not in, and with many regrets for this second failure. Satisfied that this was the result of design on the part of the governor, no further effort was made to see him. This conduct of the governor was known in the community, and afforded much merriment to some of the Mormons. We were informed afterwards that Mr. Blair had made several private applications to the governor to know if he would allow an interview to the chief justice, but he refused, declaring that "he did not wish an introduction, for none but Mormons should have been appointed to the offices of the Territory, and none others but d—d rascals would have come among them." We refer to this incident now, only to show the feelings of the governor towards the government and officers at this early period.

On the 19th of July, another of the undersigned (Secretary Harris) arrived, in company with Judge Snow and Messrs. Babbit,[7] Bernhisel, Day, and Rose, the two last-named being Indian sub-agents. A few days afterwards, the secretary was invited by the governor to be present at an interview between him and Mr. Babbit. This interview was made the occasion of a violent exhibition of his temper and abuse of Mr. Babbit, and of the government and officers, "intended for the secretary," as the governor afterwards declared, "to let him know what kind of people he had to deal with." These were but manifestations of that hostile feeling, the murmurs and mutterings of which were rife

---

7. A gifted but unstable figure in early Mormon history, Almon W. Babbitt had delivered to Washington the memorial for statehood of the State of Deseret and returned with federal funds to build a statehouse. Named territorial secretary in 1853, the New Englander three years later was killed by Indians at Ash Hollow on the Oregon Trail, near present Ogallala, Nebraska, as he was returning to Utah.

throughout the community, and intended that it should not escape our ears.

Upon the occasion of celebrating the anniversary of the arrival of the Mormon pioneers into the Valley, (the 24th July,) an immense concourse of their people were assembled from all parts of the Territory. Those of us then in the Territory were invited to be present and participate in the festivities of the occasion. We were seated upon the stand or platform, with a number of the leading men of the church, including the present delegate in Congress, (Hon. John M. Bernhisel.) The governor rose to address the audience, and a profound silence ensued, as is always the case when he rises to speak. After reflecting in terms of condemnation upon the alleged hostility of General Taylor to the Mormons, and to giving them a government, he exclaimed, in a loud and exulting tone, "But Zachary Taylor is dead, and in hell, and I am glad of it." Then drawing himself up to his utmost height, and stretching his hands towards heaven, he declared in a still more violent voice, "and I prophesy in the name of Jesus Christ, by the power of the Priesthood that's upon me, that any President of the United States who lifts his finger against this people shall die an untimely death, and go to hell." To this sentiment there came up from those seated around us, and from all parts of the house, loud and mingled responses of "Amen!" "Good!" "Hear!"

With the invitation to be present on this occasion, was an invitation to dine with the governor. Although we believed the occasion of our presence was seized upon by the governor to show us how brave and independent he could be in his declarations, and with what impunity our feelings could be outraged and insulted, we were forced, from an indisposition to produce a rupture and break off our official relations so soon after our arrival, to smother our indignation and mingle in the parade of a dinner.

Upon a subsequent occasion, (the 6th of September,) in reply to the remarks made by one of the undersigned (Associate Justice Brocchus) upon the subject, before a large audience, the governor reiterated and declared, "I did say that General Taylor was dead and in hell; *and I know it.*" A man in the crowd, seemingly to give the governor an opportunity of fixing its truth, spoke out and said, "How do you know it?" To which the governor promptly answered, "Because God told me so." An Elder, second only to the governor in the church, (Heber C. Kimball,) laying his hand on the shoulder of Judge Brocchus, added, "Yes, Judge, and you'll know it, too; for you'll see him when *you* get there."[8]

Upon the occasion before referred to, (24th of July,) another speaker, (D. H. Wells,) late chief justice of the State of Deseret, declared, that "in the winter of 1838-'39 the church was expelled from the State of Missouri by a murderous mob, under the exterminating order of Governor Lilburn W. Boggs;" that "in the year 1844, on the 27th day of June, the mob of Illinois murdered in cold blood the Prophet Joseph, and Patriarch Hyram [*sic*] Smith, while confined in jail under the guarantee of safety, and pledge of the governor, Thomas Ford;" and that when they had left their homes in 1846, in the most inclement season, and were pursuing their toilsome march westward, "the government of the United States required a battalion of five hundred men to leave their families in this precarious situation, without money, provisions, or friends, other than the God whom they serve, to perform a campaign of over two thousand miles, on foot, across trackless deserts and burning plains, to fight the battles of their country; even that country which had afforded them no protection from the ruthless ruffians who had plundered them of their property, robbed them of their rights, waylaid them in their peaceful habitations, and murdered them while under the safeguards of their pledged faith. That country that could have the *barbarity*, under such peculiar circumstances, to make such a requirement, could have no other object in

---

8. Like Brigham Young, Heber Chase Kimball was born in 1801 in Vermont, only two weeks apart from the man he served faithfully as first counselor. An original apostle of the L.D.S. Church, Kimball eventually married forty-three wives who bore a total of some sixty-five children.

view than to finish, by extermination, the work which had so ruth-
lessly begun."

Upon the same occasion, another speaker (W. W. Phelps, one
of the "Regents of the University of Deseret") declared, as a just
cause of hostility, that "the Mormons were proscribed by the
United States—he had two wives, others of his brethren had more,
and brother Brigham Young had still more, and none of them dare
return to the United States with their families; for their dirty, mean,
little, contracted laws would imprison them for polygamy."[9]

Upon the following Sunday, the mayor of the city, Jedediah M.
Grant,[10] in eulogizing the strength of the Mormons, exultingly
declared from the pulpit, in presence of the undersigned, (Mr.
Harris,) "that now the United States could not conquer them by
arms."

Brigham Young, the governor, announced, with great
vehemence, from the stand and to individuals, while the feelings of
the people were thus excited by such sentiments, "that he had
ruled that people for years, and could rule them again; that the
United States judges might remain in the Territory and draw their
salaries, but they should never try a cause if he could prevent it."

Another speaker, already referred to, standing second in the
church, (Heber C. Kimball,) encouraged by the example set him by
the governor, declared, in a speech at a public meeting, "that the
United States officers might remain in the Territory so long as they

---

9. An early convert to Mormonism, William W. Phelps, age 59, was a native
of New Jersey. He performed in many capacities as a writer and printer before
coming to Utah where he served in the territorial legislature and at the University
of Deseret.

10. A firebrand of early Mormonism, thirty-five-year-old Jedediah Morgan
Grant was mayor of Great Salt Lake City. Born in New York, he became second
counselor to Brigham Young in 1854 after delivering a scorching sermon on the
need to shed the blood of some sinners in order to save them. In 1856 he led the
great Reformation to cleanse Israel before its confrontation with the American
republic and died later that year of typhoid and pneumonia.

behaved themselves and paid their boarding; but if they did not, they (the Mormons) would kick them to hell, where they belong."

The governor announced, upon another occasion, from the pulpit, "that he was not opposed to the government of the United States, but it was the d—d infernal corrupt scoundrels at the head of it." He applied this to Congress, as he afterwards explained it, declaring "that the present administration had done them some justice; but no thanks to them, for it was God Almighty made them do it."

Upon another occasion two of the undersigned (Judges Brandebury and Brocchus) attended church on the Sabbath, and were invited to take seats upon the stand or platform. Secretary Harris had ceased to attend, to avoid hearing the government aspersed and denounced. Judge Brocchus had just recovered from a sick bed, and had not had an opportunity of attending church before. The preacher, Professor Spencer, of "the University of Deseret," among other expressions of ill feeling, declared that "the laws and policy of the United States government were intended to oppress the poor"—and turning his eyes upon us, in presence of this large audience, further declared, "the government of the United States is a stink in the nostrils of Jehovah, and no wonder the Mormons wish it down.[11] We can save it by *Theocracy;* but rather that [sic] save it any other way, we will see it d—d first." Another Mormon (Albert Carrington,) in refusing to join in firing a salute on the 4th of July, declared to Judge Brocchus and others, that ["]the United States was going to hell as fast as it could, and the sooner the better."[12]

---

11. Fifty-seven-year-old Daniel Spencer from Massachusetts was the son of a Revolutionary War veteran and one of the better educated Mormon leaders. A former mayor of Nauvoo, he was president of the Salt Lake stake.

12. Albert Carrington, age thirty-eight, was a native of Vermont and a graduate of Dartmouth College. He served as a secretary to Brigham Young and later as an editor of the *Deseret News.* He was ordained an apostle in 1870 and excommunicated in 1885.

This man arrived in the Territory with Judge Brocchus; is an Elder in the church, and expressed but the feelings and wishes of the residents there in sympathy with him.

These are but a few of the many seditious and hostile declarations, which it would be impossible to enumerate, made by Governor Young, and others in his presence, from the pulpit; and scarcely an opportunity was suffered to pass without aspersing the people and government of the United States, in language profane, and at times obscene. Indeed, the officers seemed to be looked upon as the mere toys of the governor's power—he treating them as he pleased, according to his capricious humor—sometimes encouraging a hope for a better [state] of affairs, to make the next outbreak of hostility and insult the more marked and humiliating.

The many important duties to be performed in the organization of the Territory, and the administrations of the laws, required a cordial and confidential intercourse between the officers. The governor, however, announced soon after our arrival, in the presence of Mr. Harris and others, with great temper, "that he had ruled that people for years, and could rule them again, and he would kick any man out of the Territory who attempted to dictate to, or advise him in his duty." Under such circumstances, no communication could be had with the Executive, with any regard to self-respect, or without apprehension of personal insult; especially as we were looked upon as offensive intruders rather than co-ordinate branches of the government.

He asked for no advice, and none was volunteered by any of us, and he was free to proceed in the performance of his duties as he thought proper.

The act of Congress required him to have a census taken, so as to apportion the number of representatives and councillors to each county; but he apportioned them without taking the census. We were informed that a census had been taken when the application was made by the State of Deseret for admission into the Union, but it was so false and exaggerated that a correct census would have betrayed the fraud. The act further required that he should fix the time and places, and appoint the persons, who should superintend the first election for councillors, representatives, and a delegate to Congress, and it prescribed the qualifications of voters, and who should be eligible to these offices. Regardless of these directions and of all forms, and in contempt of the organic act, he issued a proclamation, without the seal of the Territory or signature of the secretary, ordering the election to be held under "the provisional laws of the State of Deseret." This proclamation and many other papers were requested by the secretary, but never furnished, and, of course, no "executive record" could be made of the same. No notice was given in it as to the qualifications of voters, and those who were eligible to office, nor were any persons named to hold the elections. The consequence was, that unnaturalized foreigners officiated at the elections, voted, and were elected as representatives, and to offices not authorized by the act. The proclamation and election were a burlesque upon the order and decorum required by the organic act, and sprung from the determination of the church to do as she pleased in such matters.

He was also authorized and required, by the same act, to appoint all officers not provided for in the bill, who should continue in office until the end of the first session of the legislature. Yet there was not a sheriff, justice of the peace, or constable in the Territory legally qualified to act when we left, (excepting one or two justices of the peace appointed a few days before,) and criminals went at large untried and unpunished, so far as the United States judges could interfere. The church, as usual, punished some, as it was reported, and allowed others to go free. A few days before we left, we understood a posse of men were sent by the church in pursuit of some horse-thieves. Some of them were arrested, tried, and fined a hundred dollars, and others discharged. A man was tried in an adjoining county for an alleged offence, by a member of the church, purporting to be a judge, without a jury, and convicted and punished.

About the same time, a cold and deliberate murder was committed in the Territory upon the body of Mr. James Munroe, a citizen of the United States, from Utica, New York, on his way to Salt Lake City, by a member of the church, and the remains brought into the city and buried, without an inquest, the murderer walking through the streets afterwards under the eye of the governor, and in his society, some of the relatives of the deceased residing there, and members of the church, afraid or disinclined to act.[13] It was reported, and believed by many, that the murder was counseled by the church, or some of its leading members; and such an impression would paralyze the hand of any one inclined to interfere. This rumor received much force from the intimacy between the offender and the leading members of the church, before and after the commission of the offence. He was several weeks in the city, and unknown, as well as his location, to any of us; it was the common talk that he intended to kill Mr. Munroe; he was permitted to go out sixty or eighty miles to meet his intended victim, and none of these men who knew the fact lifted an arm or a voice to prevent the deed. He met Munroe, who was unarmed, invited him out of his camp, took a seat and talked half an hour with him, and then rose up, bade him farewell, and blew his brains out with a pistol! We have no doubt, however, that if he had been tried, an entire acquittal would have followed, as was the result in February last, in the case of the murder of Dr. John R. Vaughan, a citizen of Indiana, then on his way to California, and the murderer

---

13. Schoolteacher James Monroe, a former University of Nauvoo regent, was shot to death in September 1851 by noted Mormon plainsman Howard Egan, age thirty-six, for alleged adultery with one of Egan's three wives while the Irishman was looking for gold in California. In another example of theocratic justice, Apostle George A. Smith at the October trial "justified Egan for what he had done [and] said it was the duty of the nearest kin to a female who was seduced to take the life of the seducer." At this, the Mormon jury found Egan not guilty. See Brooks, *On the Mormon Frontier: The Diary of Hosea Stout*, 2:404, 407.

suffered to go unpunished. How many other crimes and offences were punished or passed by we know not. The governor was thus true to his declaration, that "the United States judges should never try a case if he could prevent it," for we had not an officer to summon a jury, or execute a warrant, subpoena, or any kind of process, except in cases in which the United States was a party, when the marshal would be bound to act.

Congress appropriated twenty thousand dollars, to be applied under the direction of the governor and legislature in the erection of public buildings. The governor no sooner received this money than he appropriated and used every dollar of it, or a greater portion of it, in payment of debts due by the Mormon church, and in a few days after its arrival in the valley it was on its way to the United States in other hands. We were not present at its actual payment, but it was a matter of public notoriety and talked of by the gentlemen who received it. This occurred about the last of July.

Those of us then in the Territory, powerless and compelled to be observers of all these things on account of the omnipotence of the church and the governor, determined to report the facts in writing to the President of the United States. Before an opportunity for a safe transmission of such a report presented itself, one of the undersigned (Associate Chief Justice Brocchus, who arrived in the Territory on the 17th of August) addressed a large meeting of the people on the 6th of September, on behalf of the Washington Monument Association, having been commissioned by the managers thereof to ask of the people of that Territory a block of marble or other stone, to be placed in that structure, "as an offering at the shrine of patriotism." As the life, character, and services of Washington were intimately blended with everything relating to the Government and institutions of the United States, the occasion was supposed to be an appropriate one to disabuse the minds of the Mormon people of the false and prejudicial opinions they entertained towards the people and Government of the United States, and thus to arrest that flow of seditious sentiment which was so freely pouring forth from their bosoms towards the country to which they owed their highest patriotism and their best affections. We had remained there up to this period, and submitted in silence to almost every species of indignity and mortification, rather than take any step that would produce discord and involve the territorial government in difficulties. It was in this spirit that we preserved silence, until the favorable opportunity, above alluded to, was presented, when we unanimously concurred in the opinion that it was not only a matter of right, but also of duty, to have the attention of the people directed to the errors of their opinions in holding the Government of the United States and her citizens as enemies to them, and the seekers of their ruin and extermination. Such opinions were daily inculcated by the leaders of the church upon the fanatical credulity of the masses of the people. They were taught to believe that the general government sympathized with those whom they regarded as their persecutors in the States of Illinois and Missouri, and desired their overthrow and utter destruction. The natural result of such convictions was a feeling of deep-seated hostility towards the Government and people of the United States, which was every day becoming more deep and invet- erate under the teachings of their spiritual leaders. We believed that to confront and remove those false impressions, thus shame- fully instilled into the popular mind, would be to dry up the fountain of seditious sentiment in the Territory, and thus revive that sense of patriotism and loyalty, the manifest absence of which was then a serious obstacle to the successful operation of the terri- torial government, and threatened, if not corrected, to become much more serious in future. It was in pursuance of this design that the address above alluded to was made. In the course of that address the speaker endeavored, in good faith, only to correct erroneous opinions in regard to the Government from which he held his commission, without indulging in terms of invective and rebuke. His remonstrances against these opinions, and the hostile feelings resulting from them, were calm and dispassionate, and in good faith intended to effect the salutary purpose of producing peace and concord between the various branches of the Government, and good will towards the United States.

The address was entirely free from any allusions, even the most remote, to the peculiar religion of the community, or to any of their domestic or social customs. It contained not a single expression of bravado or unkindness or harsh rebuke, or any sentiment that could have been tortured into a design on the part of the speaker to inflict wantonly a wound upon the hearts of his hearers.

At the close of the address, the governor arose and denounced the speaker with great violence, as "profoundly ignorant, or wilfully wicked"—strode the stage madly—assumed various theatrical attitudes—declared he "was a greater man than ever George Washington was"—"that he knew more than ever George Washington did"—that "he was the man that could handle the sword"—and "that if there was any more discussion, there would be pulling of hair and cutting of throats." Referring to a remark of the speaker, that the United States Government was humane and kindly disposed [toward] them, he said, "I know the United States did not murder our wives and children, burn our houses, and rob us of our property, but they stood by and saw it done, and never opened their mouths, the d—d scoundrels." By this time the passions of the people were lashed into a fury like his own. To every sentence uttered, there was a prompt and determined response, showing, beyond a doubt, that all the hostile and seditious sentiments we had previously heard were the sentiments of this people.

Those of us present felt the personal danger that surrounded us. If the governor had but pointed his finger towards us, as an indication of wish, we have no doubt we would have been massacred before leaving the house. The governor declared afterwards "that if he had crooked his finger, we would have been torn to pieces."

Upon the next and succeeding days, these denunciations of the officers and the Government were renewed, as we were informed by a number of citizens, and continued in their meetings, by the governor and other leading members of the church, with increased vehemence. The Government was denounced, and the officers too, in language so vulgar and obscene, that decency would blush to hear it. We were now satisfied, that with such sentiments and feelings pervading the community, towards us and the Government, the performance of our official duties were be impracticable, and to remain and be compelled to hear these offensive and seditious denunciations, disagreeable beyond endurance. The governor had been accustomed, as many of the leading men there informed us, to enter the legislative hall, under the provisional State government, and dictate what laws should or should not be passed, and the court and jury-rooms to indicate what verdicts should be rendered, and he had given us ample evidence that he was equally omnipotent and influential with the Mormon people under the territorial government. It required no over[t] act, or violence to defeat the spirit and object of the organic act, under an apparent compliance with all its requisitions. He had ordered the election of a Legislative Assembly as before described, but they were the creatures of his will, as the result shows. The other territorial officers, members of the Mormon church and under the same religious obligations, were subject to the same control. He had gone through the form of dividing the Territory into judicial districts, assigning the judges, and fixing the times for holding the courts, as one of the undersigned (Judge Brandebury) had prepared the proclamation for him. But he had declared "that the United States judges should never try a cause if he could prevent it," and it required no overt act to effect this purpose. The omission to appoint proper officers to issue and execute the various writs and warrants—to summon juries, and perform other duties in the organization of courts and administration of the laws, palsied the judiciary of itself. But apart from this, we have no doubt he would have fulfilled his own prophetic declaration, by the interposition of his power as head of the church, to repel parties and business from the courts, and force them to the disposal of the church upon its own terms—screen criminals from arrest and trial—drive off witnesses and make the court a mockery and the judge an object of ridicule. They continued their proceedings in the disposal of judicial business after our arrival the same as before, regardless of the organic act, or our authority as officers. We were fully satisfied, that what was done under the organic act by the governor tardily and carelessly, was the veriest affectation and show of obedience, to secure to himself and the Mormon church the money appropriated by Congress for territorial purposes, salaries, &c. The secretary had twenty-four thousand dollars intrusted to him by the Government, for which he had given bond to the United States for its safety and faithful application to the purposes specified according to law; and efforts had been made by the governor, as we shall show, to get this money also, in addition to the twenty thousand dollars, and for the same purpose, the benefit of himself and the Mormon church.

The legislature was not to have met until January, 1852, as was given out by the governor, a period of a year and four months after the passage of the act establishing the Territory. We know not the object of this delay, unless it was his contempt for the territorial bill, and under a supposition that, as the Secretary was bound to transmit to the President and Congress on or before the first of December, annually, a copy of the executive and legislative proceedings, no exposé of the misapplication of the twenty thousand dollars appropriated for public buildings could have been made known officially before December, 1852—more than a year after it occurred. A few days after the arrival of the secretary, (19th of July,) an attempt was made, in the interview already referred to, to browbeat and intimidate him into submission to the governor's purposes, or, as the governor said, "to let the secretary know what kind of people he had to deal with"—and soon thereafter called upon him, in a patronizing manner, to borrow eight or ten thousand dollars of it for the church. He was informed by the secretary that no consideration could induce the loan of a dollar of it, as the law made an act of the kind a felony. This effort having failed, another attempt was made by setting up a claim for daily pay and mileage for the members of the last legislature of the provisional government of the "State of Deseret"—a leading member of the church informing the secretary that this money would be of great assistance to the church in relieving her from debt, and in justice should be paid as demanded. This effort having also failed, the fixed determination of the governor to get possession of the public money in the hands of the secretary for the benefit of himself and the church, revealed itself more openly and decidedly. Although the election for members of the Legislative Assembly had been held on the first Monday in August, he had made no declaration of the result of that election, as he was specifically required to do by the organic act; and without such declaration, of course the election itself was not complete. But disregarding the plain directions of the organic act in this particular, as in almost all others, he issued secret notices to members of the Legislative Assembly, to meet on Monday, the 22d day of September. The following is a *verbatim* copy of the notice sent to one of the pretended members, the original of which is now in the possession of the secretary, to wit:

"GREAT SALT LAKE CITY.
September 17, 1851.

"Hon. Sir: The Legislative Assembly of Utah Territory will assemble in this city on Monday, the 22d instant, at precisely ten o'clock, A.M.

"This notice being shorter than might appear desirable, I have caused this notice to be forwarded to you, that you might not fail in attending this call.

"I have the honor to be, most respectfully and truly, yours,

"BRIGHAM YOUNG,
"*Governor of Utah Territory.*"

So solicitous was the governor that the secretary and other officers (not Mormons) should be kept in ignorance of this step, that on the 19th of September, two days after the date of the above notice, he most positively and emphatically denied, as communicated to the secretary, that any such notice had been issued. Immediately thereafter, however, on the same day, (Friday the 19th,) a proclamation, declaring the members elect, and convening the Legislative Assembly at ten o'clock on Monday, the 22d September, was brought to the secretary for his signature and seal. That proclamation, however, was never published. It should be borne in mind that the settlements in the Territory extend a distance of about three hundred miles north and south, and that some of the members of the Assembly resided two hundred and fifty miles from Salt Lake City, the place of the meeting. In obedience to the secret instructions of the governor, the Legislative Assembly met on the 22d. The governor transmitted to them a printed message, which was afterwards, for some reason, suppressed, and none of the undersigned were able to procure a copy. On the 25th the secretary was served with the following paper by Mr. William Kimball, (a Mormon,)[14] purporting to be the sergeant-at-arms of the Assembly, to wit:

"HOUSE OF REPRESENTATIVES,
"*Great Salt Lake City, Utah Territory, Sept.* 24, 1851.

"Sir: By a resolution passed by the Legislative Assembly this day, it was directed that an order be drawn on the secretary of the Territory for the sum of five hundred dollars towards defraying the incidental expenses of the Legislative Assembly.

---

14. William H. Kimball, age twenty-five, was the oldest son of Apostle Heber C. Kimball. He became one of the Nauvoo Legion's most capable military officers and the owner of a stage station at Parley's Park, near present Park City, Utah.

"We therefore send this order by the sergeant-at-arms of the Legislative Council, hoping that you will furnish the same for our convenience.

"Respectfully yours, &c.,
"WILLARD RICHARDS,
"*President of the Council.*
"H. CORNEY [CORAY],
"*Secretary of theCouncil.*
"W. W. PHELPS,
"*Speaker of the House of Representatives.*
"ALBERT CARRINGTON,
"*Clerk House of Representatives Utah Territory.*

"To the Hon. B. D. HARRIS,
"*Secretary of Utah Territory.*"

This paper bears upon its face evidence of an intention to get possession of the money in the hands of the secretary by any and all means. The Assembly could not have been ignorant of the obvious fact, that such an order could not be legally accepted and paid by the secretary; his duty being to pay the contingent expenses of the Legislative Council only upon the presentation of proper vouchers, showing that the expenditure had been legally incurred, was reasonable in amount, &c.; and not to furnish money in round sums to the Assembly, to be disposed of as they pleased. But more evidence of this intention to get the money remains to be told. *With the foregoing order,* Mr. Kimball, the sergeant-at-arms, placed in the hands of the secretary a copy of joint resolutions passed by the Legislative Assembly on the 24th of September, and approved by the governor, (a copy of which is herewith transmitted,) ordering and requiring the United States marshal (a Mormon) to demand this money from the secretary; and if he refused to surrender it, to seize and imprison him until he delivered over the whole amount. The marshal being absent, his deputy (Horace Eldridge, a Mormon) undertook the execution of the order. The secretary refused to comply with the demand, and transmitted his reasons therefor in writing. As Governor Young had declared he would have this money, if he had to take it by violence, the secretary applied to the supreme court for an injunction, which was granted, forbidding the marshal and others from seizing or intermeddling with the funds and other property of the United States in the custody of the secretary. It was understood the members, being all Mormons, would relinquish their daily pay and mileage to the church.

But the governor's efforts to get the money did not stop there. A warrant was issued by Aaron F. Farr, a member of the church, purporting to be a justice of the peace, but who had neither given bond nor taken the oath of office, so far as we could learn, directed "to any legal officer of the aforesaid Territory (Utah) and county of Great Salt Lake," commanding him "to restrain and to take A. W. Babbit into your possession, and also the effects of A. W. Babbit, consisting of wagons, carriages and teams, and search his wagons for a sum of money, probably gold, to the amount of twenty-four thousand dollars, and for the seal of the Territory of Utah, and bring the same before me in Great Salt Lake City, and to search all other suspected persons and places." Mr. Babbit (Honorable A. W. Babbit, late delegate in Congress from the Territory) had left the city a day or two before, with his family and household affairs, on his return to the United States. There was no one named in the warrant as complaining, no oath made, and no offence alleged. It was placed in the hands of a man, another member of the church, purporting to be a constable, but who had neither given bond nor taken an oath of office, who, with a force of thirty men or more, well armed and mounted, started in pursuit, with instructions from the governor, as we were informed, "to bring Babbit back, dead or alive." They came upon his camp about forty miles from the city, some time in the night, and in the morning Mr. Babbit and his family found themselves surrounded by a body of armed men. The carriages and wagons were emptied and the contents searched, and then reloaded to be taken back to the city. Mr. Babbit appealed to them to allow his family and teams to proceed on their journey, as a delay of a few days might overwhelm them in snowstorms, and repeated trips over the mountains he had already passed would so fatigue and break down his animals, as at that late period in the year to seriously endanger the lives of himself and family on the plains. He at the same time made known his own willingness to return with them. But their orders from the governor were peremptory, and they refused. The tent was rudely torn down over the head of his wife, then nursing a sick child, his family ordered into the carriages, and the teams turned back to the city. This extraordinary writ was executed, as above stated, *after* the injunction of the supreme court had been granted, forbidding all persons from seizing or intermeddling with the money of the United States.

Mr. Babbit applied for and was discharged from custody upon a *habeas corpus* by one of the undersigned judges. Beyond his discharge, he could procure no redress for this grievance from a Mormon community, especially as the outrage had been perpetrated by command of the governor. It may not be improper to add, in this connexion, that the secretary succeeded in keeping possession of the money, brought it over the plains, and on his arrival at St. Louis, deposited it with the Assistant Treasurer to the credit of the United States.

We deem it our duty to state, in this official communication, that polygamy, or "plurality of wives, is openly avowed and prac-tised in the Territory, under the sanction and in obedience to the direct commands of the church." So universal is this practice, that very few if any leading men in that community can be found who have not more than one wife each. The prominent men in the church, whose example in all things it is the ambition of the more humble to imitate, have each many wives; some of them, we were credibly informed and believe, as many as twenty or thirty, and Brigham Young, the governor, even a greater number. Only a few days before we left the Territory, the governor was seen riding through the streets of the city in an omnibus, with a large company of his wives, more than two-thirds of whom had infants in their arms. It is not uncommon to find two or more sisters married to the same man; and in one instance, at least, a mother and her two daughters are among the wives of a leading member of the church. This practice, regarded and punished as a high and revolting crime in all well civilized countries, would, of course, never be made a statutory offence by a Mormon Legislature; and if a crime at common law, the courts would be powerless to correct the evil with Mormon juries.

The city of Great Salt Lake is an important point in the overland route to Oregon and California, for the emigrant to replenish his stores or to winter, if overtaken by the advance of the season. But the intimidation which is produced by the denunciations and conduct of the Mormon church and people, upon citizens of the United States passing through or engaged in business there, is such, as to drive the emigrant upon another route to avoid it, and the residents to submit to all the impositions of the church to prevent a sacrifice of their business. No man dare open his mouth in opposition to their lawless exactions, without feeling its effects upon his liberty, his business, or his life. And thus, upon the soil of the United States, and under the broad folds of its stars and stripes, which protect him in his rights in every part of the civilized world, there is a spot where the citizen is brow-beaten and despoiled of his liberties as a freeman by a religious despotism. One of the undersigned (Judge Brandebury,) on his journey through the Territory, met a young man at Fort Bridger, about one hundred and twelve miles from Salt Lake City, who informed him that he had copied and forwarded to the President of the United States a letter written by James McCabe, esq., of Pontiac, Michigan, who had spent the winter in Salt Lake City, and was then on his way to Oregon, giving an account of the treatment he and others had received from the people there, and their seditious and treasonable feelings towards the United States. He stated that to give the President the facts, and conceal himself lest the Mormons should kill him if they found it out, he had signed the letter "William or George Johnston," (if remembered correctly) and thus left scarcely a mark by which an inquiry could be made into the facts. We have now before us the report of several trials which took place there before we arrived, furnished us by a respectable gentleman there at the time, and now residing in the United States, confirming the information we have received, that "gentiles" (as all are called who are not Mormons) were tried and sentenced for trivial offences to two, five, and ten years of labor upon the public highways, with ball and chain to their legs, and no shelter at night but caverns dug in the earth. We saw one of these highways cut out of the side of a mountain, and the caverns far down at its base, but the approach of the federal officers, as we were informed, was the signal for the release and banishment of these "convicts from the Territory." The account before us is too voluminous to embody in this report, but we transcribe a part of a single case, only to show the feelings there towards the government and people of the United States.

Washington Loomis was put upon trial for a larceny, and the report proceeds: "The indictment being read, defendant pleaded not guilty, when the court ordered him sworn. He testified that he knew nothing of the matter charged." George Love was then called and sworn for the prosecution, and testified "that he was positive of Loomis's innocence, for that he (Love) knew who had committed the crime, &c." Major Geo. D. Grant (a Mormon) was then called as a witness for the prosecution, for the avowed purpose of impeaching Love.[15] He stated, that he might have to tell some hearsay statements in relating his story. Defendant's counsel, James McCabe of Pontiac, Michigan, objected to this for two reasons; first, the prosecution had no right to impeach their own witness:

---

15. Born in 1812 George D. Grant was an adopted son of Brigham Young, a brother of Jedediah M. Grant, and a leading officer of the Nauvoo Legion. In 1849 he commanded the first cavalry company formed in the Great Basin. The present city of Grantsville, Utah, is named after him.

second, that hearsay testimony was wholly inadmissible. Upon this Major Grant flew into a rage, and for fifteen minutes indulged in a most outrageous tirade of profanity and abusive threats towards the defendant's counsel, (Mr. McCabe,) the Government of the United States, Missouri and Illinois mobites, &c., shaking his fists over the counsel's head, and several times threatening his life; giving vent to the most settled malignity and treasonable designs towards the United States Government; declaring that this is not a civil court, but that the military rules here, and he commanded them; and that, by the Eternal God, he would call in the "legion" and "tap the claret" of this d—d villanous [*sic*] emissary (Mr. McCabe) of that mob Government, (United States,) sent here to spy out their liberties and frighten the court with his exceptions and technicalities, and clear d—d scoundrels from punishment, &c., &c. The cries of "amen," "we are with you," "go it," "we will back you," "to the death," "we will stand by you through blood or hell," often broke from the crowd during this exhibition of extreme patriotism and bravery; and the court highly applauded the conduct of the witness, the Chief Justice (Perkins) crying, "Amen! that is the spirit of Jesus." The hearsay evidence was admitted, the defendant convicted "as accessory after the fact," for which there was no count in the indictment, and sentenced to one year's hard labor on the public works, with ball and chain. Defendant's counsel moved for the privilege of commuting by the payment of money, as had been done to others, but motion denied. Before the defendant was arrested, all his property was seized by process from this court; his counsel filed a motion to release it, that defendant might have the use of it in his trial and defence, but the motion was overruled. The material facts we have detailed in our report are known, more or less, to many other persons, and we invite the examination of almost any "gentile" who has been there, and whose person and business are secure from danger, in proof of the seditious and treasonable feelings of the leaders in the church, towards the people and Government of the United States.

These people are now living upon the soil of the United States, and drawing their sustenance from it, free of charge. The Government is paying their governor, judges, secretary, attorney, marshal, and Indian agents—allowing them to elect their own legislature and a delegate to Congress, and paying them out of the public treasury. They have received twenty thousand dollars for public buildings, and five thousand dollars for a library; and instead of the manifestation of respect and gratitude for these manifold favors, they are inexorable in their hatred, and are ready and willing to plot the destruction of their liberal benefactor. It is impossible for any officer to perform his duty or execute any law not in sympathy with their views as the Territory is at present organized. Their conduct shows that they either disregard, or cannot appreciate, the blessings of the present form of government established for them by the United States. We have no doubt the evils complained of will suggest the remedy, and that the Government has the power and the inclination to maintain its dig-nity and enforce obedience and respect to the laws, upon every part of its territory where there is not patriotism enough in the people to do it.

Aware of the solicitude of the President, that the officers appointed for that Territory should so proceed in the discharge of their official duties as to secure the confidence and amicable co-operation, and promote the welfare, of the people among whom they were sent, we were not only scrupulously careful to give no cause of offence, but equally slow to take offence at any exhibition of a want of courtesy or good will towards us. In view of these considerations, we submitted in silence and remained at our posts, until the conviction was forced upon us, that to remain longer would be to forfeit not only our own self-respect, but all claim to the approbation of the Government that had honored us with its confidence.

We have the honor to be, very respectfully, sir, your ob't serv'ts,

LEMUEL G. BRANDEBURY
Chief Justice of the Supreme Court of the United States
for the Territory of Utah.

PERRY E. BROCCHUS,
*Associate Justice of the Supreme Court of the United States
for the Territory of Utah.*

B. D. HARRIS,
Secretary of the Territory of Utah.

TO THE PRESIDENT OF THE UNITED STATES

———

Mr. Harris to Mr. Webster.

Washington, *January* 2, 1852.

Sir: I beg leave to transmit through the State Department, to the President of the United States, the accompanying papers relating to affairs in the Territory of Utah.

I have the honor to be, most respectfully, your obedient servant,

B. D. HARRIS,
Secretary of the Territory of Utah.

TO THE HON. DANIEL WEBSTER,
Secretary of State of the United States.

———

Mr. Harris to the President of the United States.

Washington, *January* 2, 1852.

Sir: I have the honor herewith to transmit to the President of the United States, copies of papers relating to affairs in the Territory of Utah, which it was not deemed important to embody in the report recently made to the President by the officers of that Territory.

The paper marked "No. 1" is a copy of a letter placed in my hands by Mr. William Kimball, representing himself to be the sergeant-at-arms of the Legislative Assembly of the Territory, on the 25th day of September last.

The paper marked "No. 2" is a copy of preamble and resolutions also placed in my hands by Mr. William Kimball, on the same occasion above mentioned, to wit: the 25th of September.

The paper marked "No. 3" is a copy of my reply to papers marked Nos. 1 and 2, which was transmitted to the persons to whom it is addressed on the day of its date, the 25th of September.

I have also the honor to state that I have not the means of making out and transmitting to the President and to Congress, copies of the "executive proceedings" of the Territory, agreeably to the original act; the governor having neglected to file in my office many of the executive papers, although I made repeated verbal requests for them. I at length addressed to him a note, of which the following is a copy, to wit:

TERRITORY OF UTAH, SECRETARY'S OFFICE,
September 22, 1851.

Sir: Will you please send me by the bearer such executive documents as you intend to file in this office, that they may be entered upon the record, and oblige,

Very respectfully, your obedient servant,
B. D. HARRIS,
Secretary

To his Excellency BRIGHAM YOUNG.

To this note no reply was ever received.
I have the honor to be, with the highest regard,
Your most obedient servant,
B. D. HARRIS,
Secretary of the Territory of Utah.

To the PRESIDENT OF THE UNITED STATES.

––––––

No 1.

HOUSE OF REPRESENTATIVES, GREAT SALT LAKE CITY,
Utah Territory, September 24, 1851.

Sir: By a resolution passed by the Legislative Assembly this day, it was directed that an order be drawn on the Secretary of the Territory for the sum of five hundred dollars towards defraying the incidental expenses of the Legislative Assembly. We therefore send this order by the sergeant-at-arms of the Legislative Council, hoping that you will furnish the sum for our convenience.

Respectfully yours,

WILLARD RICHARDS,
President of the Council.
W. W. PHELPS,
Speaker H. of Reps., Utah Territory.
H. CORAY,
Secretary of Council.
ALBERT CARRINGTON,
Clerk of the House of Representatives.

To the Hon. B. D. HARRIS,
Secretary, Utah Territory.

No. 2.

Joint resolution pertaining to the Secretary of Utah Territory.

Whereas the Hon. B. D. Harris, secretary of this the Territory of Utah, being about to leave, absent himself or abscond from said Territory, and intends, as we are authentically and credibly informed, to carry away or otherwise dispose of the territorial seal, records, papers, documents and property in his possession, and pertaining to his office, contrary to the organic act which provides (sec. 3) that said secretary shall reside in said Territory:

And whereas it is believed that said Secretary has in his possession the money appropriated by the act of Congress, approved February 27, 1851, amounting to $24,000, designed by Congress as compensation and mileage of members of the Legislative Assembly, and other expenses of said Territory of Utah—(see Statutes at Large, page 571, 31st Congress, 2d session:)

Whereas it is believed that said secretary should not be permitted thus to leave said Territory with so large an amount of government funds, and without having authority, which we apprehend nowhere exists, thereby seriously inconveniencing not only this Territory, but incurring the loss of said funds to the general government: therefore,

Resolved by the Legislative Council and House of Representatives in joint session assembled, That it shall be the duty of the United States marshal for said Territory to proceed forthwith and take into his possession all such papers, records, documents, and property of every kind, partaining [*sic*] to said office of secretary; as also all money in his possession belonging to said Territory and pertaining to said office, or intrusted by the general government, for the benefit of this Territory, in his hands, together with the seal and press of the Territory of Utah, and safely keep and preserve the same for the time being, until the Legislative Assembly shall order otherwise, or until the vacancy thus occasioned in said office shall be filled by appointment by the President of the United States, or the disabilities otherwise cease to exist.

And be it further resolved, That in case the said B. D. Harris, secretary as aforesaid, shall refuse, neglect, or anywise fail to deliver the said papers, records, seal, press, documents or money, or any other property or articles pertaining to said office, or any part thereof, then and in that case it shall be the duty of the said United States marshal for Utah Territory to arrest the said B. D. Harris, secretary as aforesaid, and him safely keep in custody until he shall comply with the foregoing resolution.

WILLARD RICHARDS,
President of the Council.
W. W. PHELPS,
Speaker of the House of Representatives.
HOWARD CORAY,
Secretary of the Council.
ALBERT CARRINGTON,
Clerk of the House of Representatives.
Approved, September 24, 1851.

BRIGHAM YOUNG,
Governor of Utah Territory
GREAT SALT LAKE CITY, *September* 24, 1851.

———

No. 3

Gentlemen: Your note, dated September 24th, communicating to me the substance of a resolution passed by the Legislative Assembly on the 24th instant, "directing that an order be drawn on the secretary for the sum of five hundred dollars, towards defraying the incidental expenses of the Legislative Assembly," has this day been placed in my hands by Mr. William Kimball. Being desirous that all official business transacted by me with other departments of the Government, and with individuals, should be placed in a form to be preserved, I have thought proper to communicate to you my decision, and some of the reasons which have induced it, in writing.

By the organic act of the Territory, the secretary is made the disbursing agent of the United States Government. This agency necessarily involves judicial powers to a limited extent, from which there is, and can be, no appeal except to the fountain-head. The secretary is not, in law, a mere machine, bound to allow and satisfy all claims presented to him for payment; on the contrary, he is expressly required to make diligent and minute examination as to the propriety, reasonableness, and legality of such claims and is clothed with ample powers to allow or reject the same, as his judgment shall dictate. No branch of the territorial government, executive, legislative, or judicial, can legally interfere to prevent the exercise of these powers. That the secretary is possessed of such powers, to the extent claimed, and is legally and morally bound to exercise them, is a perfectly clear and unanswerable proposition. Did I entertain any doubts on this point, my official instructions from the Treasury Department clearly and distinctly point at the propriety and necessity of the course I deem it my duty to pursue.

With these preliminary remarks, I proceed to assign, briefly, some of the reasons for the decision I am compelled to make.

1. The fourth section of the organic act of the Territory requires the governor, previous to the first election, to cause a census, or enumeration of the inhabitants of the several counties or districts of the Territory, to be taken, for the purpose of an equal apportionment of the members of the Legislative Assembly. In my judgment this provision has not been complied with, either literally or in accordance with its obvious intent and spirit. If I am correct in this opinion, of which I entertain no doubt, of course all subsequent proceedings, based upon this initiatory act, are null and void.

2. The proclamation of the governor, ordering an election, was, in my opinion, faulty both in form and substance. It did not bear the seal of the Territory or the signature of the secretary, and in other respects lacked the essentials of legal form. It was faulty in substance, in that it did not prescribe the qualifications of voters, or those to be voted for; it did not, as required by the organic act, prescribe rules and regulations for the government of the election; it did not designate the place where elections should be held, nor the persons by whom they should be conducted.

3. Aliens voted indiscriminately with American citizens, and those recognized as such by the treaty with Mexico.

4. Aliens acted as officers at the polls, and were elected to office.

5. Officers not authorized to be chosen were voted for and elected.

6. The fourth section of the organic act, before referred to, further requires the governor to declare the persons having the greatest number of votes for councillors and representatives, in the respective councillor and representative districts or precincts, to be duly elected to the Legislative Assembly. The obvious intent of the law in requiring the governor to make this declaration, was to give timely notice of an important fact to all parties interested, which includes not only the members elect themselves, but, in its narrowest signification, *all* the inhabitants of the Territory. In fact, the election itself could not be complete until this declaration be made.

It is perfectly clear that no declaration of the kind, coming within the letter or the spirit of the law, has been made; and, indeed, no declaration at all. A proclamation designed to accomplish that object was countersigned by the secretary, and attested by the seal of the Territory, on the 19th inst.; but that proclamation has never been published, or in any other manner made known to the public. But even if it had been published in legal form at the time it received the attestation of the secretary and his seal of office, it must obviously have been regarded as a nullity. No principle of law is more clearly established than that legal notices, when not expressly regulated by statute, must be specific in terms and reasonable in time, according to the circumstances of the case. I have said that no declaration of the important fact above referred to, has been made. A printed document, purporting to be a proclamation by the governor, and to be countersigned by the secretary, bearing date September 18, 1851, declaring the members elect, and summoning the Legislative Assembly to meet in this city on Monday, September 22, 1851, has been placed in my hands. I deem it necessary to assign but a single reason why this document is as worthless, for all legal purposes, as the paper on which it is printed. It is essentially and fatally different from any executive document filed in this office, and equally so from any ever attested by the secretary or impressed with the seal of the Territory.

7. The same section of the organic act, above referred to, makes it the duty of the governor to appoint the time and place for the first meeting of the Legislative Assembly. This duty, it is plain, has never been discharged in a manner answering the requirements of law. The printed document before alluded to contains the only appointment of the kind that has been made, and that document has already been shown to be null and void.

I have thus, gentlemen, assigned seven distinct reasons for deciding, as I am now constrained to do, to allow no claim for mileage or per diem allowance to the members of the Assembly now in session, purporting to be the Legislative Assembly of the

Territory of Utah, and to pay no contingent expenses connected therewith. No one can regret more sincerely than myself, that law, facts, and my official instructions and obligations, all conspire to render any other decision impossible. I may be permitted to add, however, that the just and legal rights of no one will be cancelled or in any manner prejudiced by this decision. Fortunately there is one appeal from it, and only one, to wit: to the Secretary of the Treasury, at Washington, and through him to the President of the United States, as may readily be ascertained by reference to the independent treasury act, passed 1846, and subsequent modifications thereof, prescribing the duties and responsibilities of disbursing agents. I shall myself so refer the whole matter, including a copy of this letter, for review. Should my decision be reversed, the well-known justice and liberality of the government whose agent I have the honor to be, will insure prompt reparation.

With your note, alluded to in the commencement of this paper, I also received from the hands of Mr. William Kimball a certified copy, approved by the governor, of a certain preamble and resolutions, passed on the 24th inst., by the bodies over which you respectively preside, setting forth in substance that I, the secretary of the Territory, it is believed, am about to abscond from the Territory with the public funds, and directing the United States marshal to take forcible possession of the money and other property pertaining to my office, and in case I refuse to deliver up the money and property aforesaid, to arrest and imprison me, the secretary, until I comply.

As a faithful officer of the United States Government, to whom I am alone responsible for my official conduct, I can have but one reply to make to this extraordinary demand. I most emphatically refuse to accede to it; and at the same time, deny the right of even a *legal* legislative assembly to exercise any control in the matter. To those who have the legal right to question and control my official conduct, I am, and ever shall be, at all times ready to render a faithful account of my stewardship.

In reply to the assertion, or insinuation, contained in the preamble above referred to, that I am about to *abscond* from the Territory, I have simply to express my unfeigned astonishment that honorable men should be willing to father it.

Very respectfully, your obedient servant,

B. D. HARRIS,
Secretary.

To WILLARD RICHARDS and W. W. PHELPS, Esqs.

————

Mr. Bernhisel to the President of the United States.

UNITED STATES HOTEL.
Washington, December 30, 1851.

Sir: On the 9th instant, I addressed to you a letter asking that "I may be informed, at the earliest convenient moment, of any allegations which the officers who had recently returned from Utah Territory may prefer, that in your judgment call for notice." On Wednesday evening, the 24th instant, I received a note from the Honorable Daniel Webster, Secretary of State, informing me that the charges of the returned officers, just referred to, were on file in the Department of State. The public offices being closed at the hour at which I received it, and the next day being Christmas, I was unable to obtain admission to the State Department before Friday, the 26th instant. Thus for the first time apprized on that day of these numerous charges, and having been on the same day informed by your Excellency that they would be communicated to the House of Representatives on Monday, the 29th instant, I cannot, of course, be expected now to make an elaborate reply to them. Nor indeed could I feel myself authorized, under any circumstances, to enter into, countenance, or admit an official discussion of either the religious faith or the moral habits of the people of Utah. But as to so much of the charges of the late officers of that Territory, against the Governor and Council thereof, as can be matter of public concern, I shall esteem it my duty, at the earliest moment, to ask for them the closest scrutiny of a Congressional committee; and, in the mean time, I take leave to place among the

executive archives my prompt, unqualified, and peremptory negation of their truth.

With sentiments of great respect, I have the honor to be, your
obedient servant,

JOHN M. BERNHISEL,
Delegate from Utah.
TO THE PRESIDENT OF THE UNITED STATES.

————

Governor Young to the President of the United States.
GREAT SALT LAKE CITY,
September 29, 1851.

Sir: It is now over one year since "An act to establish a
Territorial Government for Utah" became a law of Congress.
Information of this fact reached this place in November following;
and about the first of January authentic information was received of
the appointments of the territorial officers by the President. This
news being confirmed on the third day of February, I took the oath
of office as governor of this Territory, in accordance with the
provisions of the organic act. Owing to the great distance from this
place to the seat of the General Government, I considered it of the
first importance that the preliminary arrangements for the
organization of the Territory should be accomplished as soon as
possible, in order that a delegate might be legally returned to the
Congress of the United States before the lateness of the season
should render the (at any time) long and arduous journey
dangerous, if not impracticable; hence my anxiety to proceed with
as little delay as possible, in obtaining the enumeration of the
inhabitants, preparatory to appointing the election districts, and
apportioning the members of the Council and House of
Representatives to be elected from each.

Having been appointed census agent to take the census of
Deseret, and, owing to the total miscarriage of instructions and
blanks which had not, neither indeed have yet arrived, the taking of
that census had been delayed for a season; but now being required
to cause the enumeration to be taken for the use of the Territory,
and despairing of the blanks coming on, I proceeded to take the

census, and appointed my assistants to make out two sets of returns, one for the United States as census agent for Deseret and one for Utah, which required not the full census, but merely the enumeration of the inhabitants; this was sufficiently accomplished to enable me to make out the apportionment about the first of July, which I did, and issued my proclamation declaring the same. This being previous to the arrival of the secretary, of course his seal and signature were not attached. (See proclamation No. 1.) The reason inducing this order has been recited alone, that the election might come off in time, that whoever should be elected as delegate to Congress might be enabled to go before the inclement season should set in.

Although the appointments were made early in the fall, yet no new resident officer made his appearance until the ensuing summer, and some of them not until about the first the August.

Upon the arrival of a majority of the supreme court, I again issued my proclamation districting the Territory into three judicial districts, and assigning the judges to their several districts. This proclamation bears the impress of the seal of the Territory, and signature of Mr. Harris. (See proclamation No. 3.)

Learning to my very great regret that the secretary, Mr. Harris, and Judge Brandebury and Associate Judge Brocchus, intended to return to the United States this fall, I called upon them personally to ascertain the fact, and if possible induce them to remain. They, however, assured me it was their intention to leave, and Mr. Harris also declaring that he should carry with him all the funds in his hands for the payment of the legislative expenses of the Territory, as also the seal, records, documents, &c., pertaining to his office; plainly indicating that it was his intention to essentially vacate said office, so far as Utah was concerned, and anticipate, by leaving with the funds, the non-payment of the Legislative Assembly.

I considered this course illegal, wholly unauthorized and uncalled for by any pretext whatever; I therefore concluded that I would use all legal efforts that should seem practicable, for the retention of the property and money belonging to the United States, in the secretary's hands, designed for the use of this

Territory; I therefore issued my proclamation declaring the result of the election, and convening the Legislative Assembly on the 22d of the present month. This proclamation was dated on the 18th instant, thus showing but a hurried notice; but notices had been sent previously to the members elect, and when the day arrived, all of the Council were present, and only one member of the House absent. It is but due to myself to say, that this proclamation was delayed from the fact of a misunderstanding with the secretary, that he would make out the declaration of the members elect and prepare the proclamation; which failing to do, I caused it to be done, and sent it to him for his signature and impress of the seal of the Territory, intending for him to keep the manuscript thus furnished, and return a copy suitable for publication. Much to my astonishment, he placed the seal and signature to the manuscript thus furnished, not even filing a copy for record. It was published, however. (See proclamation No. 4.)

The legislature convened in accordance therewith, with the exception of one member of the House from Iron county. The secretary did not attend to furnish a roll of the members; I therefore had this duty to perform when they were called and qualified by his honor Judge Snow.

My message was the next document in order. (See No. 5.)

On the 24th instant, the Legislative Assembly passed a joint resolution, making it the duty of the United States marshal to proceed forthwith and take into his custody all of the aforesaid funds, property, &c. (See No. 6.) This resolution was presented to Mr. Harris, as also an order for five hundred dollars, to defray the incidental expenses of the Legislative Assembly. (See No. 7.) He refused to comply with the requirements of each, (as per No. 8.)

At this time, September 26th, I addressed a note to the supreme court, who I understood were then in session, asking their opinion in regard to my duty, having reference to the organic act, which requires the governor to see that the laws are faithfully executed, and requiring the said secretary to reside in said Territory, &c. (See No. 9.)

After awaiting a reply to this note until the day fixed for their departure had far advanced, I directed the United States district attorney to file a petition, which would cause them to give their opinion—(see No. 10 for copy of petition, and No. 11 for the opinion, and answer)—having determined to abide the decision of the judges. I accordingly stayed all further proceedings, and on yesterday, the 28th, I understand the secretary, Mr. Harris, and the two judges, Mr. Brandebury and Mr. Brocchus, left this city on their return to the United States.

For a reply to Mr. Harris's decision (No. 8.) I refer you to file No. 12.

Thus, sir, I have given you a plain, unvarnished tale of all our proceedings pertaining to governmental affairs, with the exception of report upon Indian affairs, which will be made to the proper department.

If your Excellency will indulge me in a few remarks, I will proceed and make them.

Mr. Harris informed me, in a conversation which I had with him, that he had *private instructions, designed for no eye but his own,* to watch every movement and not pay out any funds unless the same should be *strictly legal, according to his own judgment.*

The supreme court organized and held a session, as will appear by reference to the certified copy of proceedings (No. 13,) without waiting for the legislative authority fixing the time; and apparently having no other object than to shield and protect Mr. Harris, in leaving with the funds and property designed for the use and benefit of this Territory.

It has been said of myself, and the people over whom I have the honor to preside, that they frequently indulge in strictures upon the acts of men who are intrusted with governmental affairs, and that the government itself sometimes does not wholly escape. Now, sir, I will simply state what I know to be true—that no people exists who are more friendly to the government of the United States, than the people of this Territory. The constitution they revere, the laws they seek to honor. But the non-execution of those laws in times past for our protection, and the abuse of power in the hands of those intrusted therewith, even in the hands of those whom we have supported for office, ever betraying us in the hour of our greatest peril and extremity, by withholding the due execution of laws designed for the protection of all the citizens of the United States—it is for this we have cause for complaint, not the want of good and wholesome laws; but the execution of the same, in the true meaning and spirit of the constitution.

The foregoing is a case in point. What good and substantial reason can be given, that the people of this Territory should be deprived, for probably near a year to come, of a supreme court, of the official seal of a secretary of state, of the official publication of the laws, and other matters pertaining to the office of secretary?

Is it true that officers coming here by virtue of an appointment by the President, have *private instructions* that so far control their actions as to induce the belief that their main object is not the strict and legal performance of their respective duties, but rather to *watch* for *iniquity*, to catch at shadows, and make a man "an offender for a word;" to spy out our liberties, and, by manifold misrepresentation, seek to prejudice the minds of the people against us? If such is the case, better, far better would it be for us, to live under the organization of our provisional government, and entirely depending upon our own resources, as we have hitherto done, until such time as we can be admitted as a State, than thus to be tantalized with the expectation of having a legal government, which will extend her fostering care over all her offspring. In infancy, if ever, it is necessary to assist the rising State.

If it be true that no legal authority can be exercised over a co-ordinate and even a subordinate branch of the government, by the legislature thereof, then indeed we may expect the harmony of government to be interrupted, to hear the discordant sounds of irresponsible and law-defying agents desecrating by *their acts* the *very name* of *American* liberty.

In the appointment of new officers, if you will pardon me for making a suggestion, I would propose that such men be selected as will reside within the Territory, or have a general and extended knowledge of men and things, as well as of the elementary and fundamental principles of law and legislation; men who have lived and practised [sic] outside as well as indoors, and whose information extends to the duties of a justice of the peace, as well as the well-known passages and districts of the court-room. In relation to our present unfortunate position, pertaining to the supreme court, I can only hope that early the ensuing season we may be favored with a quorum.

As regards the funds, if an arrangement could be made authorizing Mr. Livingstone, a merchant in this place, to receive the money appropriated to meet the legislative expenses, he would most probably make such advances as might be necessary, after being advised of the privilege of so doing.

The Legislative Assembly are yet in session; of their acts and doings I shall take the liberty of making report, the same as would have been the duty of the secretary had he remained. I cannot conceive that it can or ought to be in the power of any subordinate officer to subvert, or event retard for any length of time, the ordinary motion of the wheels of government; although I am equally satisfied that it was, and is, the intention of a portion of those aforesaid officers to utterly subvert and overthrow this government of Utah; but of this I have no fears, as I know they can have no good and sufficient apology for the course they have and are pursuing.

The money that was appropriated for the year ending the 30th of June, 1851, should have been used to defray the expenses of the legislature of '50 and '51; and the government might have been organized, had the officers have been as efficient in coming here as they are now in going away. The legislature can now, as heretofore, do without their compensation and mileage, and find themselves; they were all unanimously elected (with one exception,) as was our delegate to Congress, the honorable John M. Bernhisel.

We have sought to obtain an authorized government, and the people have been well satisfied with the government in regard to all their acts in relation thereto, so far as I am acquainted; and if the men appointed had endeavored to be active in the discharge of their duties, all would have been well. Mr. Harris takes exceptions to every thing that has been done. Did he take hold, upon his arrival at this place, and endeavor to assist in the organization of this government as a secretary should do? Not at all; never was he the man to do the first thing, either by suggestion or otherwise, unless perhaps it was occasionally to set his hand and seal of the Territory to some document that had been prepared for him. Have either of the judges who are returning ever done any thing towards the organization of the Territory? They organized the supreme court chiefly, as I think, to assist Mr. Harris in leaving with the funds; and I believe Judge Branderbury [sic] appointed a clerk of the district. Judge Brocchus had determined on returning this fall, previous to his arrival, as I am credibly informed; and they both leaving at this time, just when the time has arrived for them to act, postpones indefinitely all courts in their respective districts. Judge Brocchus has *never been in his district,* that I know of. Thus, so far as the public interests are concerned, it would have been quite as well if neither of these gentlemen or Mr. Harris had ever troubled themselves to cross the plains.

Whatever may be your decision upon all these matters, be assured that it is and has been my intention to discharge faithfully every duty pertaining to my office; and that I shall receive very gratefully any instructions that you will please to give. Awaiting most anxiously to hear from you,

I have the honor to be, your Excellency,

Very respectfully and truly yours,
BRIGHAM YOUNG.

To his EXCELLENCY MILLARD FILLMORE,
President of the United States of North America.

———

*Memorial signed by members of the Legislative Assembly of Utah
to the President of the United States.*

GREAT SALT LAKE CITY,
September 29, 1851.

*To Millard Fillmore, President of the United States of
North America:*

The undersigned, members of the Legislative Assembly for the
Territory of Utah, do hereby most respectfully beg leave to show,
that whereas two of the honorable justices of the supreme court of
the United States for the Territory of Utah, and the Hon. B. D.
Harris, secretary of the Territory, have removed from the Territory
of Utah, and consequently vacated their offices within the same,
therefore your memorialists do most earnestly solicit and pray the
Chief Executive of the United States to fill those vacancies as
speedily as possible.

Accumulated influences of a disagreeable nature may be
regarded as our apology for trespassing upon the attention of our
highly honored Chief Magistrate at this time. The vacating of
important public offices in a manner as unwarranted as it is
unprecedented, at this peculiar crisis of our colonial settlement and
government, have created mingled sensations of an extraordinary
character, which we wish, briefly, to pour into the bosom of the
national Executive.

Immediately consequent upon the settlement of this colony, a
large and heterogeneous emigration followed upon our heels,
remaining here a shorter or longer time, imperatively requiring the
establishment of an efficient government for the speedy protection
of life, peace, virtue, and property. In addition to a transient and
ungovernable emigration, almost constant Indian depredations
have pleaded, like the irresistible maw of death, for the institution
of some formidable order and power of government among us. A
provisional government was accordingly formed, which has met the
exigencies of the people, and secured general tranquility, order,

and satisfaction. And when the announcement of a territorial government under your fostering hand reached us, it was hailed with shoutings and firing of cannon. But, sir, the officers appointed sufficiently early to have reached here last winter did not arrive till July last, when measures had been taken by the governor of Utah for taking the census, and securing an election of a delegate to Congress, and members of the legislature, without the seal of the honorable secretary of the Territory. And now, in the very dawn of the arrival of the government officers, and of our hopes of an efficient territorial government, we are most seriously embarrassed with their unprovoked departure from the limits of the Territory, taking with them the judiciary, the public seal, and the public fund, leaving us in a more crippled condition, if possible, than previous to their arrival; thereby tantalizing a people of more than Spartan integrity and fortitude, that have long been struggling against the most invincible difficulties. The first demand upon the honorable secretary for stationery, desks, and such contingent expenses as might necessarily accrue in the outset of a legislative assembly, has been peremptorily refused. Not only so, but all the authorities of the Territory, including the governor and both houses of the Assembly, and marshal, have been set at naught, as exercising their functions illegally and unconstitutionally. (See document marked No. 8.) Thus, sir, when we have looked for the fostering aid of such a functionary as the honorable secretary, and for a fellow-citizen worthy the honor conferred by our illustrious Chief Magistrate, we have been annoyed with the technics [sic] of legal quackery, and our respectful address for stationery, &c., has been responded to, not as to legislators of the undivided choice and sole representation of a sovereign people, who know the right of franchise and of self-government, under the constitution, but as to men who ape authority that does not belong to them. Although we are *ipso facto* honored with the choice of a sovereign, and free people to be their representatives in legislative assembly, and the refusal of a captious stranger to accredit us with the fact does not shake the truth; still a studious violation of etiquette, when it is designed to convey burlesque, contempt, and indignity upon a legislative body, is calculated to alienate a people from such functionaries.

Your memorialists, being aware of the difficulty of sending men from the States to fill the vacancies that have accrued from the removal of the two honorable judges, and the Hon. B. D. Harris, during the period of many months to come, and feeling cautious against any possible future removals like those which now embarrass us with the want of a Territorial seal and funds, to meet constantly accruing expenses, and also the want of a full supreme court of the United States for Utah Territory, and desirous to dwell in peace and unfeigned loyalty to the constitution and general government of the United States, do therefore pray our highly honored Chief Magistrate to appoint men to fill the aforesaid vacancies, by and with the consent of the Senate, who are indeed residents among us, in order that we may enjoy the full administration of every department of government speedily, as the prosperity of the Territory shall require; and your memorialists, as in duty bound, will ever pray.

WILLARD RICHARDS, *President of Council.*

A L. Lamereaux,	Heber C. Kimball,
John Stoker,	Daniel H. Wells,
Gideon Brownell,	Aaron Johnson,
James Brown,	Alexander Williams,
David B. Dille,	Isaac Morley,
James G. Browning,	Jno. S. Fullmer,
David Evans,	Charles R. Dana,
William Miller,	Orson Spencer,
Levi W. Hancock,	Mr. Phelps,
Charles Shumway,	Lorin Farr,

George A. Smith.

WELFA [WILFORD] WOODRUFF, *Speaker H. R.*

Nathaniel H. Felt,	Daniel Spencer,
David Fullmer,	Phineas Richards,
Albert P. Rockwood,	B. F. Johnson,
Edwin D. Woolly,	Hosea Stout,
Jos. Young,	H. G. Sherwood.

APPENDIX B

"That Sink of Perdition"
Major William Singer
on the Mormons

William Singer, a native of Pittsburgh, Pennsylvania, enlisted in the U.S. Army as a teenager in 1833 and rose to the grade of major in the War with Mexico when he served as an additional paymaster in Missouri and New Mexico. He left the army in 1849 to join the Gold Rush. The following year he started for California with his wife, Arcibella, and their three children, two girls, ages twelve and ten, and a boy, age one. At Fort Hall, near present Pocatello, Idaho, he elected to spend the winter of 1850–1851 in Mormon settlements rather than risk a late crossing of the Sierra Nevada, as described in Letter 1.

Traveling with Singer over the Fort Hall Road to Salt Lake Valley was Matthew Dalton, an adventurous, twenty-one-year-old New Yorker, also going to seek his fortune in California. Dalton described the major as "a genial man" and said he "took a liking to him at once, and our relations became quite friendly."[1] While Singer recruited his stock on Box Elder Creek, Dalton went on to the Mormon settlement at Brownsville. There he met Rosilla Whitaker, who had just arrived with her Mormon family from Fort Bridger, and soon after married her. Not far away Singer and his family settled for the winter on Ogden River, near Goodell's wagon.

In 1851 the former officer wrote about his experiences that season to a friend in Missouri, who took his letter to a St. Louis newspaper. Following is the resulting article to which Goodell referred. Also included is his obituary in 1901, which carries information on his later career in California and appears to involve him in covert American operations before the Mexican War to annex New Mexico and California from Mexico.

ST. LOUIS INTELLIGENCER
7 AUGUST 1851, VOL. 2, NO. 186, 2/3.
ABOUT THE MORMONS

The following extract from a letter, which was handed to us yesterday by a friend, describes a most deplorable state of things at Salt Lake—so much so that it might be difficult to believe some portions of the account, were it not for the unimpeachable character of the gentleman who penned it. He is well known to nearly all of our citizens as the occupant of a responsible station in the United States Army. Considering the writer, and the circumstances under which the letter was written, we are not permitted even to suppose that its statements are exaggerated. We omit some passages which

---

1. Carter, "Matthew William Dalton: 1850 Trail Account of Journey From Fort Hall To Ogden," 5, 6.

treat of domestic relations among the Mormons and the horrid licentiousness which prevails in them, not because we discredit them, but because we would not shock the sensibilities of our readers with the repulsive picture they present.

The portions which refer to the expressions and doings of Governor Young, are worthy of especial attention. We repeat that the letter is from a wholly reliable source. It was addressed to two gentlemen who reside in this city, and bears date:

CARSON VALLEY, EAST SIERRA DE NEVADA,
En Route for California, May 24, 1851

DEAR SIR—My fine and favorite horse is gone[2]—and but two yoke and a half of [my] cattle were all I had to leave Salt Lake with. When at that sink of perdition it was my expectation to write you and others of our friends, as we wished to write by the first *safe* private opportunity that would offer itself; but none such having been presented, our expectation of course was not gratified. It is true, I wrote to Dr. and M., but then I was constrained by the practice of the Mormons to destroy letters containing anything against themselves, from communicating aught in relation to my own or the grievances of other emigrants. Now that my family is out of their power, I may venture to speak of that accurst and pestilential people. And would to God that I could make myself be heard thru'-out my country and impress upon my countrymen the truth in relation to Mormonism, vile, criminal and treasonable as it insolently displays itself in the boasted security of its mountain-walled home. But no—no one would be believed were he to communicate the truth concerning the Mormons. Truly, were an angel from heaven

---

2. This was apparently the horse Goodell referred to as "the finest American mare in the company," in Letter 8.

to tell you of the wicked practices and the base, unprovoked crimes of this people, you would discredit the report. Such is the enormity of their conduct, that in a series of resolutions drawn up by a Presbyterian clergyman, and signed by the emigrants, "the truth, and the whole truth" was designedly avoided, lest it would be too shocking for belief.[3] It is hazarding nothing in saying that never, by savage horde or lawless banditti, was there exhibited such base turpitude of heart and such indiscriminate vindictiveness of purpose, as are to be seen in the conduct of the Mormons of Salt Lake Valley. With them, human feeling has been debased to worse than beastly passion and instinct, and then all sympathy is consumed by, or absorbed in lust, while sentiment there finds its lowest degree of degradation. There is no crime but has its full, free justification there, if perpetrated against a Gentile, as they term those who are not Mormons.—No matter how good a man's character may be before he becomes a Mormon, and makes common fellowship with them, after he is fairly inducted he is soon made to yield the most guilty obedience to the decrees or orders of the Twelve. All are thus rendered ready and prompt instruments in the perpetration of crime. I had supposed that, like other religious societies, there were sincere persons among them, who, believing in justice and virtuous principles, could not be made the guilty agents of crime, or commit such offences as had frequently been charged against them; but from what I have seen and heard, I am firm in the belief that the best of them will not hesitate to perform the worst bidding of Brigham Young, their "Man of God." Yes, his voice is to them more omnipotent than is the voice of God to the Christian. Let but a gentile incur his displeasure, or that of the Twelve, and soon his blood-hounds, the Danites, are scouring the

---

3. An apparent reference to the resolutions drawn up by Nelson Slater. See his *Fruits of Mormonism*, 90–94.

country in search of their prey; and woe to the Gentile who is known to give the doomed victim protection or assistance. Far different is it when emigrants first enter the valley—then all is kindness and good feeling; but no sooner does winter lock them in, than the hitherto suppressed volcano of their hate and prejudice against American citizens bursts forth. Then property is seized and confiscated, the owners thereof deprived of their liberty, loaded like the worst of felons with balls and chains, without the form of a trial, and in most cases without even any known accusation. Many emigrants beside myself heard Brigham Young from the stand declare the most treasonable hostilities against the U. States. He denied the right of jurisdiction on the part of our government, and pledged himself that if a Governor came there and attempted its extension, he would resist it to the death! The right of Governorship undisturbed by the authority of the United States, he claimed as vested in himself for life. "Yes," to use his own words, "that was about the time I was elected for." To the citizens of the United States who talked of their rights and privileges as American citizens, he would say he was not amenable to their government and said, "now as when at Nauvoo, that he defied the combined powers of the United States and all hell." Those of us who were known to speak against Mormonism or abuse the Mormons, he ordered should have their throats cut. To employ his own phraseology, he said, "Yes, cut their damned throats; if you do not I'll send the boys that will; and if they don't, I'll come myself and I'll cut their damned throats; I will slay them, by the spirit of the Almighty God!"

From that moment the emigrants became the predestined and proscribed objects of Mormon vengeance. A report was started that I was then a reporter for government, and soon my property was seized and myself arrested, and subjected to the insults of one of their prostituted functionaries, without any cause for prosecution, or any charge to plead against. Shortly after five head of my cattle were shot, and I was selected a subject to be salted down in their lake. Five of their assassins took upon themselves the pleasing duty; but I entertained no fear of them; on the contrary, I came out and declared my defiance of them. My whole solicitude was for my family and every exertion was directed toward getting it out of the valley. Being composed mostly of females, I had just cause to fear that if deprived of a protector, it would never be permitted to leave that sink of perdition—for no intelligence against Mormonism is permitted to be mailed. Dissenting Mormons and emigrants have told me that they picked up before the postoffice [sic] parts of letters they had deposited to be mailed for the United States, but in which they had expressed themselves too freely for Mormons. In truth, the basest system of espoinage [sic] prevails that ever was known to exist in the world.

So far as their religion is concerned, I never felt disposed to meddle with it. But it should be known that their teachings here, as they term their making known their abominable practices here, are greatly at variance with the preaching of the principles of Mormonism by their missionary knaves throughout the rest of the world.

❄   ❄   ❄

In nothing do their teachings correspond with Christianity. They deny the omnipotence of God, but believe in a plurality of Gods as well as of wives, and that old Brigham, part God now, will become a perfect and powerful God after his physical death.

[Major William Singer]

San Francisco Morning Call
29 June 1901, 14/3.

Major William Singer, a veteran of the Mexican war, passed away at his residence in this city last Thursday evening at the advanced age of 89 years.[4]

Deceased was born in Pittsburg[h], Pa., and entered the army in 1833. From that time until 1850, when he emigrated to California with his family, he was in the service of the Government.

During the preliminary stages of the controversy between the United States and Mexico Major Singer was called to Washington, and after being given careful instructions was ordered to go to New Mexico and California to investigate and report on their resources.

With but a small force of about fifty rather inexperienced cavalrymen, new to the tactics of border warfare, to guard the $200,000 provided to defray the expenses of the proposed research from falling into the hands of Mexican guerrillas, the major started. The Little party met with more than one thrilling and perilous adventure, but on account of the caution as well as the coolness which were among the chief features of his character Major Singer accomplished the mission intrusted to him by the Government. His report was carefully prepared and contained valuable information. It would have been recognized and appreciated more fully when laid before Congress but for the fact that the motive for the expedition and the need of his report had then become secondary in the course of politics.

Shortly after his arrival in California, in 1850, Major Singer engaged in mining, but his health failing he had to retire from that field. In 1853 he went to Marysville, then a flourishing city, and in

---

4. In the 1850 Utah census, Singer gave his age as thirty-three. This would have made him eighty-four at the time of his death.

the fall of the same year he was elected Justice of the Peace. He was re-elected to the same office twice, and shortly thereafter was elected Associate Justice of the County Court of Sessions of Yuba County, to which office he was re-elected to succeed himself until the court was abolished. In 1858 he was elected Mayor of Marysville. After his retirement from this office he practiced law until he reached the age of 75 years, when he retired.

William Singer Jr. of the Southern Pacific law department is a son of the deceased pioneer.

The funeral will take place to-morrow at 11 A.M. from the late residence, 143 San Jose avenue, thence to Mount Olivet Cemetery, where services will be held in the chapel.

APPENDIX C

"Their Mountain Stronghold" Asa Cyrus Call on the Mormons

New information about the 1851 manhunt for G. L. Turner that led to the shooting of Brigham Young's brother, Lorenzo D. Young, at the Jordan River bridge, as described in Goodell's Letter 8, came to light with the publication in June that year of the following letter in *The Daily Union* at Sacramento, Calif. The writer, Asa Cyrus Call, age twenty-five, left southern Wisconsin in March 1850 and started alone for California on foot. He reached Salt Lake Valley in August and apparently became acquainted with a Mormon relative, Anson Call.[1] He decided to spend the winter in Utah Territory. Other emigrants elected him to serve with Nelson

---

1. In a letter to Asa C. Call's son, Anson Call wrote, "We were sorry to learn of the demise of your Father, of whom we formed a favorable opinion; and whom we held in high esteem." See Anson Call to George C. Call, 5 October 1888, copy in possession of John R. Call of Derby, Kansas. Asa Call's great grandfather, James Call, and Anson Call's grandfather, Samuel Call, were brothers.

Slater on Goodell's committee to prepare a memorial to
Congress on conditions in Utah. Call left Utah on 1 April 1851
in Slater's party for California, where July that year found him
at Placerville.[2]

SACRAMENTO DAILY UNION

SATURDAY MORNING
28 JUNE 1851, VOL. 1, NO. 88, 2/2, 4.

We publish a communication from Mr. Call, in respect to the
Mormons, because we believe it right that such abuses, if they exist,
should be generally known and retribution awarded. Mr. Turner, a
person referred to in the communication, confirms the statements
and says, that he presumes that a searching enquiry [sic] will be
made in the matter by the general government.

The relation of the inhabitants of Salt Lake to the emigrants to
California, is too important and intimate to be marked by any
disposition to impose upon men and women who attempt so long
and hazardous a journey to this country.

Communicated.

THE MORMONS.

Messrs. Editors: It seems that these people in the fancied
security of their mountain stronghold, or from some other cause,
are beginning to give a pretty loose rein to their inclinations and
seem disposed to carry out publicly that line of conduct which they
have heretofore been able to practise [sic] only by stealth and in
secret, and which has caused their expulsion from every place
where they have ever tried to get a foothold.

When the emigrants came through their place last summer,
they seemed to deal fairly by them, and in some instances, even
showed kindness to persons in distress; and as the season

---

2. See John and Vanessa Call, eds., *The Diaries of Asa Cyrus Call, March
28th, 1850 – December 26th, 1853.*

advanced, they held out every encouragement to emigrants to remain amongst them during the winter. By this means, some six or eight hundred were induced to winter there; but no sooner had cold weather set in, and cut off every avenue of escape, than they began to show the cloven foot. Early in the winter, the Mormons were counselled to sell provisions to the "Gentiles," (as all dissenters are called,) only at the most exorbitant prices; and as the winter advanced, they managed to get in debt to the emigrants, and then utterly refused to pay them; and those who ventured to sue them in their own courts invariably came off losers. The emigrants complained of this treatment, and the Mormons bore down all the harder.

The liberty of speech was abridged—respectable men were arrested and mulcted in heavy fines, for expressing opinions and making remarks which were deemed disrespectful to the Church. Private letters were intercepted and opened, and those who had spoken unfavorably of the morals of the community, were boldly threatened with assassination.

Such a course on the part of the Mormons, of course aroused the feelings of the emigrants. They held meeting to consult upon their situation, and to decide upon the best mode of redress. This, in turn, incensed the "saints" more than ever. They publicly discussed the propriety of driving the "Gentiles" from the valley. The emigrants claimed the rights of American citizens, on American soil. Brigham Young declared that "God had made *him* Governor, and that while he lived, he should *govern*." That he was "the law and the order," and that "if any man stuck himself up above him, he would bring him down—*by the eternal Gods.*" That he "was not afraid of *Mr. Justice*, nor *Uncle Sam*, nor *all Hell*;" and that "if he heard another Gentile curse or abuse the Saints, he would *cut his d—d throat.*"

The sale of ammunition to the emigrants was prohibited, and a complete system of *espionage* and secret police was kept up; and every remark, and every move however slight, was instantly reported at head-quarters.

All persons who had participated in the Missouri or Illinois difficulties, whether under orders from the Governor or otherwise, were ordered to leave the valley forthwith, on pain of death.

Judge McCabe, of Michigan, was fired at in the streets, and only saved his life by secreting himself at a distance from the city.

Dr. Vaughn, of Desmoines, Iowa, was murdered with impunity by a man in high standing in the Church.

Several families intimidated by these things, packed up their effects and moved out of the settlements, and camped on Box Elder Creek, sixty-five miles north of the city; but even here they were not allowed to remain in peace. The avarice of these people was not yet satisfied. A company of militia was called out, and marched up to the encampment, and a heavy tax or contribution was levied upon what property they had remaining. This tax was assessed and collected at the same time, and without previous notice; and if not paid instantly, the property was attached, costs and mileage were charged for every man of the troops, and the property was confiscated.

In this way, several men were robbed of their teams, and but for the generous aid of their more fortunate neighbors, they would have been utterly unable to get away. But, with the exception of those who lost their lives, probably no one suffered more at the hands of those people than Mr. G. L. Turner, who has just opened Robs' Exchange on J street. It seems that this gentleman, yielding to inducements held out by the Mormons, embarked in business in the valley, and contracted with Brigham Young to furnish timber and other materials for the public works, to the amount of some twenty thousand dollars, which materials were to be furnished prior to the first day of May, 1851, until which time he (Mr. Turner) was to have exclusive control of a certain canyon, in consideration of opening roads, &c. Young further agreed to pay for this timber as it was delivered, or at least as soon after as the arrears should amount to a hundred dollars. To this contract, Brigham Young, in behalf of the Church, bound himself by a written obligation. Mr. Turner then went to work, and opened roads at the expense of over five hundred dollars—purchased teams, hired hands, and prosecuted the work to amount of nearly $2000, when his cash receipts amounted to less than $500; and the Mormons having suspended payments to all the emigrants, he deemed it advisable to discontinue operations until the arrears were settled. But no sooner did these "Saints" see that there was a probability of their getting no more out of him in that way, than they sent out an armed posse, who seized his teams, and in fact every thing they could lay their hands on, and without giving him a hearing, or even a notice, they confiscated it all, claiming a violation of the contract by Mr. Turner; and this, when it was notorious that they were deeply in his debt, and that the Mormons had been ordered to pay out no more money to emigrants.—Mr. Turner remonstrated and protested, and threatened them with a suit for the recovery of this money, and the result was, that he was obliged to make his escape in the best way he could, and conceal himself in the mountains to save his life. The emigrants, of course, sympathised [sic] with him; and the excitement became intense. Armed parties were despatched [sic] in every direction, with orders to kill him wherever he was found. Persons who were suspected of knowing his place of concealment, were arrested and placed in chains, and their property afterwards confiscated to pay the expense of their imprisonment. But all this proving of no avail, and not satisfied with all his labor, and all the capital he had invested, they seized his household furniture, his clothing, and finally followed Mrs. Turner, who had been confined to her room all winter, by sickness, and robbed her of her common wearing apparel—even her night clothes, her bonnet and veil—refusing to leave her even a cloak or a change of dress.

———————

Not many made the fortune they dreamed of in California and even fewer had the self-discipline to keep the gold they found, but Asa Cyrus Call succeeded on both counts. He boarded the side-wheel steamship *Winfield Scott* at San Francisco in December 1853 with $6,000 in nuggets quilted into his buckskin vest for the journey home via Panama. Off the California coast, the steamer ran into the shoals off Anacapa Island, west of present Oxnard. As the vessel went down, Call appeared to face a choice between his gold-laden vest and his life, but characteristically saved both. His diary became one of the few eyewitness accounts of the disaster.

On returning to the Midwest, he met Sarah Heckart on a visit to Elkhart, Indiana, in 1854 and married her after a brief courtship. The couple acquired a homestead on the northern Iowa frontier where they founded the city of Algona. They had seven children. Call devoted the rest of his life to building the Iowa city into a major center of trade and transportation. He served as county judge, surveyor, and advocate for the construction of railroads in the region among many civic and business ventures before his death in 1888.[3]

---

3. See George C. Call, "Asa C. Call, Written by His Sons, Largely From his Private Memoirs."

BIBLIOGRAPHY

This bibliography contains separate listings for books and pamphlets, periodicals, newspapers, theses, manuscripts, and public documents.

BOOKS AND PAMPHLETS

Arrington, Leonard J. *Brigham Young: American Moses.* New York: Alfred A. Knopf, 1985.

Bagley, Will, ed. *A Road from El Dorado: The 1848 Trail Journal of Ephraim Green.* Salt Lake City: The Prairie Dog Press, 1991.

———. *Frontiersman: Abner Blackburn's Narrative.* Salt Lake City: Univ. of Utah Press, 1992.

———. *The Pioneer Camp of the Saints: The 1846 and 1847 Mormon Trail Journals of Thomas Bullock.* Spokane, Wash: The Arthur H. Clark Co., 1997.

———. *Scoundrel's Tale: The Samuel Brannan Papers.* Spokane, Wash: The Arthur H. Clark Co., 1999.

———. "*A Bright, Rising Star*": *A Brief Life of James Ferguson, Sergeant Major, Mormon Battalion; Adjutant General, Nauvoo Legion.* Spokane, Wash: The Arthur H. Clark Co., 2000.

Bigler, David L. *Forgotten Kingdom: The Mormon Theocracy in the American West, 1847–1896.* Spokane, Wash: The Arthur H. Clark Co., 1998; paper back edition, Logan: Utah State Univ. Press, 1998.

——— and Will Bagley, eds. *Army of Israel: Mormon Battalion Narratives.* Spokane, Wash: The Arthur H. Clark Co., 2000.

Bitton, Davis. *Guide to Mormon Diaries & Autobiographies.* Provo, Utah: Brigham Young Univ. Press, 1977.

Brooks, Juanita, ed. *On the Mormon Frontier: The Diary of Hosea Stout, 1844–1861*, 2 vols. Salt Lake City: Univ. of Utah Press, 1964.

Brown, J. Robert. *Journal of a Trip across the Plains of the U. S. from Missouri to California, in the Year 1856: Giving a Correct View of the Country, Anecdotes, Indian Stories, Mountaineers' Tales, etc.* Columbus, Ohio: Published for the author, 1860.

Call, John R. and Vanessa, eds. *The Diaries of Asa Cyrus Call, March 28th, 1850–December 26th, 1853.* Independence, Mo: Merrill J. Mattes Research Library, National Frontier Trails Center.

Carter, Kate B., ed. *Our Pioneer Heritage*, 20 vols. Salt Lake City: Daughters of Utah Pioneers, 1961–77.

Clark, Ethel Goodell. *My Goodell Family in America, 1634–1978.*

Clark, Thomas D., ed. *Gold Rush Diary: Being the Journal of Elisha Douglass Perkins on the Overland Trail in the Spring and Summer of 1849.* Lexington: Univ. of Kentucky Press.

———, ed. *Off at Sunrise: The Overland Journal of Charles Glass Gray.* San Marino, Calif: Henry E. Huntington Library, 1976.

Collier, Fred C., ed. *The Teachings of President Brigham Young, Vol. 3, 1852–1854.* S.L.C: Collier's Publishing Co., 1987.

DeLafosse, Peter, ed. *Trailing the Pioneers: A Guide to Utah's Emigrant Trails, 1829–1869.* Logan: Utah State Univ. Press, 1994.

Eells, Myron. *History of the Congregational Association of Oregon and Washington Territory; the Home Missionary.* Portland: Publishing House of Himes the printer, 1881.

Fales, Susan L. and Chad J. Flake. *Mormons and Mormonism in U.S. Government Documents.* Salt Lake City: Univ. of Utah Press, 1989.

Firmage, Edwin Brown and Richard Collin Mangrum. *Zion in the Courts: A Legal History of the Church of Jesus Christ of Latter-day Saints, 1830–1900.* Urbana and Chicago: Univ. of Illinois Press, 1988.

Franzwa, Gregory M. *Maps of the California Trail.* Tucson: The Patrice Press, 1999.

———. *Maps of the Oregon Trail.* St. Louis: The Patrice Press, 1982; 3rd ed., 1990.

———. *The Oregon Trail Revisited.* St. Louis: The Patrice Press, 1972; 5th ed., 1997.

Gottfredson, Peter. *History of Indian Depredations in Utah.* Salt Lake City, 1919.

Gunnison, John W. *The Mormons, or Latter-day Saints, in the Valley of the Great Salt Lake: A History of their rise and progress, peculiar doctrines, present condition and prospects, derived from personal observation during a residency among them.* Philadelphia: Lippincott, Grambo & Co., 1852.

Hafen, LeRoy R. and Ann W. Hafen, eds. *Journals of Forty-niners: Salt Lake to Los Angeles.* Glendale, Calif: The Arthur H. Clark Co., 1954.

Hafen, LeRoy R., ed. *The Mountain Men and the Fur Trade of the Far West,* 10 vols. Glendale, Calif: The Arthur H. Clark Co., 1965–1972.

Hanson, Klaus J. *Quest for Empire: The Political Kingdom of God and the Council of Fifty in Mormon History.* East Lansing: Michigan State Univ. Press, 1967.

Hargrave, Helena M. Goodale. *Goodale–Goodell Forebears.* Walnut Creek, Calif., 1971; revised 1975/76.

Hill, William E. *The Mormon Trail Yesterday and Today.* Logan: Utah State Univ. Press, 1996.

History of the Pacific Northwest. Northern Pacific History Co., 1892.

Hodgkin, Frank E. and J. J. Galvin. *Pen Pictures of Representative Men of Oregon.* Portland: Farmer and Dairyman Publishing House, 1882.

Holliday, J. S. *The World Rushed In: The California Gold Rush Experience.* New York: Simon and Schuster, 1981.

Holmes, Kenneth L., ed. and comp. *Covered Wagon Women: Diaries & Letters from the Western Trails, 1840–1890,* 11 vols. Glendale, Calif., and Spokane, Wash: The Arthur H. Clark Co., 1983–93.

Jackson, Donald Dale. *Gold Dust.* New York: Alfred A. Knopf, 1980.

Jenson, Andrew. *Church Chronology. A Record of Important Events Pertaining to the History of the Church of Jesus Christ of Latter-day Saints.* Salt Lake City: Deseret News Press, 1899.

———, ed. *Latter-day Saint Biographical Encyclopedia,* 4 vols. Salt Lake City: Andrew Jenson History Co., 1901. Reprinted Salt Lake City: Western Epics, 1971.

Journal of Discourses, 26 vols. London: Latter-Day Saints Book Depot, 1854–86.

Judson, Phoebe Goodell. *A Pioneer's Search for an Ideal Home.* Bellingham, Wash., 1925.

Kelly, William. *Across the Rocky Mountains from New York to California: With a Visit to the Celebrated Mormon Colony, at the Great Salt Lake.* London: Simms & McIntyre, 1852.

Korns, J. Roderic and Dale L. Morgan, eds. *West from Fort Bridger: The Pioneering of Immigrant Trails across Utah, 1846–1850.* Salt Lake City: Utah State Hist. Soc., 1951. Revised and updated by Will Bagley and Harold Schindler, Logan: Utah State Univ. Press, 1994.

Lang, H. O., ed. *History of the Willamette Valley.* Portland: Himes & Lang, 1885.

Langworthy, Franklin. *Scenery of the Plains, Mountains and Mines: or a Diary kept upon the Overland Route to California, by way of the Great Salt Lake.* Ogdensburgh, N.Y: Published by J. S. Sprague, Bookseller; Hitchcock & Tillotson, Printers, 1855.

Ledyard, Edgar M., ed. *A Journal of the Birmingham Emigrating Company: The record of a trip from Birmingham, Iowa, to Sacramento, California, in 1850*. Salt Lake City: Legal Printing Co., 1928.

LeSueur, Stephen C. *The 1838 Mormon War in Missouri*. Columbia: Univ. of Missouri Press, 1987.

Liles, Necia Dixon, ed. *At the Extremity of Civilization: A Meticulously Descriptive Diary* [by Israel Shipman Pelton Lord] *of an Illinois Physician's Journey in 1849 Along the Oregon Trail to the Goldmines and Cholera of California, Thence in Two Years to Return by Boat Via Panama*. Jefferson, N.C: McFarland & Co., Inc., Publishers, 1995.

Long, John V. *Report of the First General Festival of the Renowned Mormon Battalion, which came off on Tuesday and Wednesday, Feb. 6 and 7, 1855, in the social hall, G.S.L. City U.T.* St. Louis: St. Louis Luminary Office, 1855.

MacDonald, G. D., III. *The Magnet: Iron Ore in Iron County Utah*. Cedar City, Utah, 1990.

Madsen, Brigham D., ed. *Exploring the Great Salt Lake: The Stansbury Expedition of 1849–50*. Salt Lake City: Univ. of Utah Press, 1989.

——, ed. *A Forty-niner in Utah: Letters and Journal of John Hudson*. Salt Lake City: Tanner Trust Fund, Univ. of Utah Library, 1981.

——. *Gold Rush Sojourners in Great Salt Lake City, 1849 and 1850*. Salt Lake City: Univ. of Utah Press, 1983.

McCall, Ansel James. *The Great California Trail in 1849*. Bath, N.Y., 1882.

McKinstry, Bruce L., ed. *The California Gold Rush Overland Diary of Byron N. McKinstry, 1850–1852*. Glendale, Calif: The Arthur H. Clark Co., 1975.

Meeker, Ezra. *Pioneer Reminiscences of Puget Sound: The Tragedy of Leschi*. Seattle: Lowman W. Hanford Stationary and Printing Co., 1905.

Morgan, Dale L. *The Great Salt Lake*. Indianapolis: The Bobbs-Merrill Co., 1947.

———. *The State of Deseret.* Logan: Utah State Univ. Press and Utah State Hist. Soc., 1987.

Mulder, William and A. Russell Mortensen. *Among the Mormons: Historic Accounts by Contemporary Observers.* New York: Alfred A. Knopf, 1958.

Paul, Rodman W. *The California Gold Discovery: Sources, Documents, Accounts and Memoirs Relating to the Discovery of Gold at Sutter's Mill.* Georgetown, Calif: The Talisman Press, 1966.

Potter, David Morris, ed. *Trail to California: The Overland Journal of Vincent Geiger and Wakeman Bryarly.* New Haven: Yale Univ. Press, 1945.

Powell, Allan Kent. *Utah History Encyclopedia.* Salt Lake City: Univ. of Utah Press, 1994.

Proclamation of the Twelve Apostles of the Church of Jesus Christ of Latter-day Saints to All the Kings of the World, to the President of the United States of America; to the Governors of the Several States, and to the Rulers and People of All Nations. New York: Pratt and Brannan, 1845.

Quinn, D. Michael. *The Mormon Hierarchy: Origins of Power.* Salt Lake City: Signature Books in association with Smith Research Associates, 1994.

———. *The Mormon Hierarchy: Extensions of Power.* Salt Lake City: Signature Books in association with Smith Research Associates, 1997.

Roberts, Brigham H. *A Comprehensive History of the Church of Jesus Christ of Latter-day Saints,* 6 vols. Salt Lake City: Deseret News Press, 1932.

Roberts, Richard C. and Richard W. Sadler. *A History of Weber County.* Utah Centennial County Series. Salt Lake City: Utah State Hist. Soc., 1996.

Sargent, Shirley, ed. *Seeking the Elephant, 1849: James Mason Hutchings' Journal of His Overland Trek to California; Including his Voyage to America, 1848 and Letters from the Mother Lode.* Glendale, Calif: The Arthur H. Clark Co., 1980.

Schindler, Harold, comp. and ed. *Crossing the Plains: New and fascinating accounts of the hardships, controversies and courage experienced and chronicled by the 1847 pioneers on the Mormon Trail.* Salt Lake City: The Salt Lake Tribune, 1997.

————. *Orrin Porter Rockwell: Man of God, Son of Thunder.* Salt Lake City: Univ. of Utah Press, 1966. Revised edition, 1983.

Sessions, Gene A. *Mormon Thunder: A Documentary History of Jedediah Morgan Grant.* Urbana: Univ. of Illinois Press, 1982.

Slater, Nelson, comp. *Fruits of Mormonism, or A Fair and Candid Statement of Facts Illustrative of Mormon Principles, Mormon Policy, and Mormon Character, by More Than Forty Eye-Witnesses.* Coloma, Calif: Harmon & Springer, 1851.

Stenhouse, Thomas H. B. *The Rocky Mountain Saints: A Full and Complete History of the Mormons, From the First Vision of Joseph Smith to the Last Courtship of Brigham Young.* New York: D. Appleton & Co., 1873.

Stewart, George R., Jr. *The California Trail: An Epic with Many Heroes.* New York: McGraw-Hill Book Co., Inc., 1962.

Tullidge, Edward W. *Tullidge's Histories; Containing the History of All the Northern, Eastern, and Western Counties of Utah, also the Counties of Southern Idaho.* Salt Lake City: Juvenile Instructor Press, 1889.

Tyler, Daniel. *A Concise History of the Mormon Battalion in the Mexican War, 1846–47.* Salt Lake City, 1881; reprinted Glorieta, N. Mex: The Rio Grande Press, Inc., 1980.

Unruh, John D., Jr. *The Plains Across: The Overland Emigrants and the Trans-Mississippi West, 1840–60.* Urbana: Univ. of Illinois Press, 1979.

Whitney, Orson F. *History of Utah,* 4 vols. Salt Lake City: Deseret News Press, 1892.

Williams, George E. *A Genealogy of the Descendants of Robert Goodale/Goodell of Salem, Mass.* West Hartford, Conn: Published by George W. Williams, 1984.

Woodfield, Floyd and Clara Woodfield, comps. *A History of North Ogden: Beginnings to 1985.* Ogden, Utah: Empire Printing, 1986.

PERIODICALS

Bigler, David, Donald Buck and Merrill J. Mattes, eds. "'O Wickedness, Where Is Thy Boundary?': The 1850 California Gold Rush Diary of George Shepard." *Overland Journal,* 10:4, 1992.

Burroughs, Burt E., ed. "Tales of the Pioneers of the Kankakee: Taken from the Diary of Henry S. Bloom." *Kankakee Daily Republic,* 27 May – 3 July 1931; typed copy made by the California State Library from the newspaper articles.

Cannon, Kenneth L., II. "'Mountain Common Law': The Extralegal Punishment of Seducers in Early Utah." *Utah Historical Quarterly,* 51:4, 1983.

Carter, Lyndia McDowell. "Matthew William Dalton: 1850 Trail Account of Journey from Fort Hall to Ogden," *Crossroads,* Utah Crossroads Quarterly Newsletter, 6:2, 1995.

Dykes, Fred W. "Cold, Hard Facts About Jeffrey's Cutoff." *Overland Journal,* 14:4, Winter 1996–97, 4–16.

Fleming, L. A., and A. R. Standing. "'The Road to 'Fortune': The Salt Lake Cutoff." *Utah Historical Quarterly,* 33:3, 1965.

Flint, Thomas. "Diary of Dr. Thomas Flint, 1851–1855." *Annual Publications of the Hist. Soc. of So. Calif.,* 1923.

Gentry, Leland H. "The Danite Band of 1838." *Brigham Young University Studies,* 14:2, 1974.

James, Eugenia Learned and Vivian K. McLarty, eds. "Three Generations in the Span of a Continent: The Zumwalt Family." Pts. 1, 2. *Missouri Historical Review,* 48:3, 4, 1954.

Kelly, Charles. "The Journal of Robert Chalmers, April 13, September 1, 1850." *Utah Historical Quarterly,* 20:1, 1952.

Little, James Amasa. "Biography of Lorenzo Dow Young." *Utah Historical Quarterly,* 14:1–4, 1946.

Morgan, Dale L. "The Ferries of the Forty-Niners." Pts. 1–3. *Annals of Wyoming*, 31, 32:1, 2, 1959, 1960.

———. "Letters by Forty-Niners Written from Great Salt Lake City in 1849." *Western Humanities Review*, 3:2, 1949.

———. "Miles Goodyear and the Founding of Ogden." *Utah Historical Quarterly*, 21:3, 1953.

Nebeker, John. "Early Justice in Utah." *Utah Historical Quarterly*, 3:3, 1930.

Quinn, D. Michael. "The Council of Fifty and Its Members, 1844 to 1845." *Brigham Young University Studies*, 20:2, 1980.

Smart, William B. "Oregon and the Mormon Problem." *Reed College Bulletin*, 26:2, 1948.

Williams, Burton J., ed. "Overland to California in 1850: The Journal of Calvin Taylor." *Utah Historical Quarterly*, 38:4, 1970.

NEWSPAPERS

Alta California, San Francisco.

Deseret News, Great Salt Lake City, Utah Territory.

The Daily Union, Sacramento, California.

Evening Daily Bulletin, San Francisco.

Kankakee Daily Republic, Kankakee, Illinois.

Latter-day Saints' Millennial Star, Liverpool.

Marysville Daily Appeal, Marysville, California.

Oregon City Spectator, Oregon City, Oregon Territory.

The Oregonian, Portland, Oregon Territory.

St. Louis Intelligencer, St. Louis.

San Francisco Herald, San Francisco.

San Francisco Morning Call, San Francisco.

Weekly Oregon Statesman, Salem, Oregon Territory.

THESES & DISSERTATIONS

Alexander, Thomas G. "The Utah Federal Courts and the Areas of Conflict, 1850–96." M.A. thesis, Utah State Univ., 1961.

Blaylock, John Q. "History of North Ogden, An Economic and Social Study." M.A. thesis, Univ. of Utah, 1922.

Jack, Ronald C. "Utah Territorial Politics: 1847–1876." Ph.D. diss., Univ. of Utah, 1970.

Kilts, Clair T. "A History of the Federal and Territorial Court Conflicts in Utah, 1851–1874." M.A. thesis, Brigham Young Univ., 1959.

O'Neil, Floyd A. "A History of the Ute Indians of Utah until 1890." Ph.D. diss., Univ. of Utah, 1973.

Reinwand, Louis G. "An Interpretive Study of Mormon Millennialism during the Nineteenth Century with Emphasis on Millennial Developments in Utah." M.A. thesis, Brigham Young Univ., 1971.

MANUSCRIPTS

Call, George C. Asa C. Call: Written by His Sons, Largely from his Private Memoirs, copy in possession of John R. Call of Derby, Kansas.

Hill, James LeRoy. Biography of James Brown. Donald R. Moorman Collection, Weber State Univ., Ogden, Utah.

Journal History of the Church of Jesus Christ of Latter-day Saints. LDS Church Historical Dept., Salt Lake City.

Love, Andrew. Journal of Andrew Love, 1852–1880. LDS Archives; author.

Moore, David. Journal and Life History of David Moore. Harold B. Lee Library, Brigham Young Univ., Provo, Utah.

Smith, Azariah. Journal of Azariah Smith. LDS Archives; author.

Young, Brigham. Collection. Marriott Library, Univ. of Utah.

Zumwalt, Solomon. The Biography of Adam Zumwalt by His Son, Solomon Zumwalt, Who Came to Oregon in 1850. Reproduced in 1959 by the Lane Co. Pioneer Hist. Soc., Eugene, Ore.

PUBLIC DOCUMENTS

U.S. Congress. "An Act to Establish a Territorial Government for Utah." *The Statutes at Large and Treaties of the United States of America from December 1, 1845, to March 3, 1851*, Vol. 9. Boston: Charles C. Little and James Brown, 1851.

U.S. Congress. "Utah Territory." *Congressional Globe* (32-1), 9 January 1852, Vol. 100, app. 84–93.

U.S. House. "Information in reference to the condition of affairs in the Territory of Utah," Exec. Doc. 25 (32-1), 1852, Serial 640.

U.S. House. "The Utah Expedition," Exec. Doc. 71 (35-1), 1858, Serial 956.

Utah Territory. *Acts, Resolutions and Memorials, passed at the Several Annual Sessions of the Legislative Assembly of the Territory of Utah, from 1851 to 1870 Inclusive.* Salt Lake City: Joseph Bull, Public Printer, 1870.

Utah Territory. Militia Records. Utah State Archives.

INDEX

The letter "n" following a page number indicates the information is found on one or more footnotes on the page.

Sacramento, Calif., 1, 12, 125n, 213

Sacramento Daily Union, 2, 117, 213, 214

St. Joseph, Mo., 8

St. Louis, 8, 24, 26, 180, 206

St. Louis Intelligencer, 25, 26, 69, 206

Salem, Mass., 4

Salem, Oreg., 131, 142

Salmon, Idaho, 97n

Salt Deseret Trail, 115

Salt Lake City, 14, 23, 24, 33, 40, 45, 53; tabernacle, 75; post office at censors emigrant mail, 78, 79, 130, 132, 133, 210; 90; guards around, 93; 101, 108, 115, 128, 129, 132, 133, 135n, 151, 152, 170, 179

Salt Lake County, 179

Salt Lake Cutoff, *See* Hensley's Salt Lake Cutoff

Salt Lake Stake, 167n

Salt Lake Valley, 1, 2, 10, 13, 18, 21, 26, 29, 38, 41, 46, 50, 59, 62; children of, 70; transients in, 87; 88, 127, 132, 142, 205, 206, 208, 213, 214

San Bernardino, Calif., 36n, 54n

San Diego, Calif., 135n

San Francisco, 129n, 218

San Francisco Morning Call, 211

Sandusky, Ohio, 8

Sanpete, 75

Santa Fe, N. Mex., 25, 120n

Sawyer, David, 72

Sevire, Augustus, 134, 135

Sherwood, H. G., 203

Shumway, Charles, 203

Sierra Nevada, 13, 25, 59, 205, 207

Silent City of Rocks, 102, 140

Singer, Arcibella, 205

Singer, William, winters in Utah, 25; 27n, 69, 78n, 120; loses horse to Indians, 121n; 140, 205, 206; letter of, 206-210; obituary of, 211

Singer, William, Jr., 212

Slater, Emily, 18

Slater Nelson, 18, compiles emigrant grievances, 19; 69; named to emigrant committee, 88, 89; 117n, 128, 208n, 213, 214

Smith, Addison, 67n

Smith, Azariah, describes Vaughn shooting, 83n

Smith, George A., 51n, 170, 203

Smith, Hyrum, murder of, 165

Smith, Joseph, Jr., 52n, reveals polygamy, 50; 61, 62, 81n; murder of, 165

Smith, Lot, 134n, 135

Smith, Louisa Catherine, 67n

Snake River, 1, 25, 28, 102, 115n, 125, 140; Three Island Crossing of, 141

Snake River Valley, 125, 126

Snow, Erastus, 22n, 129n

Snow, Willard, 128, 129n

Snow, Zerubbabel, 22n, 129n, 150; letter of to President Fillmore, 157, 158; placed over district courts, 158; 163, 196

Snowville, Utah, 140

Soda Springs, 115n

Soltmorst, Reuben, 133

Sons of Dan, 27n. *See* also Danites

South Fort (Weber), 36n

South Pass, 142

Southern Pacific Railroad, 212

Spalding, Elizabeth, 142

Spalding, Henry Harmon, 142

Spanish Trail, 114n

Spencer, Daniel, 167, 203

Spencer, Orson, 203

Stansbury Expedition, 70n

Stewart, Urban Van, shoots Chief
   Terikee, 31; 33, 39n
Stoker, John, 203
Stony Creek (Idaho), 125
Stout, Hosea, 16, 37n, 84n, 99n, 101,
   102, 115, 129, 203
Straits of Mackinac, 8
Sublette's Cutoff, 10
Suffolk, England, 4
Sutter, John A., 12
Sutter's Mill, 19

Taft, John Gilbert, 134
taxes, 56, 57n, 92, 102, 107-111, 118, 161,
   216
Taylor, Zachary, Brigham Young's
   denunciation of, 23, 153, 155, 156,
   164, 165
Templeton, Mass., 4
Tennessee, 69
Terikee (Shoshoni chief), shooting of,
   31, 33, 39n
Thurston County, Wash., 142
tithing, 54, 56-58, 76, 161
Tooele, Utah, 115
Tooele Valley, 133
Treaty of Guadalupe Hidalgo, 12
Truland, Orr, 133
Turner, Mrs., 217
Turner, George, 125n
Turner, G. L., 114-17, reportedly joined
   Mormons, 123; capture and release
   of, 124, 125; manhunt for, 213; 214;
   contracts with Brigham Young, 216,
   217

United States, 4, 6, acquires
   Southwest, 12; 13, 15, 19; officials
   report disloyalty to, 24; officers of,
   28, 42; 38, 41; alleged disloyalty
   toward, 45-52; 53; land laws of, 53n,

57n; 63, 68; denunciations of, 76; 78,
   80, 82; courts of, 99; 146, 180; as a
   mobite government, 183; power of
   denied, 209; 210
U.S. Army 25, 26, 60, 69, supply trains
   of burned, 135n; Utah Expedition
   of, 159n; 205, 206
U.S. Congress, 15, 16, 18; creates Utah
   Territory, 21, 49n; 23, 24; receives
   report on conditions in Utah, 25,
   147-203; 28, 48, 55n; emigrant
   memorials to, 73, 87-89, 91, 94, 95,
   117, 214; 110; appropriates money for
   Utah, 175; 179, 194, 211
U.S. Constitution, as stepping stone to
   higher rule, 46, 47; 161
U.S. General Land Office, 78n
U.S. House of Representatives, 193
U.S. Office of Indian Affairs, 114
U.S. Post Office, accusations of cen-
   sorship at, 78, 79, 130, 132, 133, 210
U.S. Treasury, 192
U.S. State Department, 193
University of Deseret, 166, 167
Utah, acquired from Mexico, 13; 140
Utah County, 54n
Utah Territory, 4, 8, 11, 15, 18, 19; first
   clash with U.S., 21; 24; conditions in,
   25; 26, 31; memorial of, 42; 43, 45,
   48, 49, 51; elections in, 55, 56;
   election law of, 55n; Legislative
   Assembly of, 55n, 68n, 150, 196, 199;
   60, 73, 75, 76, 79; wintering emigrants in, 87; to escape from, 88;
   U.S. marshal of, 110n; 113, 114, 115n,
   127, 129, 132, 133, 136, 142;
   Fillmore's report on conditions in,
   147-203; seal of, 169; legislative
   election, 174; lawmakers of demand
   payment, 177, 178; supreme court of

DAVID L. BIGLER

David L. Bigler is a native of Provo, Utah. A naval veteran of World War II and Korea, he graduated from the University of Utah in 1950 with a degree in journalism. He is the retired director of public affairs for U.S. Steel, now USX Corp. Since 1986 he has devoted full time to the study of Utah and western history.

Mr. Bigler is past president, Oregon-California Trails Association; a founder and first president, Utah Westerners; former member, Utah Board of State History; former director, Friends of University of Utah Libraries; and member, Utah State Historical Society, Gold Discovery Park Association, and Sacramento Westerners. He is also a former officer or director of the Utah Manufacturers Association, Utah Mining Association, and Salt Lake Area Chamber of Commerce. He received an honorary Doctor of Letters degree in 1979 from Southern Utah State College, now Southern Utah University.

Bigler has written extensively on Western history. His essay on "Garland Hurt, the American Friend of the Utahs," won the Utah State Historical Society's Dale L. Morgan Award. He edited his great-uncle's diary, *The Gold Discovery Journal of Azariah Smith*, for the University of Utah Press. Westerners International presented its Best Book Award for 1998 to his *Forgotten Kingdom: The Mormon Theocracy in the American West, 1847–1896.* His second volume for the Arthur H. Clark Company, *Army of Israel: Mormon Battalion Narratives*, won the Mormon History Association's Best Documentary prize for the year 2000.

Mr. Bigler and his wife, Evah, now reside in Roseville, California.

GEORGE MILES

Preface author George Miles is Curator of the Yale Collection of Western Americana at Yale University's Beinecke Library.

Designed and set in
Baskerville Old Face
and Franklin Gothic
at
THE PRAIRIE DOG PRESS
Salt Lake City, Utah.
Printed on #60 Gladfelter Natural Offset
Limited to an edition of 1,000 copies

The front endleaf map is Sherman & J. Calvin Smith,
"Western Territories of the United States," circa 1847,
The back endleaf map is H. O. Rogers & A. Keith
Johnston, "Territory of Utah, 1857."

Despite its title, the Sherman & Smith map does not
reflect the territorial boundaries Congress established in
1850. Rather, it uses the borders the mapmakers
anticipated when they composed the map in 1847.

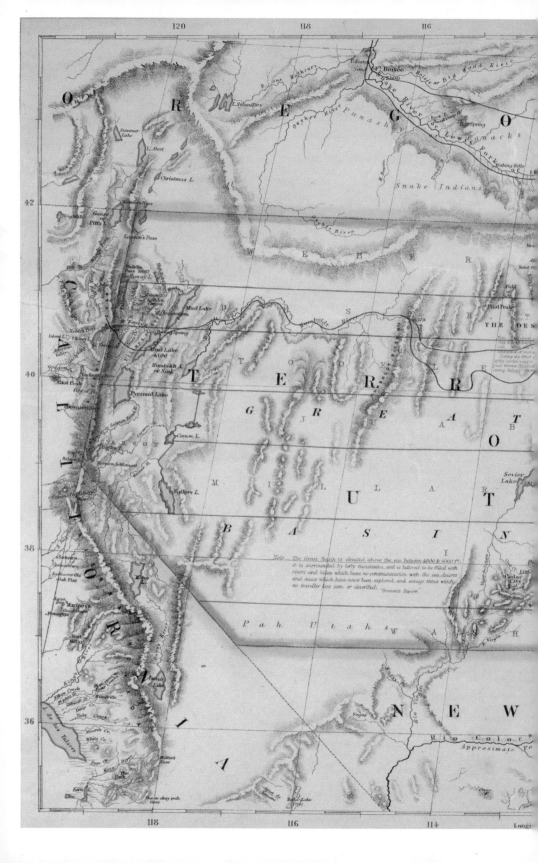